BIKERS'
BRITAIN

BIKERS' BRITAIN

3RD EDITION – 82 SCENIC ROUTES!

Simon Weir

Foreword by
Charley Boorman

Published by AA Media Limited, whose
registered office is Grove House, Lutyens Close,
Basingstoke, Hampshire RG24 8AG; registered
number 06112600.

3rd edition © AA Media Ltd 2024

Contains Ordnance Survey data
© Crown copyright and database right 2024
Distance chart contains data available from
openstreetmap.org © under the Open Database
License found at opendatacommons.org

A CIP catalogue record for this book is available
from the British Library.

A05882

978-0-7495-8425-2

The contents of this book are believed correct at
the time of printing. Nevertheless, the publishers
cannot be held responsible for any errors or
omissions or for changes in the details given
in this book or for the consequences of any
reliance on the information provided by the
same. This does not affect your statutory rights.

The maps in this book should be easy to follow.
If you're unsure where you are at any point, find
a safe place to stop and check. Never attempt to
read the route descriptions while riding.

Cartography provided by the Mapping Services
Department of AA Media Limited.

The publishers would welcome information
to correct any errors or omissions to keep this
product up to date. Please write to: The Atlas
Editor, AA Media Limited, Grove House, Lutyens
Close, Basingstoke, Hampshire, RG24 8AG, UK.

Email: roadatlasfeedback@aamediagroup.co.uk

Printed and bound by Oriental Press, Dubai.

CONTENTS

FOREWORD: Charley Boorman

I'VE TRAVELLED ALL over the world and ridden in some amazing places. There have been times when the riding has been pretty tough, from crossing Siberia's Road of Bones in the *Long Way Round* to tackling the desert in *Race to Dakar*. But a lot of it has been simply beautiful, such as crossing Ethiopia on the *Long Way Down* and exploring Canada and South Africa for *Extreme Frontiers*.

Despite all the miles I've done on two wheels, I have to admit that there's one place I could still discover more of by bike… and it's Britain. Of course, I do know some areas pretty well – especially Wales and Scotland – but too often when crossing the country I just rush along the motorways. And I know there's great riding just waiting to be discovered.

That's why I love this book, and why the first edition was so popular. No matter where you are in the country, you're never far from a route to enjoy on your bike. And in this bigger and better new edition, you know that whether you're exploring a new area or crossing the country, there will be a great ride for you contained within these pages.

There's still so much brilliant riding in Britain – it's a beautiful country and has some truly fabulous roads. Now, with the third edition of the AA's *Bikers' Britain*, we can all get straight onto them and make the most of every minute on two wheels.

Enjoy your riding – and maybe I'll see you on one of the brilliant new routes inside this great volume.

Charley Boorman

Charley's book *Long Way Back* is published by AA Publishing.
Keep track of Charley's adventures at: charleyboorman.com

INTRODUCTION

THANK YOU FOR picking up this latest edition of *Bikers' Britain*. I feel very lucky that it's been so popular – though the world has changed significantly since the first edition was published way back in 2013.

We're seeing more speed limits, more potholes, more cameras… more traffic, too. Finding a great ride can sometimes feel harder than ever – but that's where this book comes in. Once your local roads feel too closed in, head to a fresh area and discover new places to ride.

That's still possible because the important things haven't changed since the Bikers' Britain story began. This is an island blessed with fantastic landscapes – whether you like moors or mountains, forests or coastlines, or the classic quiet countryside of hedgerows and villages. The roads that cross it are still engaging, beautiful and rewarding.

But just like the speed limits, the roads are always changing – and it's important to stay up to date. This edition may not have new routes but the team at AA HQ has gone through each of the 82 rides carefully, replotting them all on the latest maps and tweaking the directions to ensure each one is as accurate as it could possibly be.

Time on the bike is precious and we aim to help you make the most of it, guiding you painlessly to the best roads.

Enjoy this updated edition of *Bikers' Britain* – and enjoy the rides.

Simon Weir

simonweir.co.uk

TOURING TIPS

There's much to be said for spontaneously jumping on the bike and heading out for a ride, but it's easy to end up on the same old roads or, worse, stuck on a dull, traffic-clogged road. If you have a day or two set aside for riding, why not plan a decent route you'll really enjoy?

THAT'S WHERE THIS book comes in. We have week-long tours, day-long and half-day routes, all accompanied by clear AA mapping and turn-by-turn directions. Check the directions before you go, then pop the book in your tank bag and follow the map. Using our routes, you should never have a dull day on the bike.

Keeping safe Although there are many other considerations to take into account when heading out to sample new roads, it can often boil down to one simple thing: keeping safe. So here are our tips for enjoying a brilliant and safe summer on undiscovered roads.

Route planning Planning a good route demands honesty about how far you really want to ride in a day and what kind of roads you enjoy. A 400-mile odyssey on tight lanes may be heaven for one rider and hell for another. Work out your ideal daily time in the saddle and build routes to that length, based on a realistic average speed.

The less time you have, the better the planning needs to be to cram in plenty of biking goodness. Avoiding towns and roads with lots of villages is a good idea, in order to minimise time spent chugging through lower speed limits. There is always a compromise with route planning –

sometimes it may be worth putting up with a couple of miles of dull dual carriageway to get quickly past an urban area and out to the good roads.

Loops versus straight runs Planning a straight ride is relatively simple. You know your start and finish points – just link up the good roads in between them. If there are awkward clumps of conurbation in the way, try to coincide them with lunch or evening stops, when it makes sense to wind down slowly and then set off again steadily. Planning a loop is trickier as it's important to keep the roads flowing.

A circle of amazing roads is the ideal, but sometimes it's necessary to fall back on the balloon approach. Here, you have one decent road from and back to your start/finish point, with a circle of other good roads at the end. Sometimes a bow loop works: a longer arc of good roads on the way out, ending on a dull but unchallenging road that makes a quick way to return to the start. And if all else fails, try the relay ride: take the roads in one direction, then turn round and ride the same ones back. But that's not very elegant, is it?

> **TIP**
> Keep types of road grouped together as much as possible – all the B-roads then all the A-roads – so the route really flows.

> **HOW FAST?**
> If you favour flowing A-roads, plan routes based on an average speed of 45mph, as that allows time for a couple of stops. If you plan to stick to minor roads, allow an average of 40mph. So if you like faster roads but only want four hours in the saddle, an 180-mile loop will give a full day's ride with time for lunch and a coffee break or two.

Stops Try to plan your stops – especially on longer rides. There's nothing worse than riding past a café, thinking you'll have a break in 20 minutes, only to find empty moorland around you for the next hour. If you can coincide fuel stops with lunch stops – at decent diners beside or near petrol stations – the route will flow better. If you have any sightseeing stops planned, time them to start or finish with lunch or a coffee stop. Always take the time that you'll spend off the bike into consideration when planning your route: if you want to spend an hour walking round a museum or castle, take 60–70 miles off your planned daily mileage.

Groups, couples or alone Always consider how many people will be riding the route you're planning. Large groups need simple routes that everyone can follow at their own pace. Big groups tend to string out, so having fewer turn-offs to look for makes a route simpler to follow.
If you're riding with only one or two mates, you can get away with a more complex route with more turnings as you're less likely to get strung out. And on your own, you can do whatever you like – just tell yourself, it's not really getting lost if you deviate from the planned route; it's exploring…

TIP
Don't use one route for every size of group. If a planned day out for three people grows into a 20-person ride-out, adapt the route so it's much simpler.

TOURING TIPS

DOs AND DON'Ts OF GROUP RIDING

DON'T ride too close together. **DO** ride in an off-set stagger on the straights. **DON'T** bunch up approaching the corners – spread out so every rider can take their own line. **DO** ride for yourself. **DON'T** follow other people's overtakes. **DO** assess corners and overtakes for yourself.

DON'T be tempted to ride at a faster speed than you normally would. **DO** wait for others when you turn. **DON'T** give anyone a hard time if they're not as quick as you. **DO** praise any safe riding you see – and try to diplomatically calm down any reckless riding you observe (but never argue:

a cross and reckless rider is worse than a calm and reckless one). **DON'T** leave the least experienced rider at the back, trying to keep up – let them ride second in the group. **DO** check your mirrors often to make sure they're okay, slowing the pace until they can happily manage to keep up with the group.

Directions It's a good idea to give everyone a copy of the route. The satnav can help with this: plot the route and email the file to everyone with a navigation device. Keep directions simple: road number, place name, turning left or right. This book has been specially designed to fit snugly inside a tank bag so that the route can be glanced at from time to time, but don't attempt to do any in-depth map-reading on the move: if you're unsure, pull over and check it properly. It's not only safer but also less likely to end up with you getting lost because you've misread the directions. The route maps in this book should be easy to follow. If you're unsure where you are or where the route goes at any point, find a safe place to stop and check – don't take your eyes off the road. Whatever you do, don't try to read the route descriptions while riding.

TIP
Sounds obvious, but write directions on white card with a thick black felt pen, not a skinny pencil. You must be able to check them at a glance.

Group riding Keeping a group together gets more difficult the bigger the group becomes, as everyone will ride at slightly different speeds. Making sure everyone has a copy of the route is a good idea. Making sure everyone has the mobile number of a couple of other people in the group is essential.

Once you are on the road, make sure everyone knows who's leading (don't follow random bikes you happen to catch up). Know which member of the group is behind you and don't take a turn if they're not in your mirrors – wait for them if you have to, and make sure they really have seen you before you set off at speed again.

TIP
Use hand signals as well as indicators in plenty of time: left forearm out for left turn, left forearm straight up for right. For straight on at a roundabout, left forearm up then chopping straight down a couple of times. Pass the signal to the rider behind you.

Luggage If you're touring, try to travel light – tricky if you're lugging camping gear as well as clothes. However, it's crucial not to overload the bike. Make sure you can sit comfortably and still have space to move around in the saddle. Allow a bit more braking distance and corner more gently with a fully-laden bike.

Even if you're just going out for a day rather than a couple of days, still take the basics: waterproofs, change of visor, maps, phone, camera and a drink. A spare pair of gloves is always a good idea.

> **TIP**
> After riding your first two or three miles with luggage, stop and check that it hasn't shifted. If it has, make it more secure before carrying on.

TOP TIPS FOR SAFE EXPLORING

New roads are more likely to catch you out than the ones you know. It's important to be safe, especially if you're riding alone.

1 **Roll off slightly** Give yourself a bit more margin, in case a bend tightens unexpectedly, a tractor emerges from a hidden entrance, there's gravel in that dip, or a sheep… or any one of 100 possible nasty surprises.

2 **Look further ahead** Especially on tight roads, it's easy to stop looking a long way in front as you deal with the bend that's right in front of you, but on unknown roads it's vital to keep looking ahead so you can always prepare for what's coming up.

3 **Don't get carried away in groups** Especially in a small group – don't let the speeds rise until you're practically racing. This is not safe riding.

4 **Stop more than you think is necessary** Not just for fuel and lunch. Make a bit of time to stop to take a picture, explore one of the places of interest on the route, or have a drink. Regular rehydration aids concentration and even five minutes off the bike every hour helps keep you more alert when you get back on.

5 **If you think you're lost, don't press on** Sometimes it's best to find someone to ask, which isn't something we're all good at. [not keen on blokes assumption]. However, it can save hours of anguish if you get back on the right road quickly. Also, frustration at being lost often leads to rash, reckless riding and that's best avoided.

6 **Don't give yourself deadline pressure** It never really matters if you're late – so don't rush to reach a destination by a fixed time. Better to take your time and stay safe.

USING THIS BOOK

THIS BOOK IS all about enjoying Britain's best roads and crossing the country from each of the four compass points in the most thrilling and enjoyable ways possible. It is split into chapters on the three nations, with a series of day trips and tours highlighting the best of each country, with the tours designed to be ridden over several days. Obviously, these longer tours are easy to adapt and do parts of as you, the rider, think fit.

Our routes are designed to showcase the best riding, with roads chosen for their scenery, excitement and sheer rideability. Some will take up to a day. However, don't be afraid to adapt or shorten them to suit you. Ultimately, they are our best recommendations but you decide where to ride.

The start point is marked on the accompanying AA road map, and on the loop rides, an arrow shows the suggested direction of travel. An approximate time is given for each ride, but this will vary according to weather, volume of traffic and other road conditions.

Although this book is designed to fit into the average-sized tank bag, we recommend that you study the route before you set off in order to minimise the need to consult the map while riding.

Some details of motorbike-friendly hotels, guesthouses and B&Bs are given here, but for a fuller list of AA-rated places to stay simply visit RatedTrips.com.

Following the routes

The route maps in this book are designed to be easy to follow. The first rule of safe riding is that you must never take your eyes off the road to study a map while you're moving and, whatever you do, don't try to read the route descriptions while riding along. They'll add detail and help confirm if you're still on the route, but reading them on the move wouldn't be safe so always stop before checking them.

M4	Motorway with number
T4 Toll	Toll motorway with toll station
5	Restricted motorway junctions
Fleet / Todhills	Motorway service area, rest area
	Motorway and junction under construction
A3	Primary route single/dual carriageway
	Primary route junction with and without number
3	Restricted primary route junctions
S	Primary route service area
BATH	Primary route destination
A1123	Other A road single/dual carriageway
B2070	B road single/dual carriageway
	Minor road more than 4 metres wide, less than 4 metres wide
	Roundabout
	Interchange/junction
	Narrow primary/other A/B road with passing places (Scotland)
	Road under construction
	Road tunnel
Toll	Road toll, steep gradient (arrows point downhill)
5	Distance in miles between symbols
	Railway line, in tunnel
	Railway station, tram stop, level crossing
	Preserved or tourist railway
628 / 637 Lecht Summit	Height in metres, mountain pass
	Snow gates (on main routes)
or	Vehicle ferry (all year, seasonal)
	Fast vehicle ferry or catamaran

or	Passenger ferry (all year, seasonal)
	Airport (major/minor), heliport
F	International freight terminal
H	24-hour Accident & Emergency hospital
C	Crematorium
P·R	Park and Ride (at least 6 days per week)
	City, town, village or other built-up area
	National boundary, county or administrative boundary
	Ride route
	Direction of route
	Lunch stop
	Tourist Information Centre (all year, seasonal)
	Visitor or heritage centre
	Caravan site, camping site, (AA inspected)
	Caravan & camping site (AA inspected)
	Abbey, cathedral or priory
	Ruined abbey, cathedral or priory
	Castle, historic house or building
	Museum or art gallery, industrial interest
	Aqueduct, viaduct
	Garden, arboretum
	Vineyard, brewery or distillery
	Country park, theme park
	Showground
	Farm or animal centre, Zoological or wildlife collection
	Bird collection, aquarium, RSPB site
	National Nature Reserve (England, Scotland, Wales)

	Local nature reserve, Wildlife Trust reserve
	Forest drive
	National trail
	City with clean air zone, low/zero emission zone
	Picnic site, hill-fort
	Waterfall, viewpoint, on route
	Prehistoric monument, Roman antiquity
1066	Battle site with year
	Preserved or tourist railway
	Cave or cavern
	Windmill, monument or memorial
	Beach (award winning), lighthouse
	Golf course
	Football stadium, Rugby Union national stadium
	County cricket ground, international athletics stadium
	Horse racing, show jumping
	Air show venue, motor-racing circuit
	Ski slope (natural, artificial)
	National Trust site (England & Wales, Scotland)
	English Heritage site, Historic Scotland site
	Cadw (Welsh heritage) site
	Major shopping centre, other place of interest
	Attraction within urban area
	World Heritage Site (UNESCO)
	National Park and National Scenic Area (Scotland)
	Forest Park
	Heritage coast

As maps of differing scales have been used throughout this book, not all features are present on every map

England

The largest country in the United Kingdom is packed with great riding

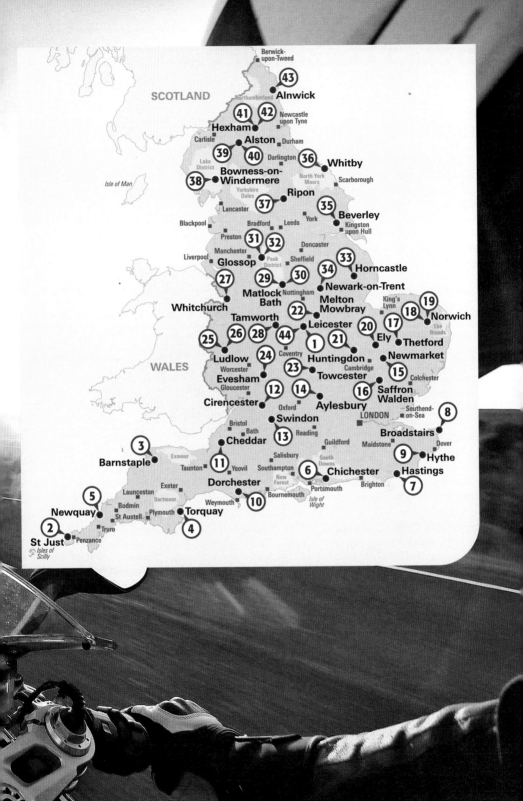

RIDE ① South Tour Day 1

DAY 1 MORNING

THERE'S SOME FANTASTIC riding on the first day, though the route starts by dodging Leicester with a bit of motorway. From Rugby on, though, it gets better and better, down across the rolling hills of the Chilterns with a lunch stop in the quiet market town of Thame. There are plenty of cafés and pubs: we'd nip into the Cornfield Bakery's café on cobbled Buttermarket.

FROM M1 Leicester Forest East Services (south)
TO Thame, Oxfordshire
DISTANCE 110 miles
ALLOW 2–2.5 hours

Route Description

➤ **M1 LFE Services** Head south on the M1.
➤ **M1 J20** Right onto A4303, then left at roundabout onto the A426.
➤ **Rugby** Continue on A426.
➤ **Southam** Left at 2 rbts, onto A423 then A425. Quick right onto Welsh Road East.
➤ **Priors Marston** Left at village war memorial, onto Hellidon Road.
➤ **A361** Right, towards Banbury.
➤ **Banbury** Turn left onto A422.
➤ **Brackley** Left onto A43, to regain A422 (right).
➤ **Buckingham** Turn right in town centre, onto Bridge Street. Continue to roundabout and go straight for A413 towards Aylesbury.
➤ **Whitchurch** Right at mini-roundabout, towards Quainton.
➤ **Waddesdon** Straight over the A41 at staggered x-roads.
➤ **Long Crendon** Left on B4011.
➤ **Thame** At roundabout go straight over (third exit) for town centre. Route ends in Thame town centre.

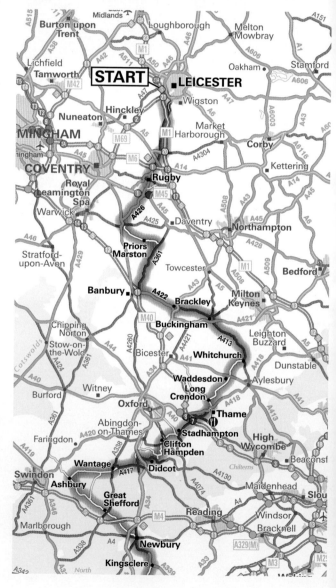

| **ROUTE TYPE** Tour | **DISTANCE** 110 miles morning | 121 miles afternoon |

DAY 1 AFTERNOON

IF YOU ARRIVE there with time to spare, it's worth having a wander around the historic city of Chichester. There are plenty of good places to stay in the centre of town, but we'd stop on the outskirts at the Bull's Head. Don't worry about filling up; the next day's route starts from the petrol station on the A27 Chichester bypass, two miles away.

FROM Thame, Oxfordshire
TO Chichester, West Sussex
DISTANCE 121 miles
ALLOW 2.5–3 hours

Route Description

➤ **Thame High Street**
Right from car park area, towards Oxford.
➤ **A418 rbt** Left on A329.
➤ **Stadhampton** Straight on A329, right on B480, then left on B4015.
➤ **Clifton Hampden** Straight over staggered x-roads.
➤ **Look out** Left turn to Didcot on B4016.
➤ **Didcot** Right on A4130, under A34.
➤ **Rowstock roundabout** Right on A417.
➤ **Wantage** Left at double-rbt on A338, straight at staggered x-roads with traffic lights onto B4507.
➤ **Ashbury** Left on B4000, through Lambourn.
➤ **Great Shefford** Right on A338, then left (straight on) at corner, towards Weston.
➤ **Newbury** Into town centre and pick up A339 to Basingstoke.
➤ **Kingsclere** Right at rbt, then right by church on B3051.
➤ **Overton** Left on B3400.
➤ **Basingstoke** Right on A340 Ringway, then right on A339.
➤ **Alton** Straight, under A31,

for B3006.
➤ **Liss** Right on A3.
➤ **Petersfield** Left on A272, right on B2199, then left on B2146.
➤ **South Harting** Left

on B2146.
➤ **Funtington** Left, still on B2146, then right for Bosham.
➤ **Bosham** Left on A259. Route ends at A259/A27 Chichester bypass roundabout.

RIDE (1) South Tour Day 2

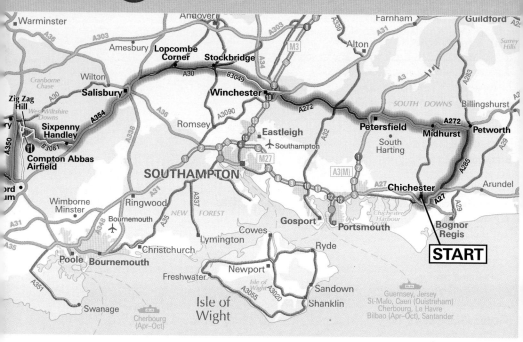

DAY 2 MORNING

SOME WONDERFUL RIDING to start the second day. A gentle warm-up with the run to Petworth is followed by the legendary A272. Don't worry about crossing Winchester – dive in (maybe stop for a coffee and see the sights if you have time) and head for the train station. From there, it's on to the A30, hurrying through Salisbury on the ring road and down towards Blandford Forum, detouring to take in the brilliantly well-named Zig Zag Hill. The lunch stop is at the bottom, at the Compton Abbas Airfield Diner.

FROM Chichester, West Sussex
TO Compton Abbas Airfield, Dorset
DISTANCE 100 miles
ALLOW 2–2.5 hours

Route Description

➤ **Chichester** A27 east, towards Brighton, then turn left onto A285 to Petworth.
➤ **Petworth** Left onto A272 heading past Midhurst.
➤ **Petersfield** Continue through town, sticking with the A272.

➤ **Winchester** Right on A31 then left for city centre on B3404. Follow signs for the railway station and pick up the B3049 to Stockbridge.
➤ **Stockbridge** Straight across roundabout on A30 towards Salisbury.
➤ **Lopcombe Corner** Turn left, still on A30.
➤ **Salisbury** Keep going straight at each roundabout, the ring road eventually feeds into the A354 to Blandford. This is the road you want.

➤ **Sixpenny Handley** Right on B3081. At the foot of Zig Zag Hill, turn left then left again, following signs for Compton Abbas Airfield. Route ends at the Airfield Diner, Compton Abbas Airfield.

| ROUTE TYPE Tour | DISTANCE 100 miles morning | 121 miles afternoon |

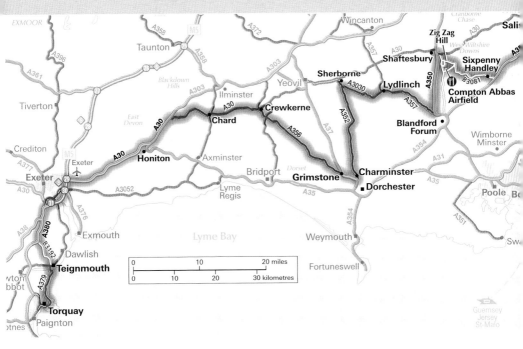

DAY 2 AFTERNOON

AFTER LUNCH, LEAVE the airfield, turn right to the A30. Turning left, then right will bring you to a petrol station. Fill up ready for the afternoon ride. The flowing section from Shaftesbury to Sherborne is a particular favourite. There is a bit of motorway towards the end of this route, just in order to avoid a dull and convoluted slog through the urban fringes of Exeter. If you're concerned at all about tank range, get a crafty top-up at the M5 services (the junction after you join the motorway). If you're feeling tired towards the end of the day, it's easy enough to drop the entertaining Teignmouth loop and just stay on the A380 to get to Torquay a bit quicker.

FROM Shaftesbury, Dorset
TO Torquay, Devon
DISTANCE 121 miles
ALLOW 3–3.5 hours

Route Description

➤ **Shaftesbury** Head south onto A350 to Blandford Forum.
➤ **Blandford Forum** Right onto A357 at the traffic lights just before town.
➤ **Lydlinch** Left onto A3030 just after village.

➤ **Sherborne** Left onto A352 just before town.
➤ **Charminster** Right onto A37, towards Yeovil.
➤ **Grimstone** Left onto the A356.
➤ **Crewkerne** Left onto A30.
➤ **Chard** Continue on A30, by-passing Honiton, to Exeter.
➤ **Exeter** Left onto M5 south.
➤ **M5 J31** Straight on for the A38, then bear left on the A380 towards Torquay.

➤ **Ashcombe Cross** Left onto B3192 to Teignmouth.
➤ **Teignmouth** Right onto A379 to Torquay. The route ends on Torquay seafront.

RIDE (1) South Tour Day 3

DAY 3 MORNING

SOME TIGHT ROADS are mixed in with the open, flowing ones. The route ends in Padstow – a great place for a wander around, with plenty of options for lunch. Rick Stein's St Petroc's Bistro might not fit the bill, so fish and chips is a good option. The afternoon route begins by retracing the route to Wadebridge from New Street – the point where you turned off the A389 for Padstow town centre.

DAY 3 AFTERNOON

SOME CLASSIC ROADS here, finishing with the steep descent down Porlock Hill after the wild beauty of Exmoor. If you have any concerns about your tank range, grab a cheeky top-up at the Barbrook petrol station, outside Lynton on the A39.

FROM Padstow, Cornwall
TO Porlock, Somerset
DISTANCE 149 miles
ALLOW 3–3.5 hours

FROM Torquay, Devon
TO Padstow, Devon
DISTANCE 86 miles
ALLOW 2–2.5 hours

Route Description
> **Torquay** Leave town on the A3022, riding past the train station.
> **Newton Abbot** Enter town centre and pick up the A382 heading past Bovey Tracey.
> **Moretonhampstead** Left on the B3212.
> **Two Bridges** Right onto the B3357.
> **Tavistock** Left on A386

Route Description
> **Padstow** Leave town the way you came in, on the A389. Don't miss the left turn back towards Wadebridge.

towards Plymouth, then right on A390.
> **Liskeard** Take the ring road around town, joining the A38 towards Bodmin.
> **Bodmin** Enter town centre, going right at double mini-roundabout on the A389 to Wadebridge.
> **Wadebridge** Forward onto A39 to head west.
> **Look out** After Whitecross take the easy-to-miss right turn for the A389 to Padstow.
> **Padstow** Follow signs for Town Centre and Docks. Route ends on the quayside in Padstow.

> **A39** Turn left, still following the signs for Wadebridge. Stay on the A39 along the coast, until approaching Bideford.
> **Abbotsham roundabout** Turn onto Clovelly Road. This short-cut misses out most of Bideford.
> **Bideford** Right on A386.
> **Great Torrington** Left at roundabout on A386, then left on A3124.
> **Winkleigh** Go straight on as the road becomes the B3220.
> **Morchard Road** Left on A377.
> **Barnstaple** Right on A361, then left on A39. Follow signs for A39 Lynton.
> **Blackmoor Gate** Straight over staggered x-roads on A39.
> **Lynmouth** Turn right to stay on A39. Route ends on Porlock High Street.

left The harbour at Padstow

RIDE ① South Tour Day 4

DAY 4 MORNING

FROM THE WILDS of Exmoor, our route cuts across the Somerset Levels, past the magical Glastonbury Tor and through the spectacular Cheddar Gorge, before arriving in Bath. Entering the city on the A4, you'll come to Queen's Square, on the edge of the city's café district – it's a perfect place for lunch. However, if you want to press on a while longer, the quieter town of Tetbury is only 22 miles into the afternoon ride. We like the Blue Zucchini Brasserie there.

FROM Porlock, Somerset
TO Bath, Somerset
DISTANCE 98 miles
ALLOW 2–2.5 hours

Route Description
➤ **Porlock** Head east on the A39 towards Minehead.
➤ **Marsh Street** At traffic lights on A39, turn right on A396 heading past Dunster.
➤ **Wheddon Cross** Left in village centre on B3224.
➤ **Methodist Church** Left at the T-junction by the chapel, on B3190, then straight on at Raleigh's Cross, where the road becomes the B3224 again.
➤ **A358** Turn right to Taunton.
➤ **Taunton** Stay on the A358 on the edge of town, picking up the A38 towards Bristol.
➤ **Look out** After about ½ mile on the A38, turn right on the A361 to Glastonbury.
➤ **A39** Turn right, still towards Glastonbury.
➤ **Glastonbury** Stay on A39 for Wells. Turn left on B3151 past Meare.
➤ **Wedmore** Right towards Wells, then left on B3151 to Cheddar.
➤ **Cheddar** Right on A371 towards Wells, then left at monument for B3135.
➤ **A39** Turn left, towards Bath. The road becomes the A37.
➤ **A37** At traffic lights after Farrington Gurney, turn right on A39.
➤ **A4** Straight over roundabout. Follow signs for city centre. Route ends in Bath city centre.

DAY 4 AFTERNOON

A REAL MIX OF roads – some small and tight, most open and sweeping. If you have any concerns about tank range, get a top-up in Princethorpe (the petrol station is opposite the junction).

FROM Bath, Somerset
TO Leicester Forest East Services (north)
DISTANCE 133 miles
ALLOW 2.5–3 hours

Route Description
➤ **Bath** Leave the city on the A46 towards Stroud.
➤ **A46** Turn right on the A433 to Cirencester.
➤ **Cirencester** Follow the ring road all the way round the town, following signs for Stow, until you can take the A429 to Stow.
➤ **After double roundabout** Cross A417 and look for traffic lights; then go straight on B4425.
➤ **A40** Turn right for Burford.
➤ **Burford** Left through town centre, over the bridge, then right on A361.
➤ **Look out** About 3 miles out of Burford, take the easy-to-miss right turn on B4437 to Charlbury.
➤ **Charlbury** Left on B4026.
➤ **Chipping Norton** Right on A361, right in town centre then go straight, on A361 towards Banbury.
➤ **Bloxham** Left turn on minor road (Cumberford).
➤ **Lower Tadmarton** Left on B4035 then first right on minor road (signed for Swalcliffe Lea).
➤ **Shutford** Straight over staggered x-roads.
➤ **A422** Left towards Stratford-upon-Avon.
➤ **Chequered signs** Turn right on the B4455 (the Fosse Way).
➤ **Princethorpe** Left on the A423.
➤ **Coventry** Take the A46 ring road to the M69 for Leicester.
➤ **M69 J3** Left onto M1 for one junction. Route ends at Leicester Forest East Services on the M1 northbound.

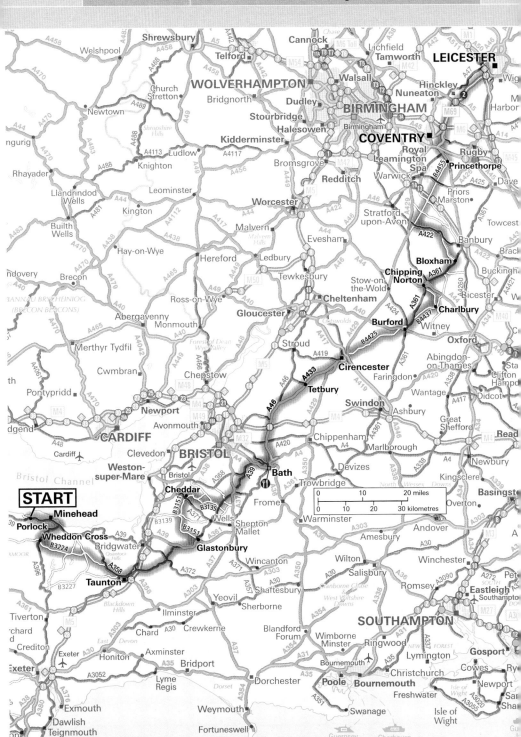

RIDE ② Land's End Loop

IT'S EASY TO become cynical about the West Country – particularly Cornwall. Clogged with caravans, torpid with tourist traffic…all the usual prejudices can blind motorcyclists to its charms. Thankfully, I have wiser friends and colleagues – one of whom swore blind that the road from St Just to St Ives was the best bit of tarmac west of London. I decided to give Cornwall another go and I'm very glad I did.

The sun beat down on deserted tarmac slicing through a sea of buttercups, sparkling off the ocean scarcely two fields away. Traffic? Well, it was midweek, term-time, and I'd made an early start, so there was practically none – in the first 10 miles it was just me, a few farmers and a little old lady walking a huge dog. Fresh salt air, rich green fields and an involving road – perfect. Even better, the fabulous B3306 fitted into a superb 90-minute loop of quiet riding. This loop has it all: proper, tight Cornish lanes as well as a few bigger roads.

Of course, Cornwall does get busy. A Bank Holiday Monday afternoon is not the best time for a brisk ride round the coast. Go midweek, before the holiday season – then the roads are quiet most of the day. Go on, give Cornwall a go – you certainly won't regret it.

FROM/TO St Just, Cornwall
DISTANCE 40 miles
ALLOW 1.5 hours

Route Description

➤ **St Just** Head north on the B3306 towards St Ives. The ride doesn't quite go into the town, though you may choose to.
➤ **B3311** Turn right onto the B3311 towards Penzance.
➤ **At the A30** Turn left towards Newlyn and head around the outskirts of Penzance.

right The famous sign at Land's End

➤ **Turn left onto the B3315** to Newlyn, then turn right in the town to continue on the B3315 towards Porthcurno.
➤ **At Sennen** Turn left on the A30 to visit Land's End itself.

Return up the A30.
➤ **A30** Continue beyond Sennen to find the B3306 on your left.
➤ **B3306** North to the A3071 and turn left, back to St Just.

Land's End This iconic place is found from a well-signposted left-turn, where the B3315 meets the A30 at Sennen. Grab a coffee in the Land's End Hotel.
landsendhotel.co.uk

Mousehole Is this Cornwall's quaintest fishing village? There's stiff competition, but Dylan Thomas called Mousehole 'the loveliest village in England' and we agree.
cornwall-online.co.uk

St Ives Bigger and busier than Mousehole, but St Ives is still a spellbinding seaside town. Whether you go for the Tate Gallery or fish and chips, it's well worth a visit.
stives-cornwall.co.uk

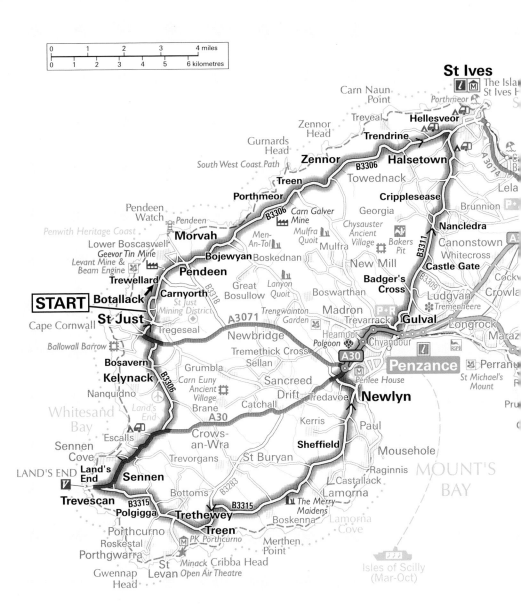

RIDE (3) West Country Loop

YOU COULD SPEND a week exploring the roads around Barnstaple quite happily, but if you only have a day then make sure you include this excellent loop. Timing is critical to your enjoyment of it – some of the roads will get busy at peak holiday times – but get a clear run and you'll be smitten forever.

The initial run from Barnstaple to Crediton on the A377 hugs the River Taw, flowing with a natural ease. The A3072 and A396 to Tiverton are even more scenic, but the landscape really goes into overdrive as the road climbs up onto Exmoor.

Turning left at Wheddon Cross, the road speeds between high hedges, bursting out to deliver immense views before the trees rise beside the road again. Joining the A39, the final descent back to Barnstaple is a shady rollercoaster. Fantastic!

FROM/TO Barnstaple, Devon
DISTANCE 98 miles
ALLOW 2.5 hours

Route Description

➤ **From Barnstaple** Head south on the A377. Stay on the road all the way into Crediton town centre.

➤ **Turn left onto the A3072** There is a bike shop further on down in Crediton town centre.

➤ **Follow the A3072 to Bickleigh** and turn left onto the A396, signed for Tiverton. Stay on this out onto the fringes of Exmoor to Wheddon Cross (there's a garage there).

➤ **Turn left onto the B3224** It becomes the B3223.

➤ **In Simonsbath** Take the left fork onto the B3358.

➤ **At the A399** Turn right towards Combe Martin.

➤ **At Blackmoor Gate** Turn left onto the A39, which will take you back to Barnstaple.

above *The view at Wheddon Cross, Exmoor*

WHAT TO SEE AND DO

The Devon Railway Centre Offers a unique railway experience and boasts a host of attractions. **devonrailwaycentre.co.uk**

Cobbaton Combat Collection, nr Cobbaton WWII British and Canadian military vehicles including tanks, trucks and armoured cars. Plus artillery, weapons and an exhibit on the Home Front. **cobbatoncombat.co.uk**

Dunster Castle There's been a castle here since the 11th century, and the inhabitants survived a 160-day siege during the Civil War. Great gardens and stunning interiors. **nationaltrust.org.uk/visit/somerset/dunster-castle-and-watermill**

RIDE ③ West Country Loop

ROUTE TYPE Loop | **DISTANCE** 98 miles

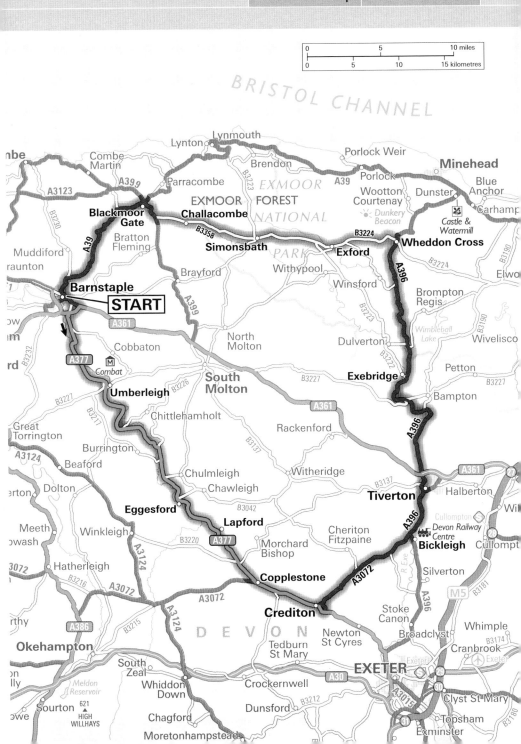

RIDE ④ Torquay Loop

THE ENGLISH RIVIERA'S been a holiday hotspot for as long as people have had leisure time and the ability to travel to the seaside. Torquay's a fantastic place for a bike-trip base. There are hotels and B&Bs to suit every budget, the town's charming and it's surrounded by brilliant roads. Like all tourist areas, it does get busier at peak times – so visit in spring or September, once the school holidays have finished, for a relaxed and grown-up biking break.

FROM/TO Torquay, Devon
DISTANCE 115 miles
ALLOW 3.5 hours

Route Description

➤ **Leave Torquay** on the A379 to Teignmouth.
➤ **Cross the bridge** and turn right into Teignmouth, then go left at the lights towards Exeter on the B3192.
➤ **Join the A380** towards Exeter for just over 2 miles, then take the exit for the services and follow the road round towards Exeter racecourse.
➤ **Join the A38** towards Plymouth for 4 miles, taking the second exit for Chudleigh Knighton.
➤ **Turn right** at the bottom of the slip road, then turn right again on the B3193 to the Teign Valley.
➤ **At the B3212 T-junction** Turn left to Moretonhampstead.
➤ **In Yelverton** Go straight over the roundabout on the A386 towards Plymouth.
➤ **After 3½ miles** in Roborough, turn left on the minor road to Bickleigh (if you get to the roundabout, you've overshot the turning by 300m).

➤ **In Bickleigh** Turn left on the minor road to Shaugh Prior and follow it all the way through Cornwood to Ivybridge.
➤ **Turn left** at the mini-roundabout to cross Ivybridge, towards the A38. Don't join it: go straight over the flyover and turn left to Ermington.
➤ **In Ermington** Turn right on the A3121 to Modbury.
➤ **Look out** After ½ mile turn left at Hollowcombe Cross towards Modbury and the A379.
➤ **At the A379** turn left to Kingsbridge. Stay on the A379 all the way to Dartmouth.
➤ **At the mini-roundabout** in Dartmouth, turn left on the A3122 to Totnes.
➤ **At the A381** Turn right to Totnes.
➤ **In Totnes** Turn right on the A385 to Paignton. Go straight over the A380 on the A3022 to Paignton and stay on this road all the way back to Torquay.

below *Great riding on the B3212 even before it reaches the wild open spaces of Dartmoor*

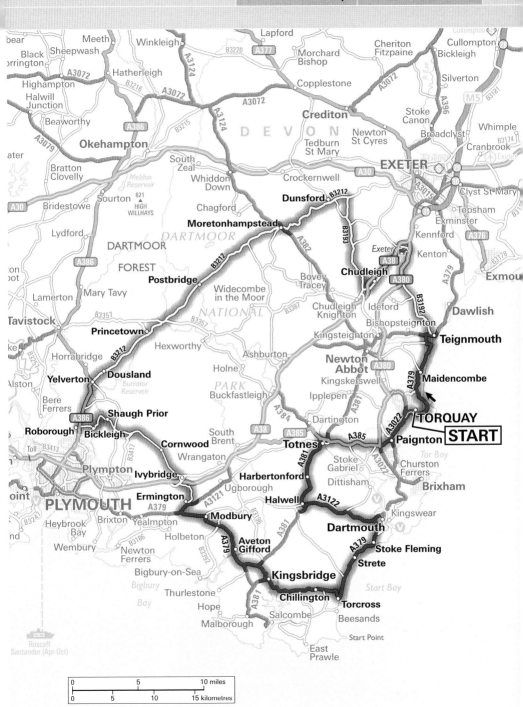

RIDE ⑤ Newquay Loop

THE SURFING CAPITAL of the West Country, Newquay has a lovely laid-back vibe to go with its golden beaches and plentiful holiday accommodation. Our equally laid-back route sets off through the north coast's quaint villages before heading to the South Coast gem of Mevagissey, passing the Lost Gardens of Heligan and heading deep into the Roseland Peninsula. It uses the King Harry Ferry (you'll need some cash for the fare) to cross the River Fal before returning to Newquay.

FROM/TO Newquay, Cornwall
DISTANCE 91 miles
ALLOW 3 hours

Route Description

➤ **Leave Newquay** on the B3276 and follow it all the way to Padstow.
➤ **From Padstow** Take the A389 to Wadebridge. Carry straight on as the road becomes the B3274 to St Columb Major.
➤ **Go straight over the A39** and the A30. At the A391 roundabout, turn right to stay on the B3274 to Carthew.
➤ **After the hairpin** in St Austell centre, turn left towards Liskeard (signed for the A390, then 'Outbound traffic').
➤ **Go straight over A390** double roundabout (next to McDonald's) on the B3273 to Mevagissey.
➤ **Stay on the B3273** as it passes through Mevagissey and eventually loops back, past Heligan to a T-junction on the B3273. Turn left to retrace your route to St Austell.
➤ **A390** This time, turn left at the double roundabout towards Truro.
➤ **After 3 miles** Turn left on the B3287 to Tregony.
➤ **In Tregony** Turn left on the A3078 to St Mawes.
➤ **In St Just-in-Roseland** Turn right on the B3289 to the King Harry Ferry. Cross the river and stay on the B3289 all the way to the A39.
➤ **Take the A39 north** to Truro. Turn right on the A390 to skirt the town and stay on this road for 4½ miles.
➤ **Turn left** on the B3275 to Probus. Don't miss the left-hand fork ½ mile later to stay on the B3275 to Ladock.
➤ **At the roundabout** Turn left on the A3058 to return to Newquay.

below *Head made from plants in the Lost Gardens of Heligan*

WHAT TO SEE AND DO

Lost Gardens of Heligan
Only a quarter of a century ago, these fabulous gardens were lost under a tangle of weeds. Now you need a whole day to do justice to the 200-acre estate and the amazing woodlands, wildlife, farm and jungle.
heligan.com

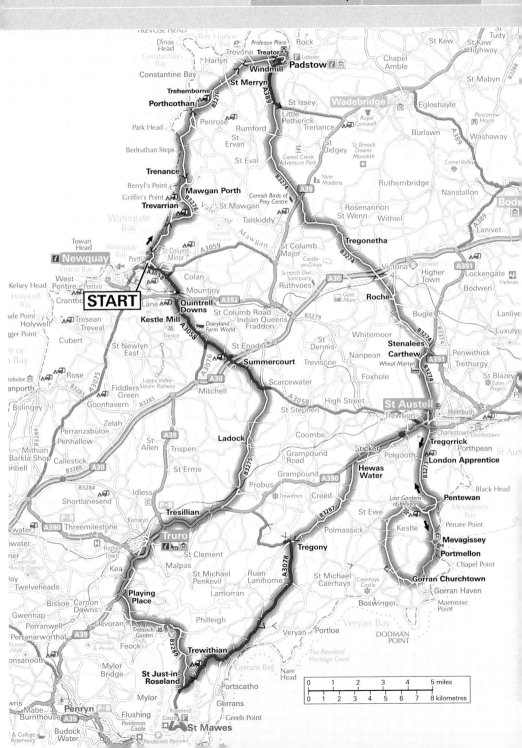

RIDE ⑥ Chichester Loop

GLORIOUS GOODWOOD – home to the Festival of Speed and the Goodwood Revival – rests at the foot of the South Downs, on the edge of the historic port of Chichester. But two-wheeled thrills aren't restricted to spectating at two great annual events, not when the riding is so great. This route uses some of our favourite roads and, even though once-legendary roads like the A272 have had increasing numbers of speed limits dropped on them in recent years, they can still deliver a glorious ride.

FROM/TO Chichester, West Sussex
DISTANCE 97 miles
ALLOW 2.5 hours

Route Description

➤ **Leave Chichester** Take the A27 and then take the A285 to Petworth.
➤ **At the second mini-roundabout** in Petworth, turn left on the A272 to Midhurst. Stay on it through Midhurst to Petersfield.
➤ **Join the A3** towards London.
➤ **At the roundabout** Turn left on the B3006 to Selborne.

➤ **At Alton** Pick up the A339 and take this all the way to just outside Basingstoke.
➤ **Look out** Take the left turn to Cliddesden (10 miles from Alton, as the A339 goes to two lanes coming into Basingstoke and you see the M3 flyover ahead). This is the B3046.
➤ **Stay on the B3046** through New Alresford until it meets the A272.
➤ **Turn left on the A272** towards Petersfield. When you get to the West Meon traffic lights, the popular biking café Loomies is just to the right on

the A32. If you don't fancy a stop, carry on along the A272.
➤ **Cross the A3** Carry on into Petersfield to pick up the B2146 to South Harting.
➤ **In South Harting** Turn right towards Emsworth and then, leaving the village, turn left on the B2141 to Chichester. When it meets the A286, turn right to Mid Lavant and keep going to return to Chichester.

below *Amazing views from the South Downs*

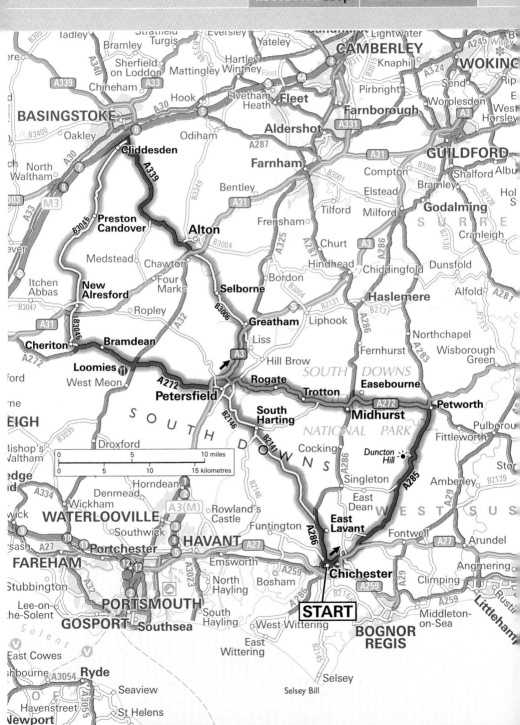

RIDE (7) Battling Round Hastings

I'VE ALWAYS STRUGGLED to find a full day's riding that satisfies me in the southeast – I've been spoiled by too many trips to Scotland, Wales and the lumpier, quieter bits of Europe. Coming back from the Alps to ride in Kent is a bit like going from a quiet country pub to a crowded, noisy rave: mind-blowing, until you adapt.

In the populous southeast there is always traffic and there are frequent speed limits – but there are still some great rides to be found. It just takes more patience and ingenuity to find them. Jumping on the first A-road you see probably won't produce the ride of the year…but turning off to explore the quieter roads might do it. You may not get an uninterrupted hour of head-down fun, but you are sure to find shorter bursts of pure riding pleasure.

FROM/TO: Hastings, East Sussex
DISTANCE: 60 miles
ALLOW: 90 minutes

Route Description

> **Take the A2690** around the edge of Hastings, from the north side of town. Go straight over the lights (as the road turns to Brighton).
> **Take the first right** for Crowhurst Road. Follow it all the way to the A2100.
> **Turn left** onto the A2100 and shortly left again, onto the B2095 to Catsfield.
> **At Catsfield** Turn right onto the B2204 towards Battle.

> **Reaching the A271** turn right onto it and quickly left onto the B2096 to Netherfield.
> **Just beyond Netherfield** at the x-roads, turn right onto a lane towards Burwash. Bear left through Brightling and to the right shortly after, to reach Burwash, and cross the A265 at x-roads.
> **Follow the lane** Ride through Stonegate, turning right at a T-junction in order to reach Shover's Green.
> **At the T-junction** Turn right onto the B2099 towards Ticehurst. Continue to A21.
> **Turn right** onto the A21, towards Hurst Green. Continue

on the A-road for 1 mile, then take a left turn onto a lane towards Bodiam.
> **Stay on the lane** through Bodiam and to Staplecross.
> **Turn left** Join the B2165 towards Rye, crossing over the A28.
> **At the A268** Turn right, to the town of Rye, and emerge on the B2089 towards Broad Oak.
> **Turn left** at the Broad Oak x-roads, onto the A28. This will lead you back to the A21 on the northern edge of Hastings.

WHAT TO SEE AND DO

Bodiam Castle This mind-blowing medieval castle rises majestically from its lake-like moat. The great gatehouse contains the original portcullis. Utterly captivating – a true must-see.
nationaltrust.org.uk/visit/sussex/bodiam-castle

1066 Battle of Hastings, Abbey and Battlefield
The site of William the Conqueror's famous victory, the abbey is a fascinating ruin. Every October sees the battle re-enacted with great aplomb.
english-heritage.org.uk/1066

Bewl Water The largest stretch of open water in southeast England, this is a great place to unwind. Fishing, watersports, a restaurant, a visitor centre and family activities are all available here.
bewlwater.co.uk

RIDE ⑦ Battling Round Hastings

| ROUTE TYPE Loop | DISTANCE 60 miles |

START

HASTINGS

Bexhill-on-Sea

| 0 | 1 | 2 | 3 | 4 | 5 miles |
| 0 | 1 | 2 | 3 | 4 | 5 | 6 | 7 | 8 kilometres |

RIDE (8) Thanet Loop

THE ISLE OF Thanet's not quite like other places. 'Planet Thanet' is how one Margate-born colleague describes it. My family are from Broadstairs, also on Thanet, so I have fond memories of sunny days on the beaches and in the arcades and ice-cream parlours when I visited as a child. It's only when you go back as an adult that you start to pay attention to its serious side

– and Thanet was the front line in the Battle of Britain. Our ride threads its way from RAF Manston and the Spitfire & Hurricane Memorial Museum down to the Battle of Britain Memorial at Capel-le-Ferne, at the top of the White Cliffs. It's a brilliant ride through the garden of England… with the finest ice-creams in Kent waiting for you back in Broadstairs.

FROM/TO Broadstairs, Kent
DISTANCE 80 miles
ALLOW 2.5 hours

Route Description

> **Take the A256** from Broadstairs to pick up the A229 towards Canterbury and London.
> **At the Monkton roundabout** go straight across on the A253 to Canterbury.
> **Don't miss** the left-hand turning 1 mile later, for Gore Street – a minor road unsuitable for HGVs. Stay on it through Plucks Gutter and on through Preston.
> **In Wingham** Turn right on the A257 to Canterbury.
> **In Canterbury** Follow the signs for Hythe and the B2068.
> **Take the B2068** all the way to the M20.
> **Go straight over** the M20 roundabout and turn left on the A20. Go straight over one roundabout – then at the next one join the M20 towards Dover for one junction.
> **Leave the M20 at J13** Take the A259 towards Folkestone Harbour.
> **Go straight over 3 roundabouts** The final one will

above *Explore the leafy lanes of Kent's quieter corners*

put you on the B2011 to Capel-le-Ferne. The Battle of Britain Memorial is at the top of the hill (a bit further on is the Clifftop Café with excellent views across the Channel).
> **From the memorial** (or café) go back down the hill towards Folkestone. Cross the first roundabout and turn right at the second one on the A260 to Hawkinge.
> **After nearly 1 mile** Turn right on the minor road to Alkham. Cross the next roundabout (don't turn left onto the A20) and continue through Alkham.

> **At the T-junction** in Temple Ewell, turn left (a tight turn) and continue to Lydden.
> **Take the first left** after leaving Lydden; the minor road to Swingfield Minnis.
> **At the A260** Turn right to Canterbury.
> **Watch out** In Barham – don't go straight, onto the A2. Turn right (after the services) and pick up the B2046 towards Aylesham.
> **In Wingham** Go straight onto the High Street – the A257 – and follow the road to Sandwich.
> **From Sandwich** Pick up the A256 to return to Broadstairs.

RIDE ⑧ Thanet Loop

ROUTE TYPE Loop **DISTANCE** 80 miles

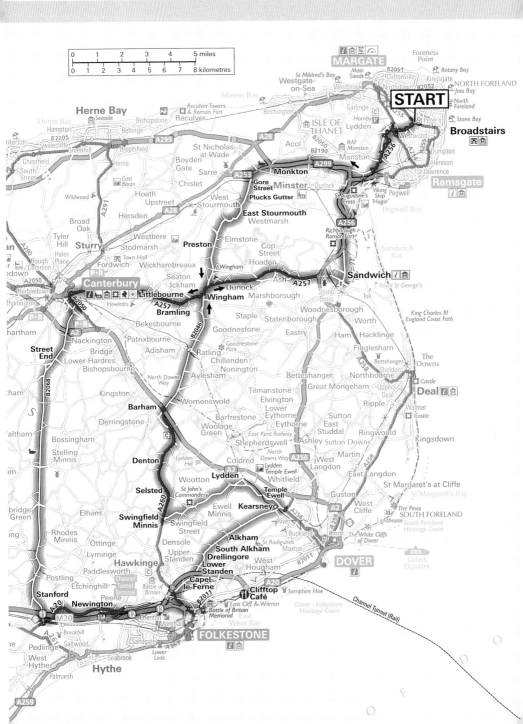

RIDE ⑨ The South Coast 500 Day 1

DAY 1 MORNING

IT SEEMED UNFAIR to us who ride bikes for a living that there was so much fuss about Scotland's North Coast 500. 'What England needs is a South Coast 500,' said tester and podcaster Simon Hargreaves, a throwaway line I picked up and filed away for future use. When the magazine I work for launched 'The Great British Ride Out' – an initiative to get readers out on their bikes a bit more by linking waypoints placed on an interactive map with good roads – I returned to the idea of the South Coast 500. I used The Great British Ride Out to create this 500-mile, two-day loop along the South Coast. It's arguably more challenging than the NC500 as there's more traffic to contend with, but we've had great feedback from people who have ridden it and written in to tell us they loved it.

FROM M20 J11
TO Lewes, East Sussex
DISTANCE 88 miles
ALLOW 3 hours

Route Description

➤ **M20 J11** Take the A20 towards Sellindge. After 1 mile, go left on the A261 to Hythe.
➤ **At Hythe** Pass the train station, go right at the lights on the A259.
➤ **New Romney** Left at lights on B2071 to Littlestone-on-Sea. At seafront, go right to Greatstone-on-Sea and follow road round.
➤ **Lydd** Left at roundabout, to Camber.
➤ **A259** Left to Rye
➤ **Rye** B2089 to Battle.
➤ **A21** Right towards London, then left at roundabout on A2100 to Battle.
➤ **Battle** Pick up the A271 to Eastbourne.
➤ **A22** Left to Eastbourne. Straight over Cophall roundabout on A27 towards Brighton, then bear left on the A2270 into Eastbourne.
➤ **After 2½ miles** turn right at the lights onto Victoria Drive, signed for Beachy Head.
➤ **A259** Right towards Seaford. In 1 mile, turn left to Beachy Head and follow the road until it rejoins the A259. Turn left to Seaford.
➤ **Newhaven** From the one-way system take the minor road to Piddinghoe. Stay on the road all the way to Lewes.

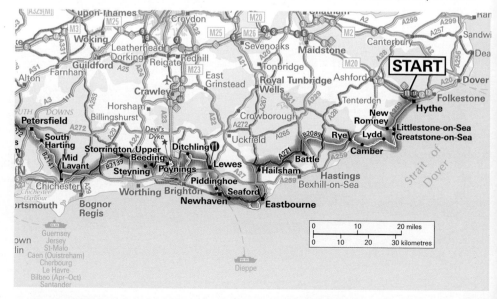

RIDE ⑨ The South Coast 500 **Day 1**

ROUTE TYPE Tour | **DISTANCE** 88 miles morning | 163 miles afternoon

DAY 1 AFTERNOON

AFTER LUNCH IN Lewes, there are spectacular roads across the South Downs and the New Forest on the way to the final destination, Weymouth.

FROM Lewes, East Sussex
TO Weymouth, Dorset
DISTANCE 163 miles
ALLOW 4.5 hours

Route Description

> **Lewes** A275 towards East Grinstead. Carry on past Offham, then turn left on B2116 towards Hassocks.
> **Ditchling** Left at mini-roundabout, then first left (Beacon Road).
> **Brighton** Join the A27 towards Worthing for 2 miles, then take the exit for Hove. At the end of the sliproad, turn right then go straight on for Devil's Dyke.
> **A281 roundabout** Left to Poynings. Follow road.
> **A2037** Left to Upper Beeding.
> **A283** Right to Steyning.

> **Storrington** Left on B2139 towards Bognor Regis.
> **A29 roundabout** Straight over on A29 towards Bognor.
> **A27** Go right to Chichester. After 3½ miles, take the exit for the A285 towards Guildford.
> **Don't miss** the left turn after ½ mile on the A285, for the minor road to Mid Lavant.
> **Mid Lavant** Left in the village, then right at mini-roundabout on A286 towards Midhurst. After 1 mile, turn left on B2141 to South Harting.
> **B2146** Right to Petersfield. Turn left in South Harting to stay on the road.
> **Petersfield** Pick up the A272 towards Winchester.
> **West Meon** Left on A32 towards Fareham.
> **Corhampton** Right at mini-roundabout on B3035 to Bishop's Waltham.
> **Bishop's Waltham** Right at roundabout on the B2177 towards Winchester.
> **Traffic lights** Left on the B3354 towards Botley.
> **Fair Oak** Right at the lights on B3037 to Bishopstoke.

> **Eastleigh** Left on A335 towards Southampton.
> **M27** Join the motorway for 7 miles, getting off at J2 for Salisbury. At the top of the ramp, turn left on A326 towards Fawley.
> **Totton** Leave A326 for the A35 to Lyndhurst.
> **Lyndhurst** Left on the A337 towards Lymington.
> **Brockenhurst** Right on the B3055 to Sway.
> **A35** Left to Christchurch. At the second roundabout, right on B3347. After 3 miles, left to Hurn on minor road.
> **Hurn** Right at roundabout on B3073 to Wimborne Minster. Go straight over double roundabout and stay on this road.
> **Canford Bottom** Left at the roundabout on the A31 towards Dorchester.
> **Bere Regis** Right on the A35 towards Dorchester. After 2 miles, exit left and take B3390 to Warmwell.
> **Warmwell** Straight over roundabout on A353 to Weymouth. To visit Portland Bill, pick up A354 to Portland.

RIDE (9) The South Coast 500 Day 2

DAY 2 MORNING

THE RETURN LEG of the South Coast 500 loops further inland, starting with some ancient wonders – from the mighty Cerne Abbas Giant to the awe-inspiring Stonehenge. However, this route is all about the riding and there's unlikely to be much time to devote to sightseeing – and who needs it, when the roads are this entertaining?

FROM Weymouth, Dorset
TO Andover, Hampshire
DISTANCE 121 miles
ALLOW 3 hours

Route Description

> **Weymouth** Take the B3157 through Chickerell.
> **Portesham** Right by the pub on minor road towards Martinstown.
> **Winterbourne Steepleton** Left on B3159 then right on A35 to Dorchester.
> **Dorchester** Left on A37 towards Yeovil. After 1 ½ miles, right on A352 to Charminster.

> **Cerne Abbas** Right in village centre to Buckland Newton (to see the giant, go ½ mile past this turning). Turn left at the T-junction and in 2 miles, take the right fork for Buckland and keep going on the B3143.
> **A3030** Right towards Stalbridge, then right on A357 to Sturminster Newton.
> **A350** Left to Shaftesbury.
> **Shaftesbury** Right on A30 to Salisbury then first right on B3081 to Melbury Abbas.
> **Don't miss** the left turn 1 mile later to stay on B3081

to Tollard Royal (this is Zig Zag Hill).
> **A354** Left to Salisbury.
> **Salisbury** A3094 to Livestock Market. Turn left on A36 and then right at the roundabout to Devizes (A360).
> **A360** Left towards Devizes, then right on the A303 (Stonehenge off to the left).
> **Amesbury** Left on A345 towards Pewsey.
> **Upavon** Right by the pub then left on A342 to Andover. At the A338, turn left then right to stay on A342 all the way to Andover.

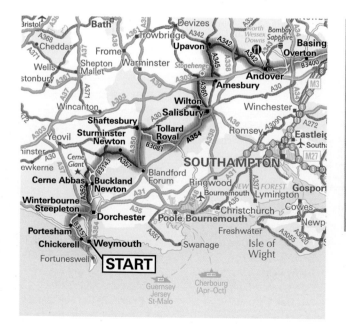

ROUTE TYPE Tour | **DISTANCE** 121 miles morning | 142 miles afternoon

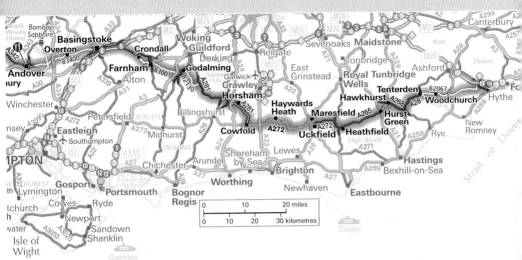

DAY 2 AFTERNOON

AFTER LUNCH IN Andover, the route continues eastwards, threading its way through bigger towns and picking out the great riding still to be found even in the busy southeast.

FROM Andover, Hampshire
TO M20 J11
DISTANCE 142 miles
ALLOW 4.5 hours

Route Description
> **Andover** Take B3400 to Basingstoke.
> **Basingstoke** Pick up the M3 for one junction, leaving at J5 for A287 to Farnham. After 5 miles, take the right turn for the minor road to Well.
> **Don't miss** the right turn to Well a few hundred yards on. Follow the road through Crondall to Farnham.

> **Farnham** Pick up B3001 to Godalming. Cross A3 to Milford and pick up A3100 to Godalming.
> **Godalming** Pick up B2130 to Cranleigh.
> **A281** Turn right to Horsham. Stick with it across Horsham town centre, all the way to Cowfold.
> **Cowfold** Left on A272 and follow this round Haywards Heath and Maresfield.
> **A267** Right to Heathfield.

Keep going straight around Heathfield as the road becomes the A265.
> **Hurst Green** Left on A21, then right after ½ mile on A229 to Hawkhurst.
> **Hawkhurst** Right on A268 towards Rye, then left on A28.
> **Tenterden** B2067 to Woodchurch. Stay on this road all the way to the A20.
> **A20** Turn right to return to the start of the route, at J11 of the M20.

WHAT TO SEE

Bombay Sapphire Distillery If gin's your tipple, take the opportunity to call in at this historic distillery at Laverstoke Mill, Whitchurch, deep in rural Hampshire. Nestled in a Conservation Area and with 1,000 years of fascinating history, an old paper mill has been transformed into a state-of-the-art distillery, where guided tours and other 'experience' packages guide you through the art of gin-making.
bombaysapphire.com/distillery

RIDE ⑩ Glastonbury Magic

THIS IS A MAGICAL RIDE, mixing A-roads and B-roads while dodging too much town riding. It was introduced to me by my mate Dan – a tough guy to follow in every sense, as he's fast, smooth, accurate – one of the most advanced of advanced riders. Trouble is, he's also a big man on a big bike – a Honda GoldWing – though he throws it about as if it is a 600cc sportsbike. He obscures much of the view ahead and, as he rarely needs to brake, that doesn't give me much warning of the corners that are coming up. And there are a lot of corners on this ride of his…We met in Dorchester, filled up and headed off for what I'd thought would be a steady tootle up to Glastonbury to see the Tor. Turns out Dan had other ideas: this is a training run on some of his favourite roads. They loop and curl past field and wood, hugging rivers then climbing hills, only to swoop down again.

Dan kept me guessing about the route. 'We'll just do the best bits of each road,' he'd promised. 'And I ain't going into Yeovil – too much traffic.'

Instead, we skirted Shepton Mallet and Sherborne, stopping for coffee in Wells. It was a magic ride, but I liked it better going back later and doing it at my own pace, without Dan spoiling the view – because that's the best bit.

FROM/TO Dorchester, Dorset
DISTANCE 105 miles
ALLOW 3 hours

Route Description

➤ **Dorchester** Take the A37 towards Yeovil and very soon turn right onto the A352 towards Sherborne.

➤ **8 miles later,** just beyond Minterne Magna, take a lane on the left towards Holywell x-roads (A37).

➤ **Turn right onto A356** and ride towards Crewkerne. Continue through the town, staying on the A356 to the major road that is the A303.

➤ **Straight across the A303** Take the B3165 towards Bower Hinton and Martock. Continue on the B-road to Long Sutton and the A372.

➤ **Cross the A372** Rejoin the B3165 to Somerton.

➤ **At Somerton** Turn right onto the B3153 for a small stretch. Turn left just outside the town and take the B3151 to meet the A361 at Street.

➤ **Turn right** onto the A361, towards Glastonbury.

➤ **Shortly turn left** onto the A39 to Wells.

➤ **At Wells** Turn right onto the A371 to Shepton Mallet. Continue through the town on the A371, passing Castle Cary to ride under the A303.

➤ **Just beyond the A303** at Lattiford, turn right onto the B3145 towards Sherborne.

➤ **At Sherborne** Turn left onto the A352 and left again onto the A3030 towards Bishop's Caundle.

➤ **At the B3143** Turn right towards King's Stag. Turn left at Duntish to continue on the B3143 all the way to Dorchester.

WHAT TO SEE AND DO

Glastonbury A lovely, quirky town crammed with historical – or should that be mystical – tourist attractions. Veggie restaurants abound. **glastonbury.uk**

Haynes Motor Museum A short detour from the route, at Sparkbrook, is this excellent automotive museum with a good café. **haynesmuseum.org**

Cerne Abbas Giant On a hillside above picturesque Cerne Abbas, the 180ft giant is thought to be a fertility symbol. It's been said that he represents the Greek god Hercules, and was probably created as a pagan idol during the Iron Age period. **nationaltrust. org.uk/visit/dorset/cerne-giant**

RIDE (10) Glastonbury Magic

ROUTE TYPE Loop | **DISTANCE** 105 miles

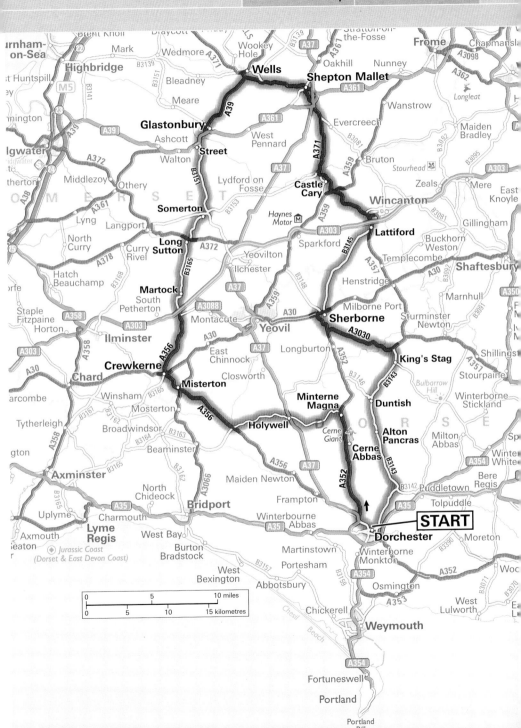

RIDE (11) Gorge-ous Cheddar

THE B3135 IS all about timing. The perfectly surfaced bends twisting tightly through the surreal natural cathedral of Cheddar Gorge should be a biking dream – but the throngs of tourists that can clog it like fat in a trucker's arteries can make it a riding nightmare. So come out of season, come in the morning – come when it's raining if you have to, because this is a spectacular road.

The gorge itself is short – not quite three miles long – and of course there may be tourists wandering around at any time, not to mention the wild goats that roam on the road as well as the verge. In other words, it's a road to ride steadily, marvelling at the views while keeping half an eye out for the unexpected.

The Mendip Hills are full of surprises. After all, you'd imagine Cheddar Gorge was a one-off – but just round the corner is Burrington Combe. Less spectacular but also less well-known, it's just as great to ride. Our route loops round through the Combe, over Cleeve Hill and down to Wells, before returning to Cheddar – though if you want something really out of the ordinary, detour to Wookey Hole. You won't regret it… just try to time it so there aren't too many tourists around.

FROM/TO Cheddar, Somerset
DISTANCE 38 miles
ALLOW 1 hour

Route Description

> **From Cheddar** Take the B3135 Cliff Road through the Gorge. Keep right to stay on this when it meets the B3371.
> **B3134** Look out for a well-signposted crossroads, where you turn left onto the B3134 to Burrington.
> **Burrington** Turn right on the A368 towards Bath.
> **West Harptree** Turn right onto the B3114 through East Harptree.
> **Chewton Mendip** Turn right on the A39 to Wells.
> **Wells** Ride into the city centre and pick up the A371 back to Cheddar.

WHAT TO SEE AND DO

Wookey Hole If you can overlook the commercial aspect of cashing in by peddling the legend of the wicked witch to kids, this place is well worth a visit for the truly spectacular caves. **wookey.co.uk**

Wells The smallest city in England is well known for its awe-inspiring 13th-century cathedral and medieval atmosphere. Plenty of good shops to browse in, too, and no shortage of quirky eating places. **wellssomerset.com**

right A rare traffic-free moment makes Cheddar's rocky scenery all the more enjoyable

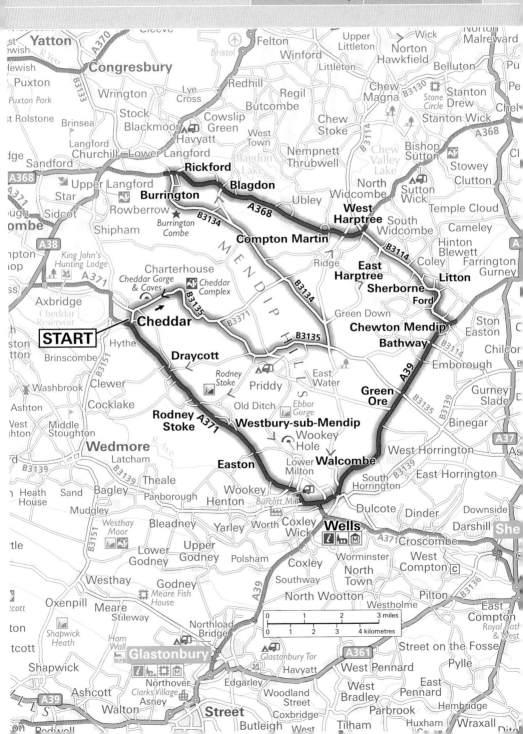

RIDE (12) Cirencester Surprise

IN MY NAIVETY (or arrogance) I thought I'd got to know the Cotswolds, because I'd bounced around between Stow-on-the-Wold and Faringdon. My mate Michael was keen to correct my ignorance (or take me down a peg or two…) so he insisted I join him for an afternoon run down to Bath from his Cirencester base. 'But why are we heading north?' I asked… Shows how little I really did know. This is my version of his route – an eye-opening blast through the quieter corners of the Cotswolds.

FROM/TO Cirencester, Gloucestershire
DISTANCE 97 miles
ALLOW 3 hours

Route Description

➤ **Leave Cirencester** on the A435 to Cheltenham.
➤ **At the double roundabout** turn left towards Gloucester on the A436.

➤ **At the next roundabout**, follow the A417 towards Cirencester.
➤ **After 1 mile** Turn right (across the dual carriageway) on B4070 to Birdlip. Don't miss the left turn after the The Royal George in Birdlip to stay on B4070 all the way to Stroud.
➤ **Cross Stroud** following

signs for Bristol A419 until (next to Sainsbury's) you pick up the B4066 to Selsley.
➤ **In Dursley** Turn right at the mini-roundabout on A4135 towards Gloucester. Cross the next one, then at the third mini-roundabout turn left on B4060 to Wotton-under-Edge.
➤ **At the war-memorial** roundabout in Wotton, go straight towards Alderley. When the road forks, bear right to Wortley.
➤ **At A46** Turn right towards Bath. After 3½ miles (a few hundred yards after the traffic lights by the Cross Hands Hotel) turn left on the minor road to Tormarton. Turn right.
➤ **At A420** Turn left towards Chippenham. Stay on the road for 6 miles, then turn left on B4039 to Castle Combe.
➤ **In Acton Turville** Turn right opposite the pub on B4040 to Malmesbury.
➤ **Stay on B4040** across Malmesbury and continue through Minety.
➤ **At the traffic lights** Turn left on B4696 and then continue on minor road to return to Cirencester.

left There's brilliant riding in the quiet corners of the Cotswolds

RIDE (12) Cirencester Surprise

ROUTE TYPE Loop | **DISTANCE** 97 miles

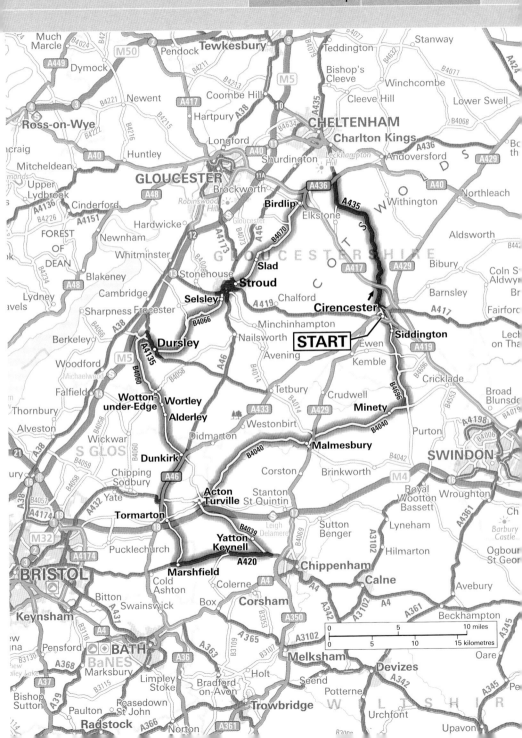

RIDE (13) Swindon Sights

SIGHTS? IN SWINDON? The sprawling town on the M4 is perhaps more famous for its connections with a certain David Brent, its Victorian railway works, modern Mini factory and its legendarily complicated 1970s dual-circulation roundabout, but the countryside around it is rich in sights from Britain's most ancient history. This pleasant ride heads out to Uffington, with its stunning White Horse, Iron Age hill fort and Wayland's Smithy, before looping its way south. On the way back to Swindon, it passes several other galloping white horses, the West Kennett Avenue and Avebury ring of megalithic standing stones.

FROM/TO Swindon, Wiltshire
DISTANCE 90 miles
ALLOW 2.5 hours

Route Description

➤ **Take the A419** along the northern edge of Swindon, turning off onto the B4019 through Broad Blunsdon to Highworth. Take the B4019 all the way to Faringdon.

➤ **Cross Faringdon** Pick up A417 towards Wantage.

➤ **After 5 miles** Turn right on B4001 towards Lambourn.

➤ **Don't miss the right turn** 2½ miles later (just after leaving Childrey) for the B4507 to Ashbury.

above *Discover white horses and Neolithic monuments on this route*

➤ **After 4 miles** Turn left on Dragon Hill Road (there's a White Horse sign on the corner pointing down the B4507; ignore it and turn left here).

➤ **Follow the road round,** pass the White Horse, turning right past Wayland's Smithy. When it meets the B4507 again, turn left and continue to Ashbury.

➤ **Turn left** in Ashbury on the B4000 to Lambourn. Turn right in Lambourn to stay on the B4000.

➤ **At Ermine Street** Turn left towards Newbury on the B4000 and after just under 1 mile, turn right on the B4001 to Chilton Foliat.

➤ **Turn left** in Chilton Foliat on the B4192, then right on the A4 towards Marlborough.

➤ **Don't miss the left turn** 5 miles later for Great Bedwyn. In 1½ miles turn right on minor road to Savernake and Burbage.

➤ **In Burbage** At the roundabout go straight on the A338 towards Salisbury.

➤ **After 6 miles** Turn right on the A342 towards Devizes.

➤ **In Upavon** Turn right on A345 towards Marlborough.

➤ **Go straight over** the roundabout on a minor road to Woodborough and stay on the road for 7 miles.

➤ **Don't miss the left turn** to East Kennett.

➤ **Go straight over** the staggered crossroads on the B4003 to Avebury.

➤ **In Avebury** Go straight, joining the A4361 to Swindon. After 4 miles, turn left on the minor road to Broad Hinton and Broad Town.

➤ **In Royal Wootton Bassett** Pick up the A3102 to return to Swindon.

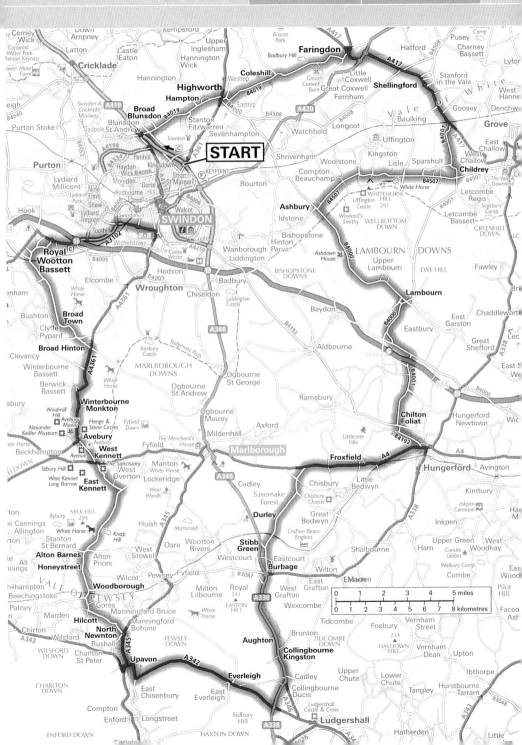

RIDE (14) Charlbury TT

THE HEART OF this route is the triangle of roads known affectionately as the Charlbury TT – the B4437, A361 and B4026. Tight in places, open and flowing in others, rushing beneath shady trees and out across open hilltops, it's the essence of all that's great about riding a bike in rural England, distilled down to a 20-mile loop.

FROM/TO Aylesbury, Buckinghamshire
DISTANCE 105 miles
ALLOW 2.5 hours

Route Description

➤ **Aylesbury** A413 to Buckingham.
➤ **Buckingham** Go left on A421 towards Brackley.
➤ **A43** Straight across A43 rbt on the B4031 to Aynho. Turn right when road meets B4100.
➤ **Aynho** Left in village, after sharp bend, to regain B4031. Carry on through Deddington.
➤ **A361** Turn left at A361 T-junction, then take next left onto B4022 signed Enstone.
➤ **A44** Across staggered x-roads on B4022 to Charlbury.

➤ **Charlbury** Right on High Street, then left towards the train station on the B4437.
➤ **A361** Turn right at the A361 T-junction.
➤ **Chipping Norton** As soon as you enter the 30 limit, turn right on the B4026 to Charlbury.
➤ **Charlbury** Turn left after the small riverside park, then straight over the x-roads on the B4437 towards Woodstock.
➤ **A44** Straight across staggered x-roads to Wootton.
➤ **Wootton** Ride past church, turning right at T-junction on the B4027 to Islip.
➤ **A4260** Straight over A4260 at staggered x-roads, staying on the B4027. For a stretch,

the road number changes to the A4095, but keep straight on as it becomes the B4027 again.
➤ **Woodperry Hill** At the chequered road signs, turn left on minor road to Horton-cum-Studley.
➤ **Horton** Turn left in the village towards Boarstall.
➤ **B4011** Turn right at T-junction with the B4011 through Oakley.
➤ **Long Crendon** Turn left at mini-rbt, towards Waddesdon. Where main road goes right in Chearsley, go straight on to Waddesdon.
➤ **A41** Turn right on the A41 to return to Aylesbury.

below *Charley Boorman and the author, Simon Weir, enjoying the B4437 on this route*

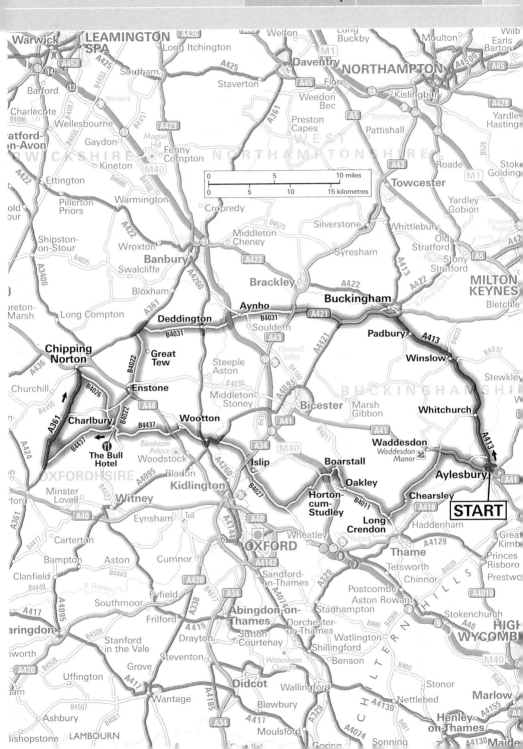

RIDE (15) Newmarket Loop

IT'S ALWAYS TEMPTING when writing about riding around Newmarket to use words like 'racing' but the reality is that only the racehorses should be looking to break records round here. The riding is outstanding but, as well as being well-policed, is deceptively demanding. The roads on this route look open and inviting, but there are any number of tight and tightening corners ready to catch out the gung-ho. This loop is best enjoyed at a sensible speed, soaking up the sunshine and enjoying the beautiful bends without scaring the horses.

FROM/TO Newmarket, Suffolk
DISTANCE 80 miles
ALLOW 2.5 hours

Route Description
> **Leave Newmarket** on B1063 towards Clare.
> **At A143** Turn right towards Haverhill.
> **After 5½ miles** Turn left on B1061 to Kedington.
> **At A1017** Turn left towards Braintree.

> **After 1 mile** Turn right on B1054 to Steeple Bumpstead.
> **In Steeple Bumpstead** Turn left on B1057 to Finchingfield. Stay on the road all the way to Great Dunmow.
> **In Great Dunmow** Turn right towards Saffron Walden on B1008. Stay on the road as it becomes B184.
> **In Thaxted** Turn left on B1051 to Stansted Mountfitchet.

> **Turn sharp right** and then take B1383 to Newport.
> **At B1052 roundabout** Turn right to Saffron Walden. Stay on B1052 across Saffron Walden to Linton.
> **Follow one-way system** through Linton, staying on the B1052 through Balsham. Stay on the road as it becomes the B1061 to return to Newmarket.

above *Storm clouds and golden fields around Saffron Walden*

WHAT TO SEE AND DO

Saffron Walden
The attractive town of Saffron Walden bustles with specialist shops and historic buildings built by the Quakers. There are the remains of a small castle, the church of St Mary (the largest parish church in Essex) and a wealth of pubs, restaurants and tea rooms at which to wet your whistle. Bridge End Garden is perfect for a leisurely post-lunch stroll.
visitsaffronwalden.gov.uk/2020/03/bridge-end-garden

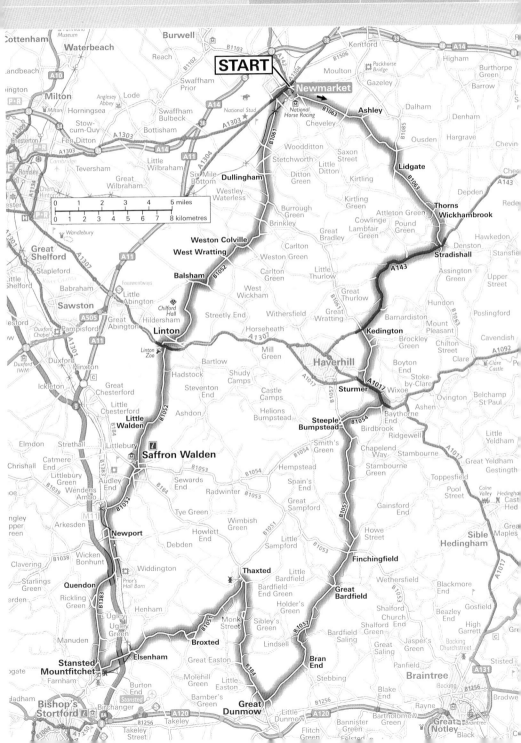

RIDE (16) The Best of Essex

WHEN MY MATE Tony moved from London to Essex, he surprised me by getting rid of his beloved sportsbike. Instead, pride of place in his new garage in suburbia went to a brand-new KTM 950 Supermoto. 'They've got the best B-roads in the world round here,' he boasted, promising to show me. Now, East End boys are often prone to exaggerating, but in this case Tony might just have got it right. In other places they'd call them A-roads: wide and well-surfaced, well signed…and definitely A-grade riding roads. Tony's staple short weekend blast is a loop out to Newmarket (he's a big fan of the horses, though you'd never guess from the shouty exhausts on the KTM). With a bit more time, it's a seaside ride to Frinton for an ice cream from a van on the esplanade (though the route shown here doesn't go all the way to the town).

'Have you ever ridden better corners?' insisted Tony after we explored Essex together for the first time. Not within such easy reach of London, I assured him. There's a beautiful flow to the roads here, great corners feeding seamlessly into open sections – and there's very little traffic.

FROM/TO Saffron Walden, Essex

DISTANCE 135 miles

ALLOW Half a day

Route Description

> **From Saffron Walden**
Take B1053 towards Radwinter and on through Steeple Bumpstead. At the A1017 turn right.

> **Turn left** on the A1092 to Clare and follow it to its end.

> **At Long Melford** Turn left onto the A134 towards Bury St Edmunds. Shortly turn right on a minor road to Lavenham.

> **Turn right at Lavenham** onto the A1141 to Hadleigh.

> **Hadleigh** Take the B1070 towards Manningtree, crossing over the A12.

> **At the A137** Turn right to Manningtree and quickly left onto the B1352, which takes you all the way to Harwich.

> **Leave Harwich** on the B1414 towards Clacton-on-Sea.

> **At Thorpe-le-Soken** Turn right on B1033, then right again on the B1035 back to the A137 near Manningtree.

> **Turn left** onto the A137 towards Colchester.

> **At Ardleigh** Turn right onto the B1029 towards Dedham and continue straight across the A12 to join a lane to Higham.

> **Turn left** onto the B1068 in Higham village and follow it through Stoke-by-Nayland, to the A134 at Leavenheath.

> **A134** Right to Sudbury.

> **At Sudbury** Take the A131 towards Halstead, shortly turning right onto a minor road to Castle Hedingham.

> **Go straight over** the A1017 x-roads and take the lane towards Finchingfield, turning right onto the B1053 to reach the village.

> **B1053** to Great Sampford. Left turn onto the B1051 will take you to Thaxted.

> **Thaxted** Turn right onto B184 to Saffron Walden.

WHAT TO SEE AND DO

Lavenham Calling itself England's finest medieval village, this beautifully preserved wool town makes a fantastic half-timbered stop.
lovelavenham.co.uk

Frinton-on-Sea This sleepy seaside town is known as a 'dry' town due to the fact it only has one pub. There are other attractions, though.
frinton.org/tourism/frinton-beach.php

Audley End One of the grandest stately homes, Audley End and its impressive gardens and miniature railway are definitely worth a visit.
english-heritage.org.uk/visit/places/audley-end-house-and-gardens

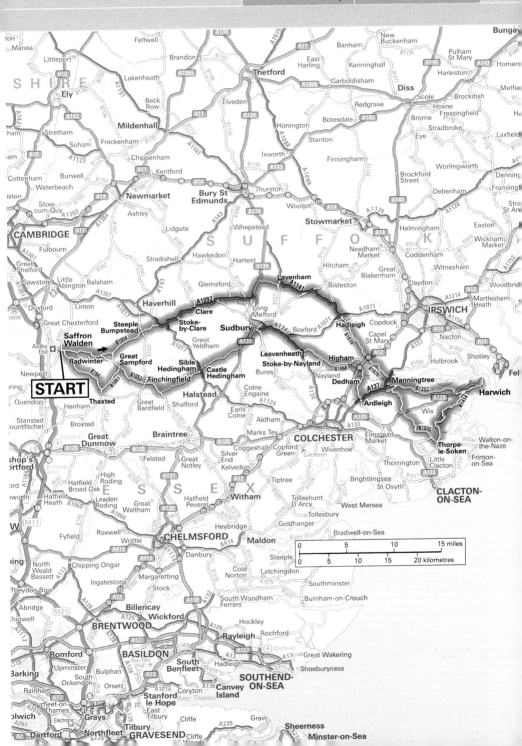

RIDE (17) A Breckland Loop

SNETTERTON MAY DRAW race fans, but how many motorcyclists visit Norfolk for the riding? Traditionally, it's the driest county in the UK so fans of riding in sunny weather should see the appeal – but how are the road conditions?

True, there are no mountains in East Anglia, but it's not all flat fenlands. This route circling Snetterton has hills, sweeping bends, shady forest roads and demanding twisty sections so it should suit every riding taste. I have a great affection for these roads – I grew up in Snetterton and learned to ride round here. Nostalgia doesn't disguise bad roads, though – nothing redeems the A11, which is functional but dull. The good roads, however, are still very good – the sweeping A1066, the tight B1077, the fantastic A134 through the forest… The riding in Norfolk may lack mountains, but it still hits some impressive highs.

FROM/TO Thetford, Norfolk
DISTANCE 66 miles
ALLOW 90 minutes

Route Description

> **Thetford** Take the A1088 towards Bury St Edmunds.
> **Ixworth** Left at the rbt on the A143 towards Diss.
> **Stanton** Turn left on the B1111 to Garboldisham.
> **Garboldisham** Turn right on the A1066 to Diss.
> **Diss** Turn left at the mini-rbt on the B1077 to Attleborough.
> **Attleborough** Follow the one-way system, turning left at the war memorial to stay on the B1077.
> **Rockland All Saints** Turn right to stay on the B1077 towards Watton.
> **B1108** Turn left at the T-junction with the B1108, taking this road straight through Watton. When you reach the roundabout go straight to stay on the B1108.
> **A1065** Turn left at the A1065 T-junction, towards Newmarket.
> **Mundford** Turn left on the A134 for the return route to Thetford.

WHAT TO SEE AND DO

Thetford Forest Park
30 miles of trails in 5,000 acres of forest as well as the chance to swing among the trees on high wires and zip wires at Go Ape.
forestryengland.uk/ thetford-forest

Bressingham Steam & Gardens Has several narrow gauge rail lines and a number of steam engines and vehicles in its collection and is also the home of a Dad's Army exhibition.
bressingham.co.uk

Dad's Army at Thetford
Many external scenes for the BBC series *Dad's Army* were filmed in Thetford, and there is a statue of Arthur Lowe as Captain Mainwaring, sitting on a park bench near the River Ouse in the town.

left *Don't panic! There's time for reflection at Pitt Mill, Thetford*

RIDE (17) A Breckland Loop

ROUTE TYPE Loop | **DISTANCE** 66 miles

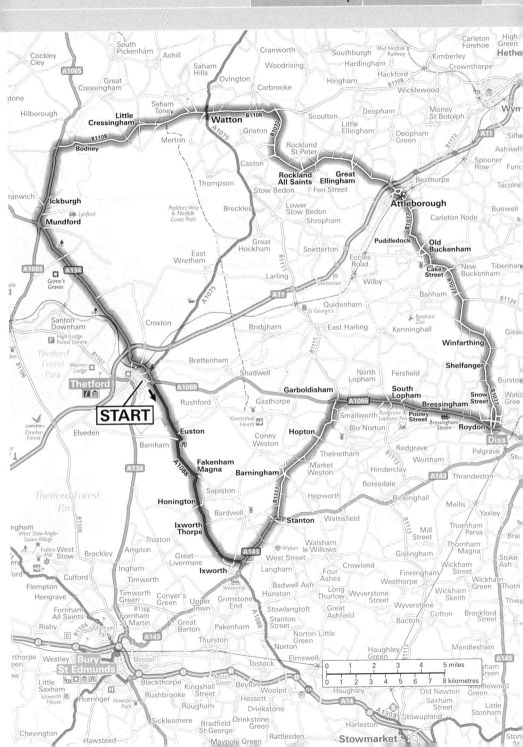

RIDE (18) Norwich North Circuit

NORWICH IS AN absolute gem of a city: compact, friendly, full of character. With only a few major A-roads in Norfolk, there are miles of quiet, twisting roads across a quintessentially English countryside, where steepled churches and cricket on the village green seem not merely natural but almost mandatory.

This route heads out from the city to the beautiful North Norfolk coast – scenic, but potentially busy, especially in summer (particularly the main A149). So approach it in a relaxed manner, enjoy the sights, stop for an ice cream, then make a bit more progress on the quieter roads back to the city.

FROM/TO Norwich, Norfolk
DISTANCE 105 miles
ALLOW 3 hours

Route Description
➤ **From Norwich** Take the B1108 to Watton.
➤ **At the lights** in Watton town centre, turn right on A1075 to Dereham.
➤ **Cross Dereham** and pick up B1146 to Fakenham.

➤ **Don't miss** the left turn 2 miles later to stay on B1146. At B1145, turn right/left at the staggered crossroads to continue on B1146.
➤ **At Fakenham** Turn right towards King's Lynn (A148), then left at the roundabout on A148 and take the first right, the B1355 to Burnham Market.
➤ **Cross Burnham Market** on B1355 and at A149 turn right

to Wells-next-the-Sea. Stay on A149 all the way through Cromer to North Walsham.
➤ **From North Walsham** Turn right on B1150 to return to Norwich.

below *The A149 can be busy at times – but is a great ride when it's quiet*

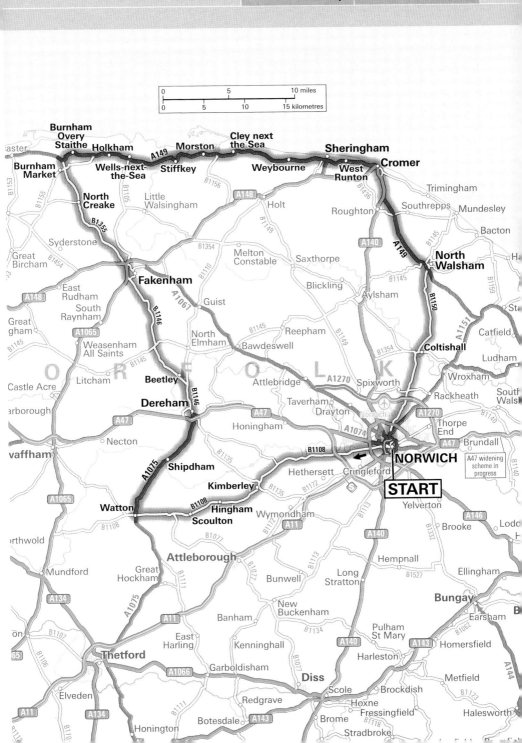

RIDE (19) Norwich South Circuit

THIS RUN OUT to the Suffolk coast and the charming town of Aldeburgh consists of two loops, so is easily shortened to return to Norwich from Harleston if you're short of time. It's worth doing the full ride, though: I was at sixth form in Diss when I got my full licence and would find any excuse to ride the roads between Harleston and the coast. Even more so on powerful modern bikes, rather than the rattly old things I first rode, these are deeply satisfying roads with a near-ideal corner-to-straight ratio – and still with a blissful lack of traffic to spoil the ride.

FROM/TO Norwich, Norfolk
DISTANCE 110 miles
ALLOW 3.5 hours

Route Description

> **Leave Norwich** on the A146 towards Loddon. At the first set of lights after the A47 Norwich Bypass, turn right on the B1332 to Poringland.
> **At A143 roundabout** Turn right, then at the next roundabout turn left to go into Bungay. Cross the town centre and pick up the B1062 to Homersfield.
> **Rejoin A143** for 1½ miles and at the roundabout turn right to go into Harleston.

> **At the end** of Harleston high street turn left to Fressingfield and Halesworth (B1123).
> **Go under the A143** and take the second left the B1123 to Halesworth. Cross Halesworth following signs for Southwold to stay on B1123.
> **Turn right on A145** then right on A12.
> **In Blythburgh** Take the left fork after the pub (signed for village only). Stay on the road as it becomes B1125 to Leiston.
> **Turn left at B1122** to Leiston. Turn left at the lights for Leiston town centre and follow B1122 to Aldringham.

> **Turn left on B1353** to Thorpeness and stay on the road along the seafront to reach Aldeburgh.
> **From Aldeburgh** Take A1094 towards Ipswich.
> **Don't miss the right turn** after about 3 miles for the B1121 to Saxmundham.
> **Turn left** at the lights in Saxmundham. Turn right then left at A12 to take the B1119 to Framlingham.
> **Go straight over** the mini-roundabout in Framlingham and keep going straight on the B1116 to Dennington. Stay on this road all the way to Harleston.
> **In Harleston** Turn right at the T-junction, then take the first left for the minor road to Starston. Stay on the road through Pulham Market, all the way to the A140.
> **At roundabout** go straight across onto B1134 to Attleborough. Turn right when it meets the B1077.
> **After 1 mile** Turn right at the crossroads on the B1113 and take this road back to Norwich.

left *Suffolk's roads have a near-ideal corner-to-straight ratio*

RIDE ⑲ Norwich South Circuit

ROUTE TYPE Loop | **DISTANCE** 110 miles

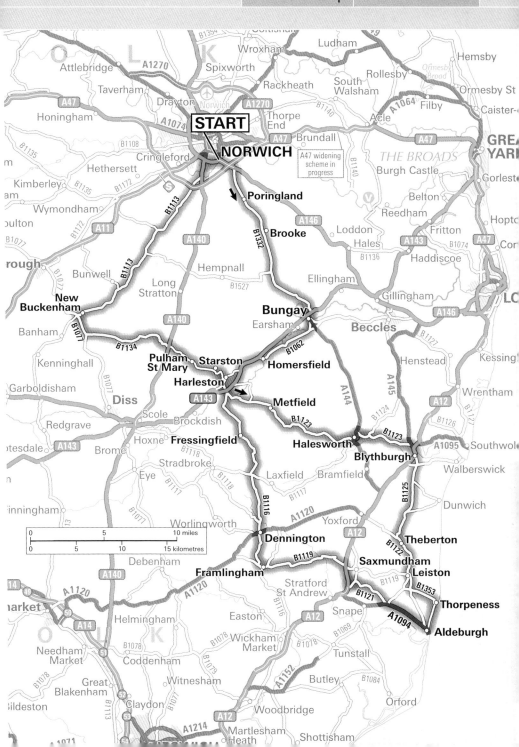

RIDE (20) The Fenland TT

THE FLATLANDS OF the Fens hold a riding challenge that is uniquely their own: it's not the elevation but the undulation that make these roads so demanding. Roads that look arrow-straight on the map turn out to be rippled like a rucked-up carpet, waves of tarmac frozen in lumps and troughs capable of kicking a speeding bike (or indeed Transit van) into the air. Speeds have to be moderate or bike and rider can be hurled into one of the deep dykes that run beside the roads.

Then there are the corners. Cambers and road conditions vary vastly but tightness is pretty uniform: there are more 90° bends than MC Escher's plumbing. When you find a tight turn at the end of a long, bumpy straight, the riding can be taxing, to put it mildly.

In other words, this is proper biking country – but needs to be approached sensibly. This route around the Isle of Ely showcases all the brilliant but very different riding to be found on the Fens.

FROM/TO Ely, Cambridgeshire
DISTANCE 80 miles
ALLOW 2.5 hours

Route Description
➤ **Leave Ely** on the A142 towards March.
➤ **At Chatteris** Turn right on the A141 to March.
➤ **After 3 miles** Turn left on the B1093 towards Wimblington. Then turn left towards Doddington and stay on the B1093 all the way to Whittlesey.
➤ **In Whittlesey town centre** Turn left at the first roundabout, then right at the second one on the B1040 to Thorney. Continue on the B1040 to Crowland.
➤ **At Crowland** Turn right on A16 towards Spalding, then take the first right for the B1166 to Wisbech.
➤ **Turn left** in Parson Drove on to the B1166 and then the B1169 to Wisbech.
➤ **In Wisbech** Pick up A1101 towards Downham Market.

above *Breathtaking Ely Cathedral*

➤ **At the mini-roundabout** in Outwell turn right, then turn left past the church to stay on the A1101. Take this road all the way to Littleport.

➤ **Cross the A10** into Littleport and turn right at the town centre roundabout to return to Ely.

RIDE 20 The Fenland TT

ROUTE TYPE Loop | **DISTANCE** 80 miles

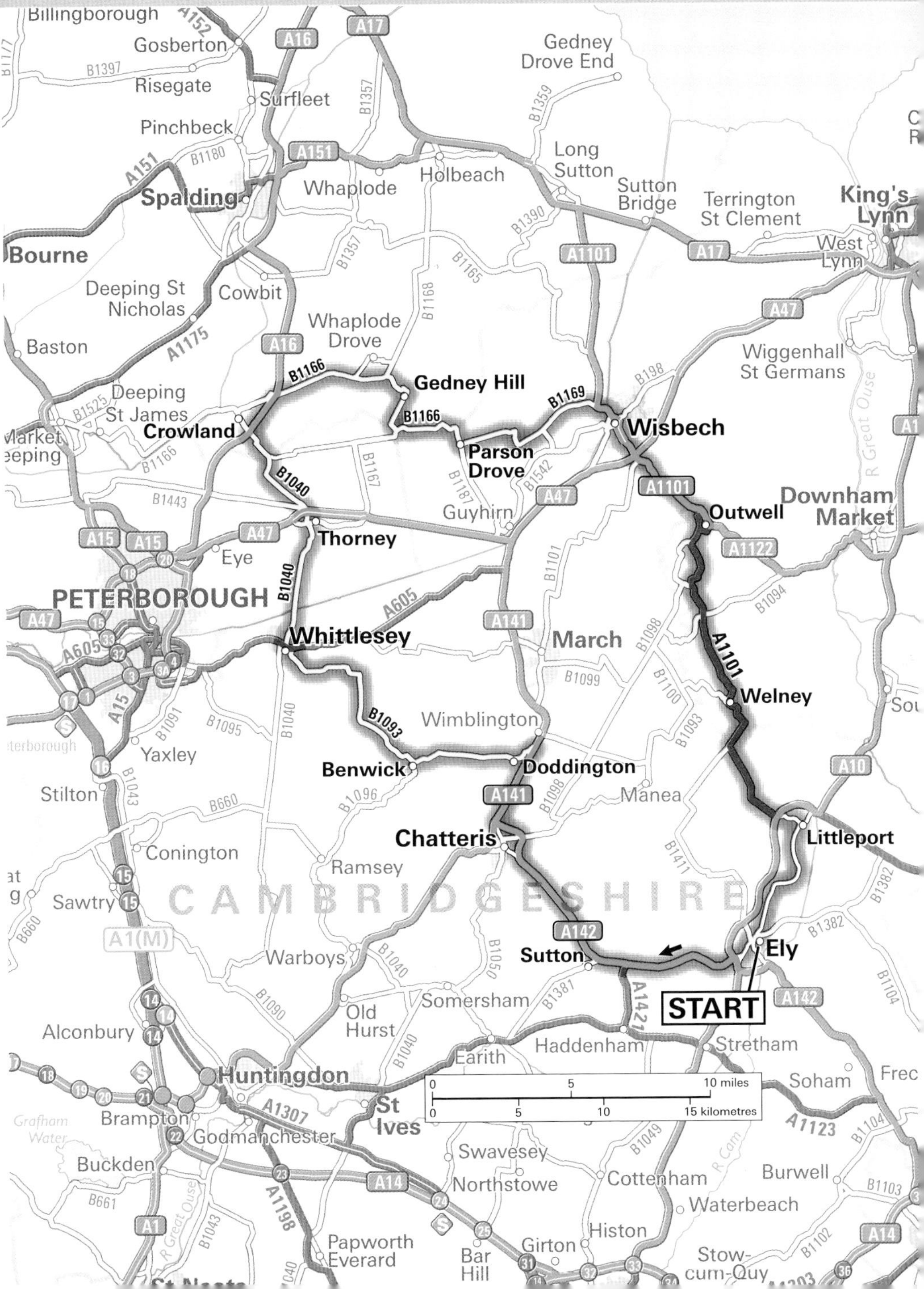

Billingborough
Gosberton
Risegate
Surfleet
Pinchbeck
Spalding
Bourne
Whaplode
Holbeach
Gedney
Drove End
Long
Sutton
Sutton
Bridge
Terrington
St Clement
King's
Lynn
West
Lynn
Deeping St
Nicholas
Cowbit
Baston
Market
eeping
Deeping
St James
Crowland
Whaplode
Drove
Gedney Hill
Wisbech
Wiggenhall
St Germans
Parson
Drove
Guyhirn
Outwell
Downham
Market
Thorney
Eye
PETERBOROUGH
Whittlesey
March
Welney
Benwick
Wimblington
Doddington
Manea
Littleport
Yaxley
Stilton
Chatteris
Ramsey
Conington
Sawtry
CAMBRIDGESHIRE
Warboys
Sutton
Ely
Alconbury
Old
Hurst
Somersham
Haddenham
Stretham
Soham
Frec
START
Huntingdon
Brampton
Godmanchester
St
Ives
Swavesey
Northstowe
Cottenham
Burwell
Waterbeach
Buckden
Papworth
Everard
Bar
Hill
Girton
Histon
Stow-
cum-Quy

0   5   10 miles
0   5   10   15 kilometres

RIDE (21) Huntingdon Loop

THIS ROUTE IS built around one of the best biking roads in Bedfordshire: the B660. It's one of those unexpectedly brilliant roads that manages to take the job of linking sleepy villages and elevate it to an art form expressed with elegant curls of tarmac, getting the best out of the very gently rolling hills to deliver more smiles per hour than is strictly decent. Even the 50mph limit dumped on it south of Kimbolton doesn't spoil the fun. The best thing about the B660, though, is the way it links so effortlessly with other great roads for a brilliant afternoon of riding.

FROM/TO Huntingdon, Cambridgeshire
DISTANCE 98 miles
ALLOW 3 hours

Route Description

➤ **From the Tesco roundabout** on the A141 on the north side of Huntingdon, take the minor road to Abbots Ripton, where it becomes the B1090.

➤ **1½ miles** after the railway bridge in Abbots Ripton, turn right to Wood Walton to stay on the B1090.

➤ **At the roundabout** Turn right on B1043 to Conington. Cross three more roundabouts then, after 1½ miles turn right then left on B660 to Glatton.

➤ **At the T-junction** after Winwick turn left, then ½ mile after leaving Old Weston turn left again to stay on B660.

➤ **Turn left on the B645**, cross Kimbolton then turn right to continue on the B660.

➤ **At the first roundabout** in Bedford, turn left. Keep going straight until there's no straight-ahead option, turn left ('Other routes') on A4280.

➤ **At A421** double roundabout turn right on the minor road to Great Barford.

➤ **Turn right** in Great Barford. Cross the river and turn right to Willington.

➤ **In Willington** Turn left on A603 to Moggerhanger.

➤ **At T-junction** Turn right towards Upper Caldecote. Stay on this road as it becomes the B658 all the way to Shefford.

➤ **At roundabout** Turn left onto A600 and at next roundabout turn left onto the A507. Follow the A507 towards Baldock.

➤ **Go straight** over the A1 roundabout, turn right by the services then take the first left on the minor road to Newnham.

➤ **At the T-junction** Turn right through Newnham. Cross Ashwell and at the T-junction turn right towards Ashwell station.

➤ **At the next T-junction** Turn left towards The Mordens and after Steeple Morden turn left into Trap Road. Stay on this road to Wrestlingworth.

➤ **Go straight** over the x-roads, through Wrestlingworth, on the B1042 to Potton.

➤ **In Potton** Turn right on the B1040. Turn right then left on the A428 to continue on the B1040.

➤ **At A1198** roundabout, turn left to return to Huntingdon.

left *Dazzling riding on the Huntingdon Loop*

RIDE ㉑ Huntingdon Loop

ROUTE TYPE Loop | **DISTANCE** 98 miles

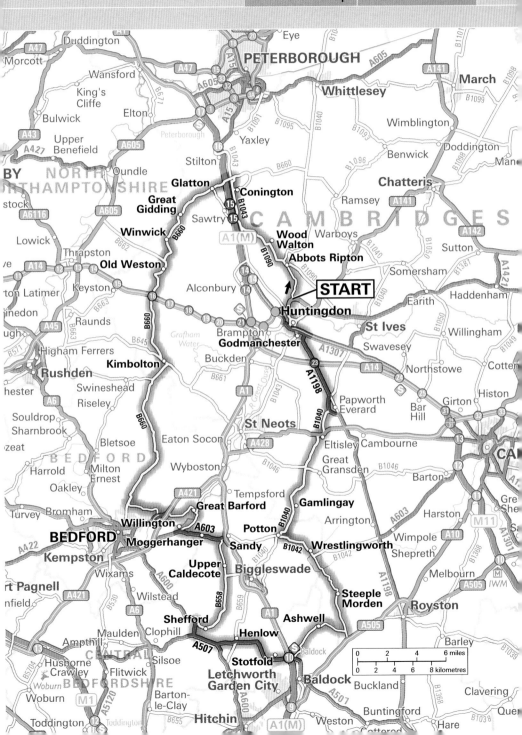

START (near Abbots Ripton / Huntingdon)

RIDE (22) The Rutland TT

SOME OF THESE roads may look oddly familiar if you read a lot of motorcycle magazines. This is because the heart of the UK's motorcycle-magazine business is in Peterborough – not a million miles from Rutland. Over the years, there have been countless road tests conducted and photographed on these roads (and others in the area). As you ride round it, you may not remember which bike you saw scraping its footpegs on the Uppingham hairpin, but there might be the merest tingle of déjà vu as you wonder where you've seen that corner, that viaduct, that invitingly flowing road before…

The Latin motto for the tiny county of Rutland is *Multum in Parvo* – which very loosely translates as 'lots in a small space'. It's appropriate, as this quiet corner of the country is crammed with lovely countryside and excellent roads. So what are you waiting for?

FROM/TO Melton Mowbray, Leicestershire
DISTANCE 95 miles
ALLOW 2.5 hours

Route Description

> **From Melton Mowbray**
Take B6047 south, towards Market Harborough.
> **At the A6** Just before Market Harborough, turn left to by-pass the town.
> **Turn left onto A427** Almost immediately turn left again, onto B664 towards Uppingham.
> **At Uppingham** Turn right onto A6003 towards Corby.
> **At Caldecott** Turn left onto the B672 to Morcott and follow signs to stay on the road all the way to the outskirts of Morcott village.
> **Cross the A47** to the right. Take the A6121 towards Stamford.
> **Telegraph Hill roundabout** Turn left, following the road all the way to Edith Weston.
> **At Edith Weston** Turn right at the mini-roundabout.

> **A606** When the road past Rutland Water meets the A606, turn right towards Stamford. After about 4 miles, look for the x-roads (the first junction along this road) and turn left towards Ingthorpe. If you reach the A1, you've missed it.
> **At Great Casterton** Go straight over the x-roads, past the school.
> **At Ryhall** Turn left on the B1176 towards Careby. In Swinstead, turn left to stay on this road.
> **At Corby Glen** Turn left on the A151. Leave the village and turn right at the top of the hill on the B1176 towards Burton Coggles.
> **Spitalgate roundabout** Turn left on the B6403 to Colsterworth. About 4 miles after the railway bridge (as you see the A1) turn left to cross the A1 and go into Colsterworth.
> **Colsterworth** Turn right at the end of the High Street on the B676 to return to Melton Mowbray.

WHAT TO SEE AND DO

The OK Diner A slight detour at Great Casterton, where the route first crosses the A1, will lead you to the finest burgers and milkshakes around. okdiners.com

Woolsthorpe Manor One for history and science buffs: Isaac Newton's home, complete with historic apple tree. Decent visitors' centre makes an interesting stop. nationaltrust.org. uk/visit/nottinghamshire-lincolnshire/woolsthorpe-manor

Rutland Water One of the largest artificial lakes in Europe, a good place to indulge in some water sports or a spot of birdwatching. anglianwaterparks.co.uk/rutland-water

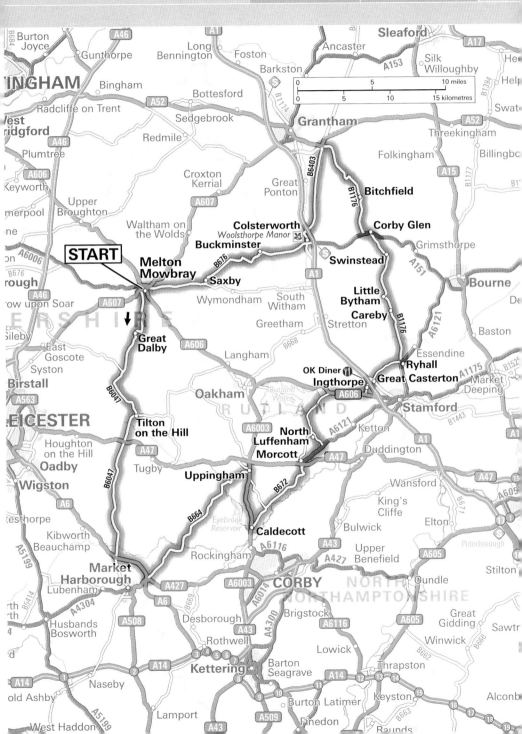

RIDE (23) Towcester Loop

THERE MUST BE something in the water around Towcester. There's a greyhound racing track and there's a motor racing circuit: Silverstone, home to the British Grand Prix. Coincidentally, it's also where the headquarters of the UK arms of KTM and Ducati are based. After a morning meeting, I decided to get off the main A43 and start exploring the country lanes – I had all afternoon to play with and the sun was shining… I set off gently but gradually found myself enjoying the twisting back lanes more and more. Not racing about, for sure, but definitely having more fun than I'd expect to have on an average weekday afternoon. There's indesputably something very special in the water around Towcester.

FROM/TO Towcester, West Northants
DISTANCE 116 miles
ALLOW 3 hours

Route Description
> **From Towcester services/ McDonald's** on A43, take the minor road to Abthorpe.
> **After 8 miles** Turn right on B4525 to Middleton Cheney.
> **At A422 roundabout** Turn right to Banbury. At the next roundabout, take the fourth exit: A361 to Daventry.
> **Bear right** on the road round Daventry, then from the roundabout follow signs for Daventry Country Park until picking up B4036 to Long Buckby.
> **Stay on the road** through Long Buckby as it becomes the B5385.
> **At A428** Turn left towards Rugby.
> **Join A5** to Hinckley.
> **In Hinckley** Pick up A47 towards Earl Shilton (this passes the Triumph factory).

> **After 5 miles** Turn right on B581 to Elmesthorpe. Go left at B4114 then instantly right at the lights to stay on B581 to Dunton Bassett.
> **In Dunton Bassett** Turn right at the traffic lights on A426 towards Rugby.
> **Cross Lutterworth** and turn left on A4304 towards Market Harborough.
> **In Husbands Bosworth** Turn right on A5199 towards Welford (A14).
> **In Chapel Brampton** Turn right on the minor road to Church Brampton.
> **At A428** Turn left to Northampton.
> **At first set of lights** in the town centre, turn right then right again on A4500 then left onto A5076. At roundabout for Pineham Village, take the minor road signed for Pineham, then turn left at the lights to Rothersthorpe.
> **At A5** Turn left to return to Towcester.

WHAT TO SEE AND DO

Triumph Visitor Experience This spectacular immersive museum traces historic and modern motorcycle design and showcases legendary iconic motorcycles. **triumphworld.co.uk/ triumph-factory-visitor-experience**

Daventry Country Park Is a 160-acre local nature reserve and country park in Daventry. Includes a bird hide, a nature trail, an adventure playground and a café. **westnorthants.gov.uk/ daventry-country-park**

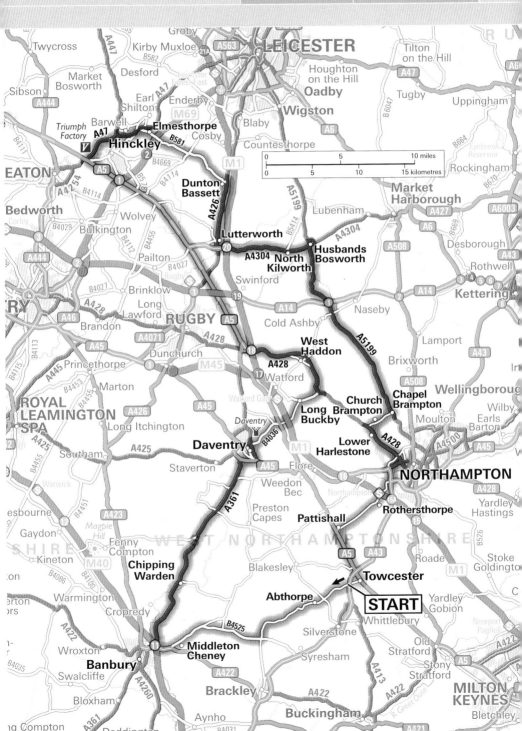

RIDE (24) Evesham Loop

WHAT DOES THE essence of England look like? For plenty of people, it looks very much like these thatched cottages of honey-coloured stone clustered within earshot of the bells of a serene-looking church. Villages are surrounded by rich, well-tended farmland dotted with woods and criss-crossed by clear streams. Better for bikers, this idyllic countryside is traversed by a network of brilliant roads. On most bikes this compact ride represents less than a tankful of pure pleasure – 110 laid-back miles swooping and twisting through the heart of the Cotswolds. Just take care on the descent of Fish Hill (the A44) as the notorious hairpin bend has caught out more than its fair share over the years.

FROM/TO Evesham, Worcestershire
DISTANCE 110 miles
ALLOW 3 hours

Route Description

➤ **Leave Evesham** on the B4035 to Badsey.
➤ **In Weston-sub-Edge** Turn left towards Stratford-upon-Avon on the B4632.
➤ **In just over ½ mile** (after a tight right) go straight – effectively a right turn – when the road bends hard left, taking B4035 to Chipping Campden.

➤ **Go into Chipping Campden** village centre and pick up the B4081 towards Moreton-in-Marsh.
➤ **At the A44** Turn right towards Evesham.
➤ **At the second roundabout** Turn left on the B4632 to Childswickham.
➤ **Don't miss the right turn** in Broadway village to stay on B4632 towards Winchcombe.
➤ **In Toddington** Turn left at roundabout on B4077 to Stow.
➤ **In Stow-on-the-Wold** Turn right, then left at the lights on

the A429 towards Stratford.
➤ **After 9 miles** Turn right on the B4035 to Shipston-on-Stour and stay on the road all the way to Banbury.
➤ **From Banbury** Take the A422 past Drayton.
➤ **At the Ettington roundabout** Turn right on the A429 towards Warwick.
➤ **At M40 roundabout** Take the first exit. Go straight over next roundabout on B4463 to Henley-in-Arden.
➤ **At the A4189** Turn left to Claverdon.
➤ **At the lights** in Henley-in-Arden, turn left towards Stratford on the A3400.
➤ **After 1½ miles** Turn right on the B4089 to Great Alne. Shortly turn left to Little Alne.
➤ **At Alcester** Follow the 'through traffic' signs to A435 then the A422 to Evesham.
➤ **At the A441** Turn left to Evesham and go straight as it becomes the B4088. Turn right in Dunnington to stay on the B4088 and take it all the way back to Evesham.

left You don't need a big engine to enjoy these roads

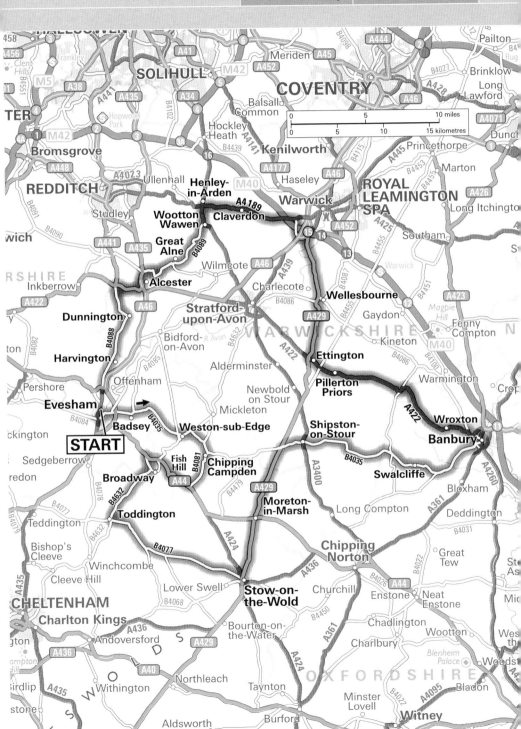

RIDE (25) Ludlow North Loop

THE LAND BETWEEN Birmingham and Wales is rich in spectacular riding, but how many people go there? With the Welsh biking honeypots of the Brecon Beacons and Eryri (Snowdonia) so close – little more than another hour away – it's easy for touring riders to buzz straight past, heading for the famous roads. No harm in that, of course, but it does mean missing some real gems along the way. The next two rides are centred around Ludlow, an unspoilt market town in the Welsh Marches. This first one goes north up to Shrewsbury and back again, while the southern route takes you down to Hereford before returning to Ludlow.

FROM/TO Ludlow, Shropshire
DISTANCE 90 miles
ALLOW Half a day

Route Description

> **From Ludlow** Take A4117 towards Kidderminster, soon turning left onto B4364 to Bridgnorth.
> **At Bridgnorth** Go through town centre to emerge on B4373 towards Ironbridge.
> **Stay on the B4373** around outskirts of Broseley and cross River Severn, bearing left.
> **At next main junction** go straight across, signed Coalbrookdale Museums.
> **Turn right onto A4169** and soon left, onto the B4380 towards Shrewsbury.
> **At T-junction** Turn left onto B5061 towards Shrewsbury, continuing straight on as it becomes B4380 again and meets A5.
> **Turn left onto A5,** the Shrewsbury by-pass, leaving it at A488 to ride to and through Bishop's Castle.
> **In central Clun** Carry straight on to follow signs for B4368 towards Craven Arms.
> **At Purslow x-roads** Turn right onto the B4385 towards Leintwardine.
> **Continue towards Leintwardine** Stay on road as it becomes B4367.
> **Through Bucknell** Turn left onto the A4113 towards Ludlow and Leintwardine.
> **At the T-junction** Turn left to continue towards Ludlow on the A4113.
> **In Bromfield** Turn right onto the A49 to complete the short ride back to Ludlow.

WHAT TO SEE AND DO

Ludlow Castle One of the finest medieval ruins in England. The castle has superb views over the Shropshire countryside. **ludlowcastle.com**

Attingham Park An 18th-century estate for all seasons with 200 acres of parkland and Regency Mansion. **nationaltrust.org.uk/visit/shropshire-staffordshire/attingham-park**

Clun Castle One of the many castles in the area, Clun is now just a picturesque ruin. **english-heritage.org.uk/visit/places/clun-castle**

left Beautiful Ludlow Castle

RIDE 25 Ludlow North Loop

ROUTE TYPE Loop | **DISTANCE** 90 miles

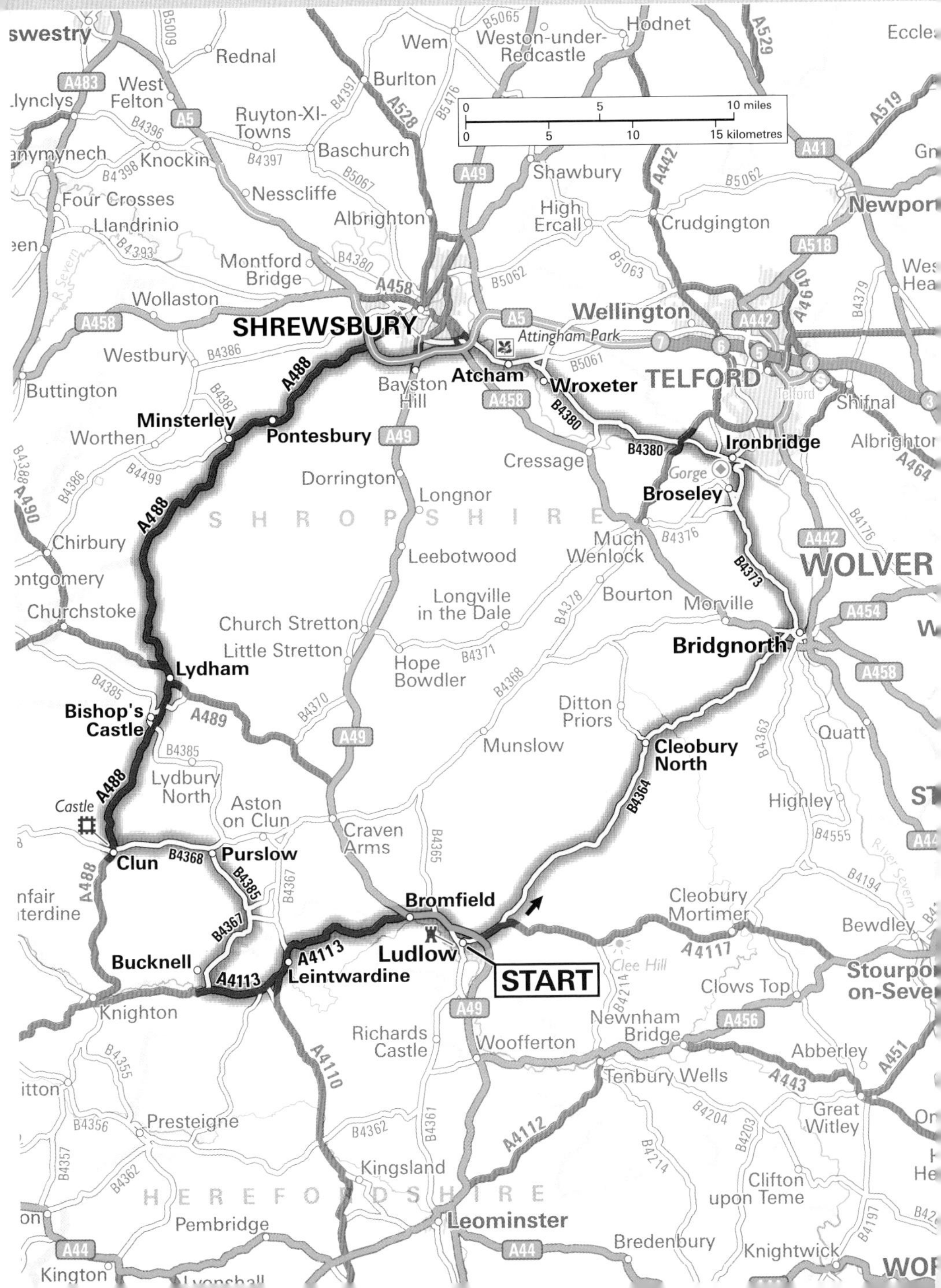

RIDE (26) Ludlow South Loop

AT FIRST GLANCE, Ludlow might seem like an odd town to use as a base for a riding holiday. It's a sleepy, unspoilt market town in the Welsh Marches, studded with Tudor buildings and crammed with character (if you like historic castles, Ludlow's a cracker). It's a small town, easy to explore in the evening without getting lost. But it's the roads *around* Ludlow that make this town such a good base for exploring on

a motorbike. The scenery is breathtaking – rolling hills draped with superb tarmac offering huge views, until the next bend drops down between trees or tall hedges, demanding all your concentration. There are none of the blanket speed limits that blight the southeast and very little traffic – just engaging roads, quiet countryside and fresh, fresh air. Lovely.

FROM/TO Ludlow, Shropshire
DISTANCE 96 miles
ALLOW Half a day

Route Description

➤ **From Ludlow** Take A4117 towards Kidderminster, staying on it through Cleobury Mortimer.
➤ **At Callow Hill** Turn right onto A456 towards Leominster.
➤ **At Newnham Bridge** Go left onto A443 towards Worcester.
➤ **Great Witley** Bear right at

fork in road to stay on A443, then take right turn on B4197 through Martley.
➤ **A44** When road meets A44, turn left towards Worcester.
➤ **Just before city** Right at rbt onto A4103 towards Hereford.
➤ **Approaching Hereford** Stay on A4103 towards Holmer.
➤ **Continue** straight across the A49 signed Stretton Sugwas.
➤ **At the A4110** Turn right towards Canon Pyon.
➤ **Stay on the A4110** crossing

the A44, to Wigmore. At x-roads in Wigmore signed castle and Ludlow, follow the narrow lane back to the start at Ludlow.

WHAT TO SEE AND DO

West Midlands Safari Park A 200-acre site with all your favourite creatures. There's a drive-through safari and a gang of amusing meerkats.
wmsp.co.uk

Museum of Cider Explore the fascinating history of cider: cider-making equipment, cooper's workshop, cider cellars and more.
cidermuseum.co.uk

Clee Hills A range of hills including Brown Clee Hill and Titterstone Clee Hill. A great place to stop and eat your sandwiches and gaze out over miles of landscape.

left *Early evening at Clee Hills*

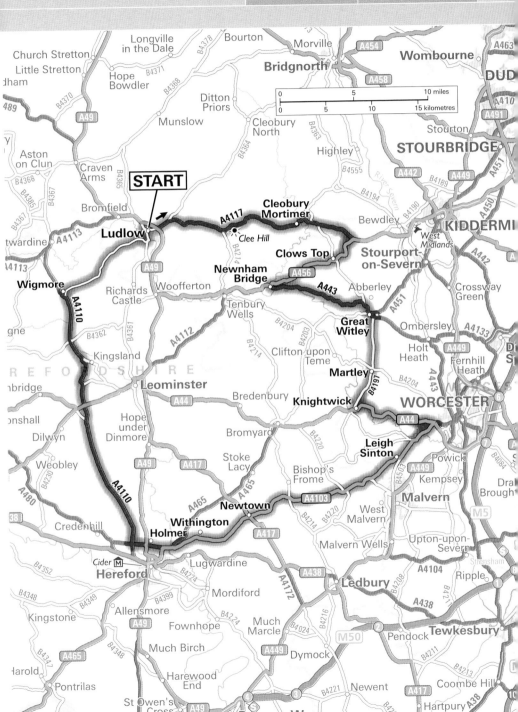

RIDE (27) Whitchurch Loop

YOU DON'T NECESSARILY need to pile on the miles to have a great ride. This Midlands cracker is an easily enjoyed 73 miles long – a cheeky little Saturday morning blast if you're local, or simple to tack on to the journey to and from the start point if you're not. And though it was pieced together from a Whitchurch base, it's not at all hard to adjust it to run from Stafford, Crewe or even – at a push – Stoke-on-Trent, if that's where you'll pick it up.

FROM/TO Whitchurch, Shropshire
DISTANCE 73 miles
ALLOW 2 hours

Route Description

> **Leave Whitchurch** on the A525 towards Newcastle-under-Lyme.
> **Stay on the road** as it becomes the A530 to Nantwich.
> **Nantwich** Turn right on the A529 to Audlem.
> **Audlem** Turn left at the war memorial on the A525 towards Newcastle-under-Lyme.
> **In Woore** Turn right at the lights on the A51 towards Stone.
> **In ¾ mile** Turn right on the B5026 to Eccleshall. Go straight over the staggered crossroads in Loggerheads to stay on the road.
> **In Eccleshall** Turn right at the first mini-roundabout then left at the second on the A5013 towards Stafford.
> **In Great Bridgeford** Turn right on the B5405 to Woodseaves.
> **In Woodseaves** Turn left on the A519 to Sutton.
> **Straight over A41 rbt**, taking the B5062 into Newport. When it reaches a T-junction, turn right then left to stay on the B5062 towards Shrewsbury.
> **In Crudgington** Turn right on the A442 to Whitchurch.
> **At the A53 roundabout** Go straight over on minor road to Hodnet. Follow the road (which eventually becomes the B5063).
> **At the A41** Turn left to Whitchurch.
> **At the A49 roundabout** Turn right to complete the loop.

below *Three's not always a crowd*

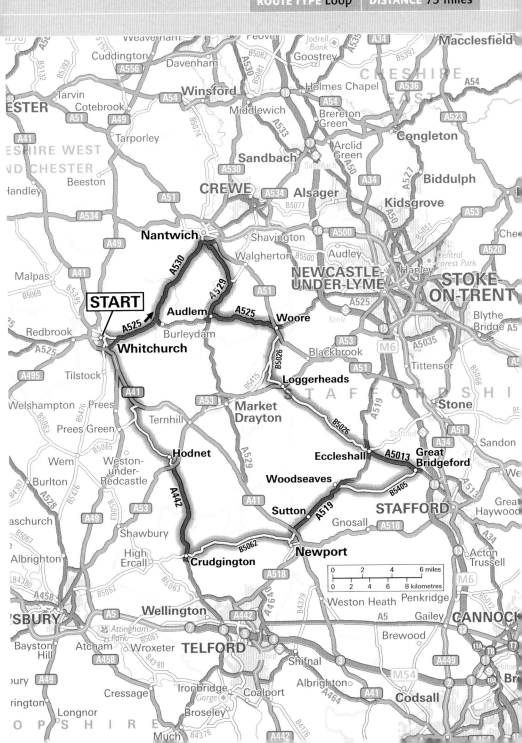

RIDE (28) The Midland 300 Day 1

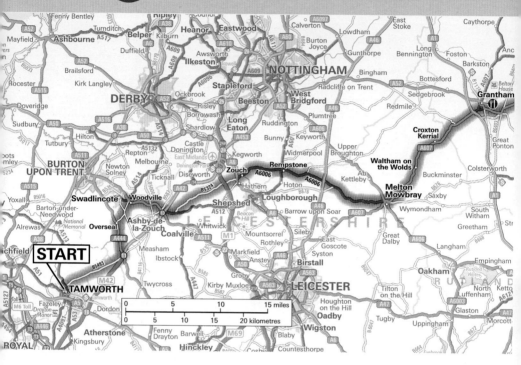

DAY 1 MORNING

THE CURSE OF the Midlands – or perhaps their real blessing – is that so few people realise how great the riding is. So many hurry past from the south, intent on reaching the Peak District, Yorkshire or Scotland… when in fact there are some astonishing roads hidden in the leafy heart of England. Experienced high-mile riders looking for a challenge might pack our Midland 300 ride from Tamworth to the coast into one long sunny day in the height of summer, but it's better as a relaxed two-day tour – an ideal weekend break.

FROM Tamworth, Staffordshire
TO Grantham, Lincolnshire
DISTANCE 60 miles
ALLOW 2 hours

Route Description

> **Leave Tamworth** on the B5493 towards Ashby-de-la-Zouch and Nottingham.
> **At M42 roundabout** turn left on the A444 towards Burton upon Trent.

> **After 4 miles** Turn right at the roundabout on the minor road to Albert Village. Go over the crossroads by the clock tower.
> **At the first roundabout** Turn right, then turn left at the next one, on the minor road towards Swadlincote.
> **At the Woodville roundabout** Turn right on the high street – A511 towards Leicester.

> **At A42 roundabout** Take the third exit for the A512 towards Loughborough.
> **After 1 mile** Turn left on the B5324 towards Hathern.
> **At A6 lights** Turn left then right onto the A6006 to Melton Mowbray. Stay on A6006 all the way to Melton.
> **Melton Mowbray** Through town centre and pick up the A607 to Grantham.

| ROUTE TYPE Tour | DISTANCE 60 miles morning | 90 miles afternoon |

DAY 1 AFTERNOON

W E'D SUGGEST BREAKING the first day's journey at Grantham: go into the town centre following signs for 'Boston A52'. There's still a street market on Wednesdays and Saturdays in the town centre, so there's likely to be a pleasant bustle as you get lunch. The rest of the afternoon is spent on the quiet roads of Lincolnshire – often there's very little traffic, though at peak summer times there may be a bit more near the coast as people head out to make the most of the broad, sandy beaches and traditional seaside resorts.

FROM Grantham, Lincolnshire
TO Skegness, Lincolnshire
DISTANCE 90 miles
ALLOW 2.5 hours

Route Description

➤ **Leave Grantham** on the A52 towards Boston. Turn left at the roundabout at the top of the hill to stay on the A52.
➤ **At the next roundabout** Turn left on A15 to Sleaford.
➤ **At major roundabout** Take the third exit for the A17 towards King's Lynn.

➤ **Take the first exit** from A17 for the A153 to Sleaford and Horncastle. At the bottom of the ramp, turn left to Horncastle.
➤ **Stay on A153** all the way through Coningsby.
➤ **Tumby** At the roundabout, turn right on A155 to Mareham le Fen.
➤ **After 4 miles** Coming into Revesby, turn left on B1183 to Horncastle.
➤ **At A153** Turn right to go into Horncastle. Stay on the road through town and out past Cadwell Park.
➤ **At the A16** Turn right towards Boston.
➤ **At roundabout** Go straight over on A157 to Mablethorpe. Turn right at the next roundabout and stay on the A157 and then the A1104 all the way to Mablethorpe.
➤ **At the traffic lights** on Mablethorpe High Street, turn right on the A52 to Sutton on Sea and follow it all the way to Skegness.

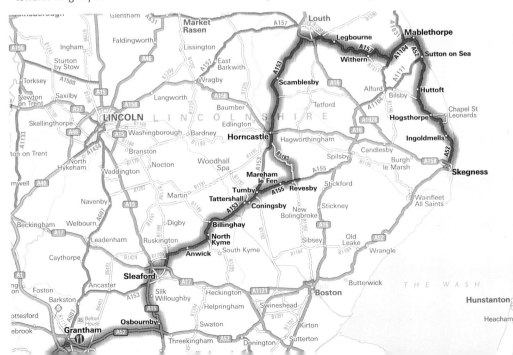

RIDE ㉘ The Midland 300 Day 2

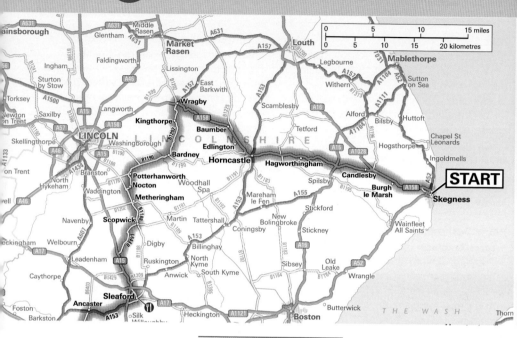

DAY 2 MORNING

FROM THE COAST back to the heart of the country, the second leg of the Midland 300 is an absolutely cracking ride. Heading back inland, through Horncastle from Wragby, it takes one of Lincolnshire's most famous biking routes: Bardney Bends (followed by the arrow-straight Bardney Causeway) before heading into the quiet market town of Sleaford – an ideal place to stop for a bite to eat.

FROM Skegness, Lincolnshire
TO Sleaford, Lincolnshire
DISTANCE 55 miles
ALLOW 1.5 hours

Route Description

➤ **Leave Skegness** on the A158 to Horncastle and continue to Wragby.
➤ **At the traffic lights** in Wragby, turn left onto B1202 to Kingthorpe.
➤ **Bardney** Turn right on B1190 towards Lincoln.
➤ **Don't miss** the left turn, on the corner at the end of the causeway, for the B1202 to Potterhanworth.
➤ **At the B1188** Turn left to Metheringham.
➤ **After 4 miles** Turn right in Scopwick on B1191 to Ashby-de-la-Launde and RAF Digby.
➤ **At A15** Turn left to Sleaford.

DAY 2 AFTERNOON

YOU COULD STOP at the A15 services by the Holdingham roundabout, but we'd recommend crossing the roundabout and going into Sleaford for lunch. The afternoon run gets even further off the beaten track, twisting through Rutland and Leicestershire as the Midland 300 heads back to Tamworth. There may be a little traffic as the route skims the northern suburbs of Leicester, but for the most part the roads are quiet and gloriously twisty.

RIDE (28) The Midland 300 **Day 2**

| **ROUTE TYPE** Tour | **DISTANCE** 55 miles morning | 95 miles afternoon |

FROM Sleaford, Lincolnshire
TO Tamworth, Staffordshire
DISTANCE 95 miles
ALLOW 2.5 hours

Route Description

> **Leave Sleaford** on the A153 towards Grantham.
> **At the traffic lights** in Ancaster, turn left on B6403 to Colsterworth.
> **Turn right** at A52.
> **At the roundabout** Turn left on B1176 past Old Somerby and towards Bourne.
> **At A151** Turn right to Colsterworth.
> **At the roundabout** Turn left to cross over A1, and at the next roundabout turn left (into Colsterworth) on B676 towards Melton Mowbray.
> **Don't miss** the left turn 3 miles later (1 mile outside Stainby) for the minor road to Sewstern.

> **Thistleton** Take the first right to Market Overton.
> **Teigh** Turn left to Ashwell and Oakham.
> **Go straight over** the roundabout into Oakham town centre and follow signs for the station. Cross the railway line and turn left. Take the second left, signed to Braunston.
> **Tilton on the Hill** Go straight by the church then right on the B6047 towards Melton Mowbray.
> **After 3 miles** turn left on minor road to Barsby. Go through Queniborough to join the A607 towards Leicester.
> **Turn right onto A46** and then join A6 towards Loughborough. After 6 miles on the dual carriageway, turn left at the roundabout and then right into Quorn.

> **At the lights** in Quorn, turn right to Woodhouse and the Great Central Railway.
> **B591** Turn left towards Coalville and M1.
> **A511 roundabout** Turn right, then turn left at the next roundabout on B585 to Ellistown.
> **Nailstone** Turn left on the A447 towards Hinckley.
> **Bull in the Oak** Turn right to Market Bosworth on the minor road.
> **Enter Market Bosworth** town centre and pick up the road to Wellsborough.
> **Cross A444** at staggered crossroads, on B585 to Sheepy Magna.
> **Turn left** in Sheepy Magna on the B4116 to Pinwall.
> **Pinwall** Turn right (by the garage) on B5000 and stay on this road all the way back to Tamworth.

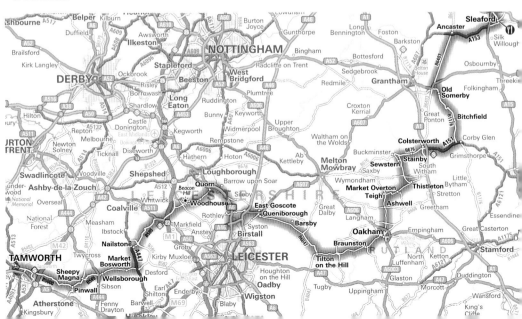

RIDE ㉙ Peak District Part 1

THERE ARE SO many brilliant roads in the Peak District – and this can sometimes be a curse. Sunny weekends see riders from the surrounding cities of Manchester, Leeds, Sheffield and Derby flocking to the Peaks, along with walkers, sightseers, coach parties… put off yet? Don't be. Just pick your time to visit and choose one of the four rides on the following pages, tailor-made to help you get the best out of the area. The first two loops focus on the popular bike-meet venue Matlock Bath, an attractive Victorian spa town. This ride climbs to Whaley Bridge, swinging back to Buxton along the famous Cat and Fiddle road – the sublime A537.

FROM/TO Matlock Bath, Derbyshire
DISTANCE 80 miles
ALLOW 2.5 hours

Route Description

> **Matlock Bath** Head south on A6 towards Derby.
> **Cromford** Right at the lights, then right again on the A5012 to Newhaven. This is the Via Gellia, one of the Peak District's legendary biking roads.
> **Newhaven** Turn right on the A515 to Buxton.
> **Buxton** Cross the town centre to pick up the A5004 towards Whaley Bridge.
> **Horwich End** Turn left on the B5470 to Macclesfield.
> **Macclesfield** Left and left again to pick up the A537 towards Buxton – the famous Cat and Fiddle road.
> **A537** About 4 miles past Cat and Fiddle pub, turn right on the A54 towards Congleton.
> **Allgreave** At the hairpin bend, carry straight on along the minor road to Flash and Quarnford.
> **Look out** Take the easy-to-miss right turn signed for Royal Cottage. Look out for an old stone bridge.

> **A53** When the lane meets the A53 turn left for 100 yards or so, then take the first right to Longnor.
> **Longnor** Straight through the village, carrying on through Crowdecote.
> **A515** Cross the main road, taking the B5055 through Monyash.
> **Bakewell** Into the town centre, taking the A6 towards Matlock.
> **Haddon Hall** Just after passing the hall, turn right on the B5056 towards Ashbourne.
> **Via Gellia** When the road meets the A5012 again, turn left and return to Matlock Bath.

below Snake Pass looking even more sinuous by night

WHAT TO SEE AND DO

Haddon Hall
Is one of England's most elegant and timeless stately homes and a magnificent example of a fortified manor house.

Poole's Cavern Spectacular limestone caverns in the beautiful Buxton Country Park. Good guided tours.
poolescavern.co.uk

The Heights of Abraham
Up in the air and under the ground in one attraction. Catch a cable car to the park, then tour the underground show caves.
heightsofabraham.com

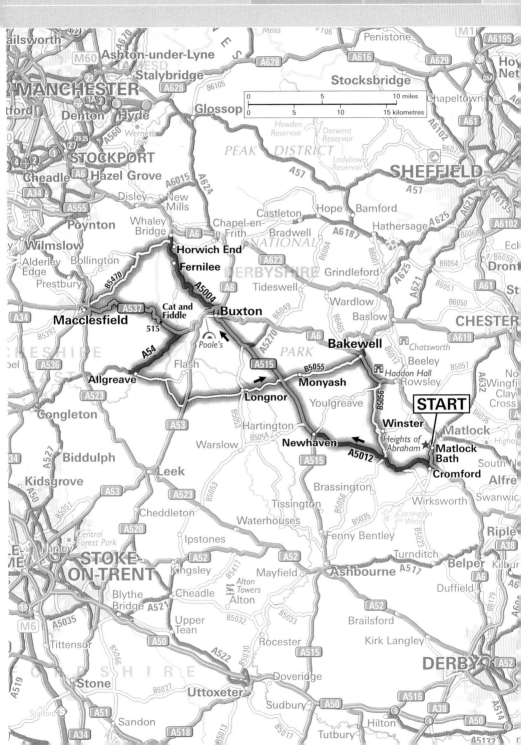

RIDE (30) Peak District Part 2

IN AN IDEAL world, we'd take a few days off for a mid-week trip to the Peaks. At that time, this lovely corner of Britain is comparatively quiet and there's a chance to enjoy the fantastic riding without the heavy weekend traffic. If you don't have so much time, you could incorporate one of the four loops in this section into a day trip to the Peaks.

Like the previous ride, this slightly shorter loop begins and ends at Matlock Bath, but this one offers a more relaxed blend of great riding and spectacular rural views.

FROM/TO Matlock Bath, Derbyshire
DISTANCE 67 miles
ALLOW 2.5 hours

Route Description
➤ **From Matlock Bath**
Ride south on A6 towards Derby.
➤ **Cromford** Turn right and follow signs to B5035 towards Ashbourne.
➤ **Ashbourne** Go into the town centre to pick up the A52 towards Leek. Be patient – there are speed limits with cameras. After the first camera in the 50 limit, turn left to stay on the A52 towards Stoke.

➤ **A52** After about 3 miles, turn left on the B5417 through Oakamoor.
➤ **Cheadle** Turn right in the town centre to pick up the A522. As it leaves Cheadle, turn right on the A521 to Froghall.
➤ **Froghall** Turn right on the A52, then left on the B5053 through Ipstones. Cross the A523 and stay on the B5053 all the way through Warslow and Longnor.
➤ **A515** When the road reaches the A515 T-junction, turn right towards Ashbourne.
➤ **Newhaven** Turn left by the garage at Newhaven, returning to Matlock Bath on the A5012.

WHAT TO SEE AND DO

Carsington Water
Enjoy a fun-filled day engaging in walking, cycling or watersports at this award-winning location on the edge of the Peak District National Park. Best of all, most of the facilities are free.
carsingtonwater.com

Wirksworth Heritage Centre An old silk and velvet mill houses displays on the town's history as a lead-mining centre. Also information on well-dressing, local memories of WWII and round-the-world yachtswoman, Dame Ellen MacArthur.
wirksworthheritage.co.uk

Middleton Top Engine House A beam engine built in 1829 for the Cromford & High Peak Railway, in an octagonal engine house. It hauled wagons up the Middleton Incline, and was last used in 1963.
middleton-leawood.org.uk

left *Busy day in Matlock Bath*

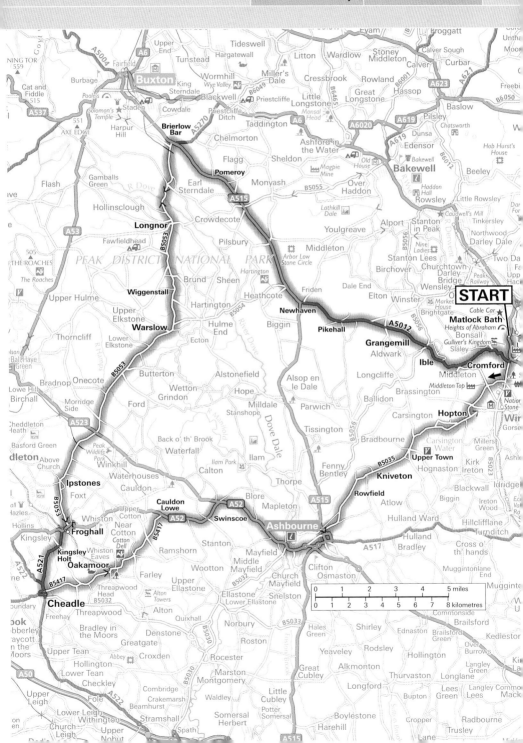

RIDE (31) Peak District Part 3

IN THE NORTHERN part of the Peak District, this more southerly route starts and ends in Glossop – an unexpectedly charming town complete with its own opera house. It takes in the fabulously well-named Snake Pass in the shadow of Kinder Scout before dropping down, past Chatsworth and returning to Glossop again along the stunning Hope Valley. Is this the most scenic ride you can have in the Peak District? Possibly… But keep looking, as there are so many great roads that our four routes merely scratch the surface of what this glorious area has to offer.

FROM/TO Glossop, Derbyshire
DISTANCE 68 miles
ALLOW 2.5 hours

Route Description

➤ **Glossop** Take A57 towards Sheffield. This is Snake Pass.
➤ **Ladybower Reservoir** At traffic lights at end of reservoir, turn right across the bridge on the A6013 through Bamford.
➤ **A6187** Turn left at A6187 T-junction through Hathersage, turning right on A625 to Calver.
➤ **Calver** Turn left on the A623 to Baslow.
➤ **Baslow** Turn right on A619 towards Bakewell. As the road turns to the right, head towards Matlock on B6012, following signs for Chatsworth House.

➤ **A6** Turn right at T-junction with A6, through Bakewell.
➤ **Ashford in the Water** Turn right on A6020 towards Chesterfield then shortly turn left on B6465 signed for Monsal Head.
➤ **A623** After Wardlow, turn left on A623. After just over 1 mile turn right on B6049 through Bradwell.
➤ **A6187** Turn left on A6187 through Castleton and Hope. At T-junction on the high moor, turn right to Chapel-en-le-Frith.
➤ **Chapel-en-le-Frith** Enter town centre and turn right on A624 towards Glossop.
➤ **A624** After leaving Hayfield, look for the minor road on the left, signed for Charlesworth.

➤ **Charlesworth** Turn right on the A626 back to Glossop.

WHAT TO SEE AND DO

Blue John Cavern Into scenic Edale, this is a fascinating cave and mine complex. Make sure your riding boots are comfy for walking.
bluejohn-cavern.co.uk

Upper Derwent Valley The visitor centre below the wall of the Derwent Dam tells the story of the drowned villages of Derwent and Ashopton, the Dambusters, and the rest of the popular valley.
visitpeakdistrict.com

Chatsworth House Explore the historic house for fascinating stories and one of Europe's most significant art collections. In the garden, discover water features, giant sculptures and beautiful flowers.
chatsworth.org

left The glorious Snake Pass

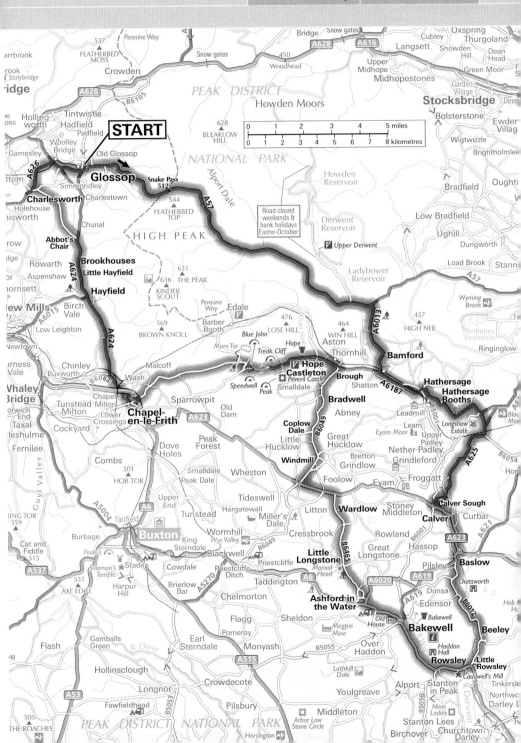

RIDE (32) Peak District Part 4

THE NORTHERN HALF of the Peak District has a slightly different character to the southern end. Hope Valley is perhaps the most beautiful part of the Peak District National Park, but the whole area is higher, more rugged, wilder… Like the ride on pages 86–87, this more northerly route starts from Glossop. From there, it heads out across Howden Moor on the sweeping, almost Alpine Woodhead Pass, looping back across Saddleworth Moor before crossing Holme Moss on the A6024 – a road loaded with enough hairpins to match any Pyrenean pass.

FROM/TO Glossop, Derbyshire
DISTANCE 38 miles
ALLOW 90 minutes

Route Description

➤ **Glossop** Leave town on the B6105 towards Woodhead Reservoir.
➤ **A628** When the road crosses the reservoir and meets the A628, turn right towards Barnsley. After ¾ mile, turn left on the A6024 to Holmfirth.
➤ **Holmfirth** Turn right on the B6106 towards Hade Edge. Go straight across at the A616 x-roads, staying on the B6106.
➤ **Millhouse Green** Turn right on the A628 towards Manchester. This is Woodhead Pass.
➤ **Hollingworth** Turn left at the traffic lights by The Gun Inn on the A57, to return to Glossop.

WHAT TO SEE AND DO

Pennine Way Get off the motorbike and try walking a stretch of the famous Pennine Way. This ride crosses over it at Crowden. **thepennineway.co.uk**

Holme Moss This high moorland has stunning views. The transmitting station is the highest in England.

Peak District Beautiful upland area that includes Kinder Scout, where on a clear day you can see Manchester and Snowdonia/Eryri.

left *Far-reaching views of the Peak District from Holme Moss*

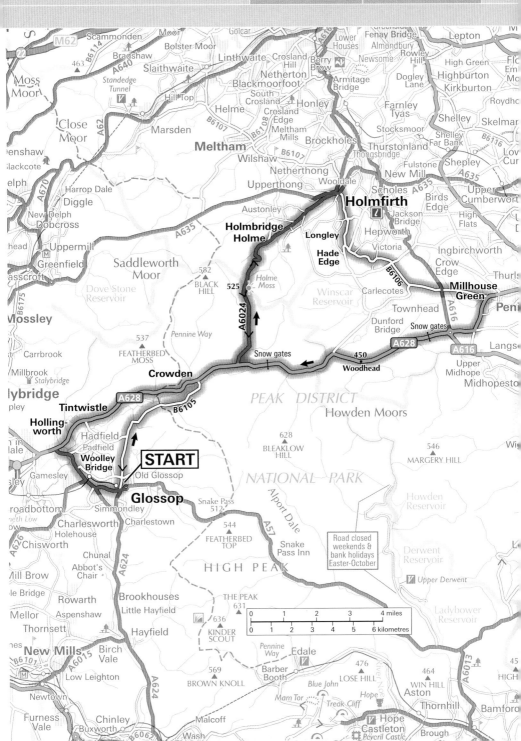

RIDE 33 Lincolnshire Bends

SOME OF THESE roads are local Lincolnshire legends – they have their own nicknames and their own fearsome reputations. Fearsome? These are roads to respect, not rag the bike on. Roads that have caught out many a reckless and unready rider, just as they reward the cautious and skilful. The run up from Horncastle to Louth, past the Cadwell Park race circuit, is a straightforward, brilliant road. Twisting, turning and sweeping along, it climbs the Wolds and sweeps down again. From Louth to Market Rasen, past the excellent Willingham Woods tea stop, it's the same story: sweeping bends, great elevation changes – easy to see the appeal, easy to ride.

It's from Market Rasen to Bardney that things get trickier. These are the Bardney Bends, a selection of fiendishly tight turns connecting some spectacularly open straights. Hooking left in Bardney, it's onto the Bucknell Bends, which are even tighter (and in places bumpier too). Lincoln riders will argue their merits, some preferring Bardney, others Bucknall, but all of them agreeing: you don't get roads this good very often – and you won't get so many challenging bends so close together anywhere else in Lincolnshire.

FROM/TO Horncastle, Lincolnshire
DISTANCE 52 miles
ALLOW 1.5 hours

Route Description

➤ **Horncastle** Take A153 to Louth (passing Cadwell Park).
➤ **Louth** Turn left on the A16 Louth bypass. At the first roundabout, turn left on the A157 towards Lincoln.

➤ **A157** After about ½ mile, take the right fork on the A631 towards Gainsborough. As you enter the woods after North Willingham, keep a look out for the Willingham Woods tea stop and bike meet on the right, and make a stop if you fancy it.
➤ **Market Rasen** Turn left at the traffic lights on the B1202 to Wragby.

➤ **Wragby** Go straight across at the lights, sticking with the B1202 to Bardney.
➤ **Bardney** In the centre of the village, turn left, joining the B1190 through Bucknall and Thimbleby.
➤ **Horncastle** Turn right on the A158 to return to the centre of town.

WHAT TO SEE AND DO

Wragby Maze Where you can get lost in the conifer maze and be amused at the variety of topiary sculptures along the way.
thewragbymaze.weebly.com

Cadwell Park Racing Circuit One of Britain's most scenic circuits, Cadwell has always got something going on. Superbikes and vintage sports cars, track days and championships.
cadwellpark.co.uk

Bardney Heritage Centre Popular location to have a pit stop and enjoy the views of the River Witham.

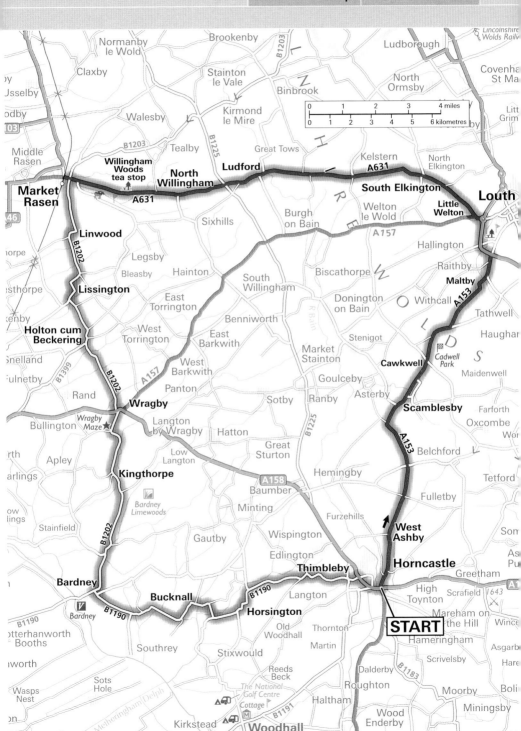

RIDE (34) Newark Loop

IMOVED FROM LONDON to Lincolnshire many years ago and a big part of the attraction was the quality of riding on the doorstep. There's no such thing as a dull ride around here (okay, apart from maybe the A52 from Grantham to Nottingham – but you won't find that in this book). The starting point for this route may be in Nottinghamshire – in the surprisingly charming market town of Newark-on-Trent – but that's just to make it easy to reach for anyone visiting the area, as it's bang on the A1. The ride itself is in Lincolnshire and is basically one of my favourite local rides.

FROM/TO Newark-on-Trent
DISTANCE 135 miles
ALLOW 3.5 hours

Route Description

➤ **Newark-on-Trent** Take the A46 towards Lincoln.
➤ **At the first roundabout** Turn left on the A1133 to Gainsborough. Go straight over the staggered crossroads at Newton on Trent.
➤ **Torksey Locks** Turn left on the A156 to Gainsborough.
➤ **Gainsborough** Pick up the A631 towards Rotherham.
➤ **From Beckingham** Take the A161 towards Goole.
➤ **At the A18** Turn right to Scunthorpe.
➤ **On the outskirts** of Scunthorpe pick up the A1077 towards Winterton.
➤ **In South Ferriby** Turn right on the B1204 to Brigg. At the B1206 turn right, and right again at the A18, to continue to Brigg.
➤ **At Brigg roundabout** Turn left on the A1084 to Caistor.
➤ **From Caistor** Take B1225 to Rothwell and Horncastle.
➤ **Turn left on the A158** into Horncastle.
➤ **At traffic lights** in Horncastle turn right on the

B1191 to Woodhall Spa.
➤ **At the B1189** Turn right to Metheringham.
➤ **Metheringham** Turn right on B1188 then first left on B1202 to Metheringham Heath. Go straight over A15.

➤ **Boothby Graffoe** Turn left on the A607 towards Grantham.
➤ **At the lights** in Leadenham turn right towards Newark. At the A17, turn right to return to Newark-on-Trent.

above You don't need a Brough Superior to enjoy the flowing bends of the Lincolnshire Wolds – they're great on all bikes

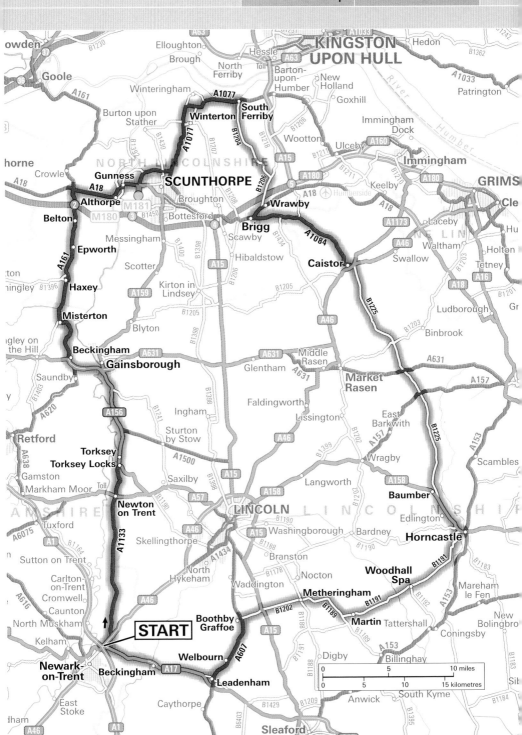

RIDE (35) Beverley Loop

THERE'S AN OLD expression: it's not what you know, but who you know… and when it comes to finding great roads that's certainly true. My good friend Hoody used to ride police bikes on this side of the Humber. Now he's retired, it's easier to pick his brains about the best roads for a ride – the ones in prime condition, with the least traffic… He helped refine this route, which heads out to the wonderful lighthouse at Flamborough Head before returning to Beverley on one of the greatest roads in the East Riding – the B1248. It's an outstanding ride with the added bonus of having a good café in the woods at the Fimber roundabout or, for a more substantial bite to eat, you could try the Deep Blue fish and chip shop in Wetwang.

FROM/TO Beverley, East Yorkshire
DISTANCE 93 miles
ALLOW 2.5 hours

Route Description

➤ **Leave Beverley** on A164 to Driffield.
➤ **Cross Driffield** (past the train station) and pick up B1249 towards Hornsea.
➤ **Beeford crossroads** Turn left on A165 to Bridlington.
➤ **Bridlington** Pick up B1255 to Flamborough. It's worth taking the B1259 out to the lighthouse at Flamborough Head (then return to the village to continue the route).
➤ **Flamborough** Take the B1229 towards Filey.
➤ **At A165 roundabout** Turn left to Bridlington.
➤ **Turn right** on the A165 at Bridlington roundabout then after ½ mile turn right on B1253 to Rudston and Sledmere House.
➤ **Turn right** in Sledmere then right again, to stay on B1253 towards Malton.
➤ **At the B1248** Turn left to Beverley. NB: It's a nasty, tight off-camber left – it may be easier to turn right, ride down to North Grimston and turn around there.
➤ **At the A166** Turn left to ride into Wetwang, then turn right to continue on the B1248.
➤ **At the roundabout** Go straight over on the A614.
➤ **In Bainton** Turn left to continue on the B1248.
➤ **At the A1035 roundabout** Turn left to return to Beverley.

below The B1248 at Tibthorpe

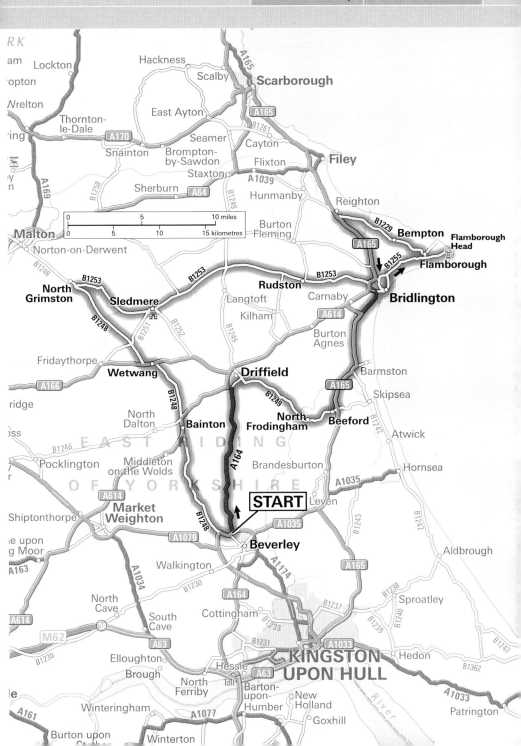

RIDE (36) North York Moors Loop

TOURISTS WANDER ACROSS the perfectly preserved 1960s village green, incongruous in their modern clothes, ice cream melting in cones as the sun beats down. This is Goathland, where the TV series *Heartbeat* was filmed – a perfect time capsule on the North York Moors.

We're not here for the postcards and nostalgia, though. This is great riding country, whether you want open, flowing roads or tighter, more testing lanes.

Down the A169, past the majestic Hole of Horcum, the ride uncoils over the course of a day. We probe quiet B-roads, through the sleepy villages of the East Riding. Then we're climbing again, north from Malton, crossing the A170 and up, back across the moors on wild and windswept roads, the only vehicles out there. We continue up to the coast, sunset shining romantically on the North Sea, then we're back in Whitby, exhausted and exhilarated.

FROM/TO Whitby, North Yorkshire
DISTANCE 150 miles
ALLOW 4.5 hours

Route Description

> **Whitby** Head north on A174 towards Redcar.
> **Loftus** Turn left onto B1366, towards Liverton.
> **Continue to the A171** Turn right to Guisborough.
> **Just beyond Guisborough** Turn left onto A173 to Stokesley.
> **At A172** Stokesley by-pass rbt, turn left onto B1257 and follow it to Helmsley.
> **At Helmsley** Turn right on A170 towards Thirsk.

> **After 3 miles** Turn left opposite Duncombe Park stately home's gatehouse on the B1257 to Malton.
> **At the level crossing** at Malton, turn right onto a minor road signed Stamford Bridge.
> **Stay on minor road** from Malton until it meets the A166. Turn left towards Bridlington.
> **At Fridaythorpe** Turn left onto B1251 by Seaways café towards Scarborough.
> **Go through Sledmere** and turn left onto the B1253, towards Bridlington.
> **Beyond Cowlam** At rbt, turn left onto B1249 towards and through Foxholes.

> **At the A64 traffic lights** Turn left towards Malton.
> **Sherburn** Turn right at the traffic lights, towards Brompton-by-Sawdon.
> **Brompton-by-Sawdon** Turn left on the A170 to Pickering.
> **Continue to Pickering** town centre. Turn right, onto the A169 towards Whitby.
> **High on the open moor** Turn left on a lane signed for Goathland. Follow the lane round the village and back out across the moor to A169.
> **Turn left** onto the A169.
> **At A171 roundabout** Turn right to return to Whitby.

WHAT TO SEE AND DO

Seaways No frills, no fuss bike café in Fridaythorpe does a good line in home-made cakes. Good value, great atmosphere.
seawayscafefridaythorpe.co.uk

Sledmere House Superbly maintained stately home with park, gardens (including a walled rose garden) galleries, visitor centre and a café.
sledmerehouse.com

Flamingo Land Resort Enjoy a dozen stomach-churning white-knuckle rides, take a monorail ride and stroll through the extensive zoo, where you'll find tigers, giraffes, hippos and rhinos.
flamingoland.co.uk

RIDE ③⑥ North York Moors Loop

ROUTE TYPE Loop | **DISTANCE** 150 miles

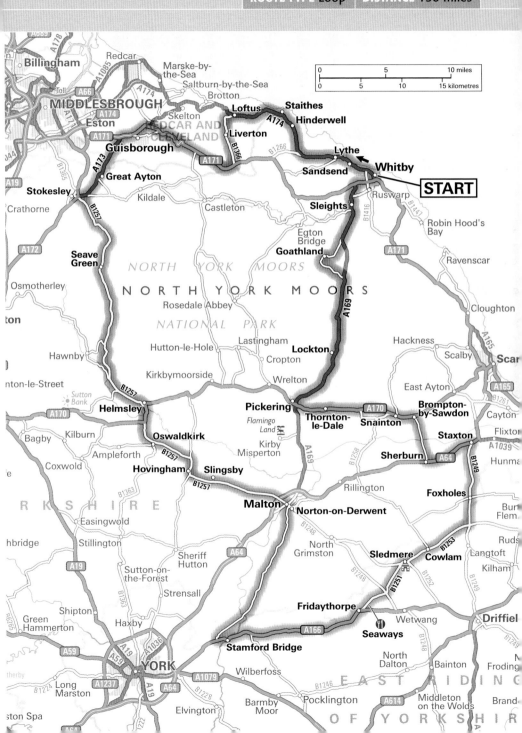

RIDE (37) Yorkshire Dales Loop

RIDE THIS 100-ODD-MILE loop once, and you'll be looking for excuses to come back and ride it again and again. True, Ripon is a typical traffic-clogged town, but once you escape onto the road to Masham and Leyburn, that's all forgotten.

There's very little traffic up here in the Dales, but there are many safe and easy opportunities to overtake anything that does threaten to hold you up. Judge it carefully, though – there are plenty of tightening turns and small crests that can turn into jumps, and with dry-stone walls beside many of the roads, you don't want to make a mistake up here.

The highlight of the loop is the B6255 out of Hawes – a rollercoaster of a road seemingly designed to delight bikers. Turning south at Ribblehead, this route swings off at Stainforth, on the even quieter single-track roads across Malham Moor to Pateley Bridge, but it's nearly as much fun (and less demanding) to take the B6479 all the way to Settle, then take the A65 back to Ripon. Whichever way you go, you'll want to come back for more.

FROM/TO Ripon, North Yorkshire
DISTANCE 97 miles
ALLOW 3 hours

Route Description
> **From Ripon** Take the A6108 towards Masham.
> **In Masham** Continue on the A6108 towards Leyburn.

below Upper Wensleydale

> **Beyond the turreted bridge** over the River Ure, turn left onto a lane signed for Wensley.
> **At its end** in Wensley, turn left onto the A684 towards Hawes.
> **Turn left** in Bainbridge to stay on the A684.
> **Go straight on** through Hawes, possibly stopping at the Penny Garth Café. Turn left at the fork at the far end, onto the B6255 towards Ingleton.
> **Nearing Ribblehead Viaduct** Turn left onto the B6479 towards Settle.
> **At Stainforth** Turn left onto a lane signed for Halton Gill.
> **Continue on the lane**

Often narrow, it bends through Halton Gill, Litton and Arncliffe, towards Kilnsey. This is a tricky minor road across Malham Moor – if you don't fancy it, carry on to Settle and take the A65 to Skipton, then the B6265 to rejoin the route in Threshfield.
> **Emerge onto B6160** and turn right, towards Grassington.
> **Continue to Threshfield** Turn left onto the B6265 towards Pateley Bridge.
> **Through Pateley Bridge** Near the village of Glasshouses, turn left to stay on the B6265 and follow it all the way back to Ripon.

WHAT TO SEE AND DO

Penny Garth Café A famed biker's café, the Penny Garth has been feeding hungry riders in Hawes for years. It's the ideal place for a cuppa and a butty after a long ride through the Dales.
pennygarthcafe.co.uk

Stump Cross Caverns Near Pateley Bridge, these caverns were discovered in 1860 and have been open to visitors since 1863. The limestone showcaves have some remains of wolverines.
stumpcrosscaverns.co.uk

RIDE (37) Yorkshire Dales Loop

ROUTE TYPE Loop   **DISTANCE** 97 miles

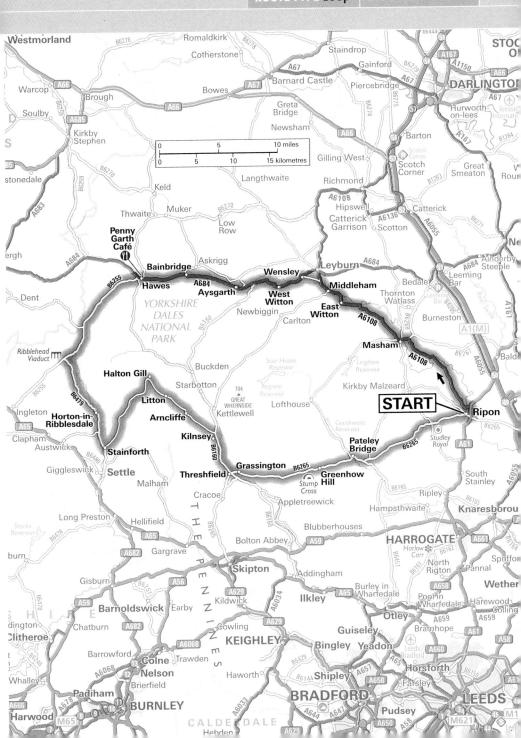

RIDE (38) Lakeland Loop

YOU DON'T NEED a big adventure bike to enjoy Hardknott Pass – it's an adventure on any bike. It's narrow, incredibly steep, indifferently surfaced… yet something about the way it twists irresistibly through the quiet wilds of the Lake District makes it as magical as it is challenging. It's not a road for everyone, though. Luckily, the Lake District is equally rich in relaxed, perfectly surfaced, involving yet easy-to-ride roads – the sublime A595 round the coast or the A593 past Coniston Water, for instance. For the full, intense Lakeland riding experience, try this fabulous route, taking in Wrynose, Hardknott, Honister, Newlands, Whinlatter and Kirkstone Passes.

Now that's an adventure…

FROM/TO Bowness-on-Windermere, Cumbria
DISTANCE 129 miles
ALLOW 4 hours

Route Description

➤ **Leave Bowness-on-Windermere** on the A591 to Ambleside.
➤ **Ambleside** Follow the road round to the left and then turn left, following signs for the A593 towards Coniston.
➤ **Clappersgate** Turn left onto B5286 to Hawkshead.

➤ **Approaching Hawkshead** Turn right onto a small road, the B5285, signed towards Coniston.
➤ **In the centre of Coniston** Turn right onto the A593 towards Ambleside.
➤ **Before Skelwith Bridge** take a left turn down a lane signed for Wrynose. Follow it through both Wrynose and Hardknott Passes.
➤ **Stay on the road** to ride through Boot, and turn right at a T-junction to reach Eskdale Green.

➤ **Keep straight on** through the village and beyond, eventually turning left at the road end to reach the centre of Gosforth.
➤ **Leaving Gosforth** turn right onto A595, towards Workington.
➤ **From Egremont** Take A5086 to Cockermouth.
➤ **Go over A66 roundabout** into Cockemouth. At the lights, go straight then turn right on B5292 to Lorton. After 3 miles, take the left fork for the B5292 towards Keswick, Whinlatter Pass.
➤ **In Braithwaite** Turn right by the pub and follow signs for Newlands and Buttermere.
➤ **In Buttermere** Turn left on B5289 to Keswick, Honister Pass.
➤ **From Keswick** Take A66 towards Penrith.
➤ **At A592 roundabout** Turn right to Ullswater and Kirkstone Pass. Stay on this road all the way back to Windermere.

left Coniston Water is one of the Lake District's treasures

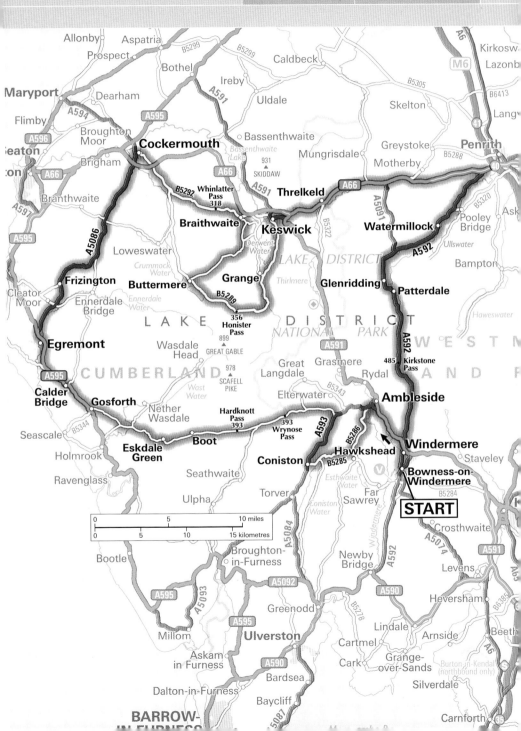

RIDE (39) Alston North Loop

WHAT IS BRITAIN'S best biking town? Racing towns like Castle Donington or Louth, with Cadwell Park, Hinckley with its Triumph factory, or Brighton with the speed trials on Marine Drive may come to mind. Forget them – it's Alston in Cumbria. No, hear me out… Alston is perfectly positioned as a base for exploring other riding pleasure zones: the Yorkshire Dales, the Scottish Borders, the Lake District… There's simply no better town to base yourself in for bike riding in Britain.

On this and the following pages we have two day-long rides starting from Alston. The ride on this page heads north, into Kielder Forest and the Scottish Borders. But the best bit? There's plenty more great riding around there. So when there's a poll on Britain's best biking town, you know what to do: vote Alston.

FROM/TO Alston, Cumbria
DISTANCE 160 miles
ALLOW A full day

Route Description

➤ **Alston** Leave town on the A686 towards Penrith, but before leaving the speed limit (after crossing the bridge) turn right on the A689 to Brampton.
➤ **Brampton** Cross the A69, going into Brampton town centre to pick up the A6071 to Longtown.
➤ **Longtown** Turn right on the A7 towards Edinburgh.
➤ **Canonbie** Turn right on the B6357 to Newcastleton.
➤ **Stay on the road** and when it forks, stay left as it becomes the B6399 to Hawick (the B6357 turns off to the right).

➤ **Hawick** Go into the town centre, bear right at mini-roundabout then at next roundabout turn right on the A698. Leaving town, take the first right turn for the A6088 to Bonchester Bridge.
➤ **After Bonchester Bridge** look for the right turn onto the B6357 towards Newcastleton again.
➤ **Saughtree** Easy to miss – look for an isolated handful of farm buildings and a left turn signed for Kielder Forest.
➤ **Bellingham** After riding through the forest and around Kielder Water, turn right in Bellingham on the B6320 towards Hexham.
➤ **Chollerford** Turn right on the A6079 to Hexham.

➤ **Hexham** Pick up the A69 towards Carlisle.
➤ **Haydon Bridge** Leave the A69 for the A686 towards Alston, but after just over 1 mile turn left to continue with the B6295 through Allendale and Allenheads.
➤ **A689** Turn right when the road meets the A689, returning to Alston over Killhope Summit.

WHAT TO SEE AND DO

Chesters Roman Fort
Don't pass Hadrian's Wall without a stop at the best-preserved Roman cavalry fort in the country.
englishheritage.org.uk/visit/places/chesters-roman-fort-and-museum-hadrians-wall

Kielder Water Birds of Prey Centre Beautiful birds of prey flown twice a day in one of the most stunning settings imaginable.
kielderbopc.com

left *The strongroom at Chesters*

RIDE (39) Alston North Loop

ROUTE TYPE Loop | **DISTANCE** 160 miles

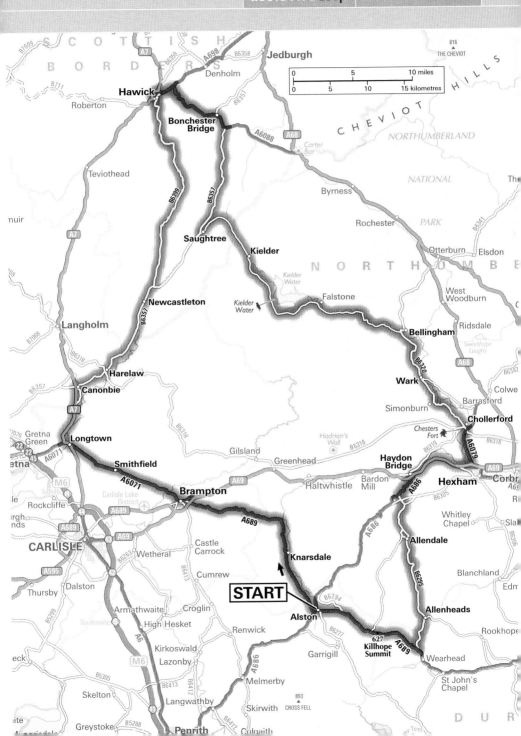

RIDE (40) Alston South Loop

MEMBERS OF THE AA once voted the A686 the most beautiful road in Britain. It's easy to see why. This route heads off along its most magnificent aspect – Hartside Pass, which descends to Penrith in a cascade of well-surfaced bends and hairpins. From Penrith the route heads south over Shap Summit on the A6 – the parallel M6 is Britain's highest motorway, but the A-road is a better ride. From Kendal, a dash to Ingleton leads to the Yorkshire Dales and the spectacular B6255 through Ribbledale, followed by the magnificent Buttertubs Pass from Hawes to Kirkby Stephen, which you'd think were about the best pair of roads as you'd ever find. Until, that is, at Brough you pick up the B6276 to Middleton-in-Teesdale, followed in short order by the B6278 to Stanhope... We return to Alston on the A689, over Killhope Cross – England's highest A-road. Which is the most beautiful road on the route? It's impossible to say – there are simply too many.

FROM/TO Alston, Cumbria
DISTANCE 155 miles
ALLOW A full day

Route Description

> **Alston** Leave town on the A686 for Penrith, over Hartside Pass.
> **Penrith** Go straight over the A66 roundabout, taking the A6 through Shap to Kendal.
> **Kendal** Go straight through the town centre to pick up the B6254 to Kirkby Lonsdale (in Kendal, look out for signs for Westmorland General Hospital).
> **Kirkby Lonsdale** Take the A65 towards Skipton.
> **Ingleton** Turn left on the B6255 to Hawes.
> **Hawes** Turn left on the A684 towards Sedburgh.
> **After 1 mile** Take the first right turn, on a minor road signed for Hardraw. Take the next left, signed for Simonstone.
> **B6270** After crossing Buttertubs Pass from Simonstone, turn left at the T-junction onto the B6270, towards Kirkby Stephen.
> **Nateby** Turn right on the B6259 to Kirkby Stephen.
> **Kirkby Stephen** Turn right on the A685 to Brough.
> **Brough** Turn right at the clock tower in the town centre, taking the B6276 to Middleton-in-Teesdale. When it descends from the moor and comes to a T-junction, turn left to reach the town centre.
> **Middleton-in-Teesdale** Turn right along the high street, turning right on the B6282 to Eggleston.
> **Eggleston** Turn left on the B6278 to Stanhope.
> **Stanhope** Turn left to return to Alston.

left *Ribblehead Viaduct*

RIDE ④ Alston South Loop

ROUTE TYPE Loop | **DISTANCE** 155 miles

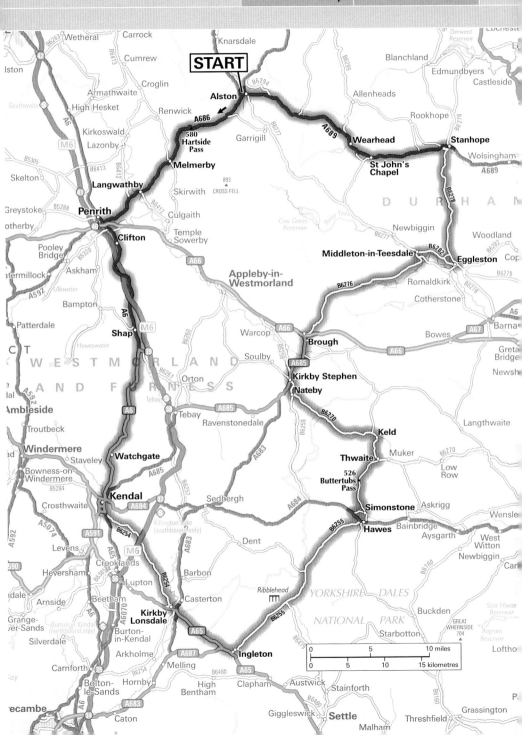

RIDE (41) Hexham South Loop

THIS IS ANOTHER ride that passes through Alston, so it could be amended if you like the idea of basing yourself there and making it into three day trips. However, by basing yourself further north in the market town of Hexham there's a whole world of other opportunities open to you – some in this route and others in our Hexham North loop (next page). The highlight of this route is the B6277 between Middleton-in-Teesdale and Alston – truly one of the best biking roads in the country. Just be sure to keep a sharp eye out for sheep…

FROM/TO Hexham, Northumberland
DISTANCE 78 miles
ALLOW 2.5 hours

Route Description
➤ **Leave Hexham** Take the B6306 to Blanchland.
➤ **In Edmundbyers** Turn right on the B6278 to Stanhope.

➤ **In Stanhope** Turn right on the high street then left towards Eggleston and the community hospital to continue on the B6278.
➤ **Don't miss the right turn** 8 miles later, signed for Alston and High Force.
➤ **Middleton-in-Teesdale** Turn right on the B6277 to Alston.

➤ **Alston town centre** Ride down the steep, cobbled centre – take care if it's wet. At the T-junction, turn right on the A686 to Hexham.
➤ **After 13 miles** Turn right on B6305 to return to Hexham.

below *The B6277 is biker heaven*

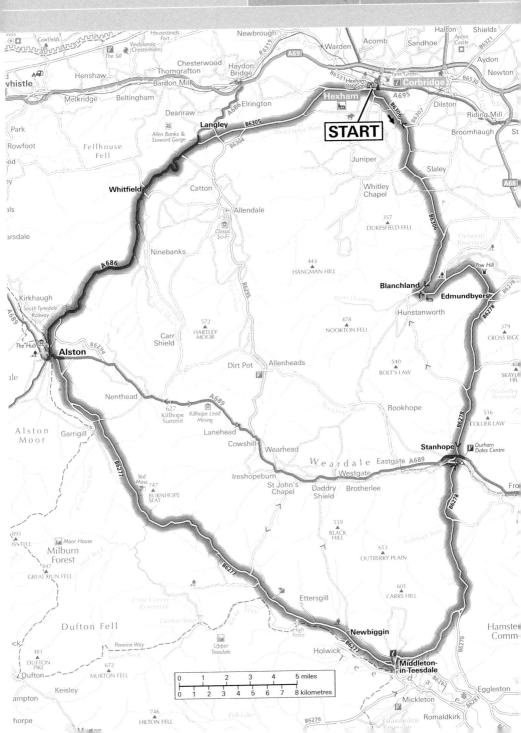

RIDE (42) Hexham North Loop

THIS IS A longer ride, heading north from Hexham to the magnificent A68 into Scotland (pausing for the obligatory pic with the standing stones at the Carter Bar border crossing – a burger from the van is optional). From Jedburgh it heads back to Northumberland – sharing the flowing A697 with the Alnwick route (next page) before cutting across to the truly epic A696 and the challenging B6309. It's a real rider's route, with a grin-factor that's off the charts.

FROM/TO Hexham, Northumberland
DISTANCE 147 miles
ALLOW 4 hours

Route Description

➤ **Take the A69** towards Carlisle for 1 mile, then turn right on the A6079 to Acomb and Chollerford.

➤ **At the A68** Turn left to Jedburgh. Turn left at T-junction to stay on the A68, past Carter Bar, to Jedburgh.

➤ **In Bonjedward** Turn right on the A698 towards Kelso.

➤ **After 4 miles** Turn right on the B6401 to Morebattle. Stay on the road through Town Yetholm, as it becomes B6352.

➤ **At the crossroads** Turn right to stay on the B6352 to Kirknewton.

➤ **Don't miss the right turn** 2½ miles later for the B6351 to Wooler.

➤ **At the A697** Turn right to Wooler and follow the road for 18 miles.

➤ **Don't miss the right turn** for Rothbury on the B6341. Follow this road all the way though Rothbury and Elsdon.

➤ **At the A696** Turn left towards Newcastle upon Tyne.

➤ **After 15 miles** Turn right on the B6309 to Stamfordham. Turn left after 1 mile to stay on this road.

➤ **In Stamfordham** Turn right to Whittledean on the B6309.

➤ **At the crossroads** by the reservoirs, turn right on the B6318 to Chollerford.

➤ **At the roundabout** Turn left on the A68 to Corbridge.

➤ **Cross the A69** into Corbridge and pick up the A695 to return to Hexham.

left *Amazing riding in the Cheviot Hills*

| ROUTE TYPE Loop | DISTANCE 147 miles |

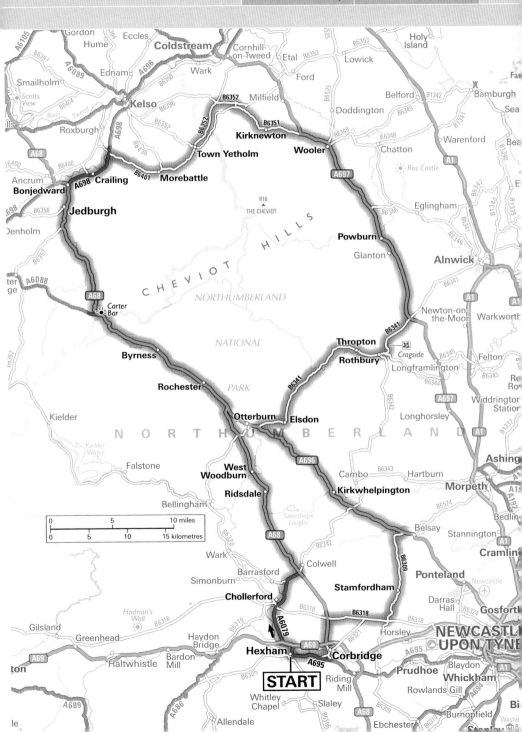

START

RIDE (43) Amazing Alnwick

THERE'S SOME AMAZING riding to be had north of Newcastle upon Tyne before you hit the Scottish border. If you don't fancy basing yourself in the heaving Geordie metropolis, head to the quieter town of Alnwick, in the heart of the brilliant roads. The Northumbrian coast is a real treat – quiet and windswept, achingly beautiful. It's rich in fascinating places to visit, as well, as you ride past the magnificent Bamburgh Castle and spectacular Lindisfarne, on to the fascinating walled town of Berwick-upon-Tweed. Each one is worth a day trip. Or head inland, through the Northumberland National Park and across the border at Carter Bar – the riding into Jedburgh and Kelso is sublime. The route returns to Alnwick on the A697, which might be the north of England's best-kept secret.

FROM/TO Alnwick, Northumberland
DISTANCE 123 miles
ALLOW 3 hours

Route Description

> **Alnwick** Take the A1068 towards Alnmouth.
> **Lesbury** Turn left onto B1339 through Embleton.
> **Stay on the road** beyond the village, as it becomes B1340 towards Seahouses.
> **Turn right in Seahouses** to stay on the B1340 towards Bamburgh, along the coast.
> **Ride beneath Bamburgh Castle** Bear right, joining the B1342 towards the A1.
> **Turn right onto A1** Ride towards Berwick-upon-Tweed (option to take the road to Lindisfarne/Holy Island – tide permitting). Continue on A1 past Berwick-upon-Tweed.
> **A few miles after the dual carriageway** turn right onto the A1107 through Eyemouth, following this road until it rejoins the A1.
> **Turn left onto A1** Ride south towards Berwick-upon-Tweed.
> **At Grantshouse** Turn right onto the A6112 through Preston to Duns.
> **Turn left at Duns** to stay on the A6112.
> **Cross straight over B6460** and turn left in Swinton to take the A6112 all the way to Coldstream.
> **At Coldstream** Turn left onto the A697 and continue to Cornhill-on-Tweed. At rbt turn right to continue on the A697.
> **After Glanton** Look out for left turn onto the B6341 to return to Alnwick.

WHAT TO SEE AND DO

Bamburgh Castle
The seat of the kings of Northumbria is one of the most impressive castles you'll ever see, dominating the skyline as you approach.
bamburghcastle.com

Lindisfarne/Holy Island
Timing is crucial if you're to get across the causeway without getting stuck by the tide. Loads to see and do on Holy Island – well worth a visit. **lindisfarne.org.uk**

left Riding over to Lindisfarne

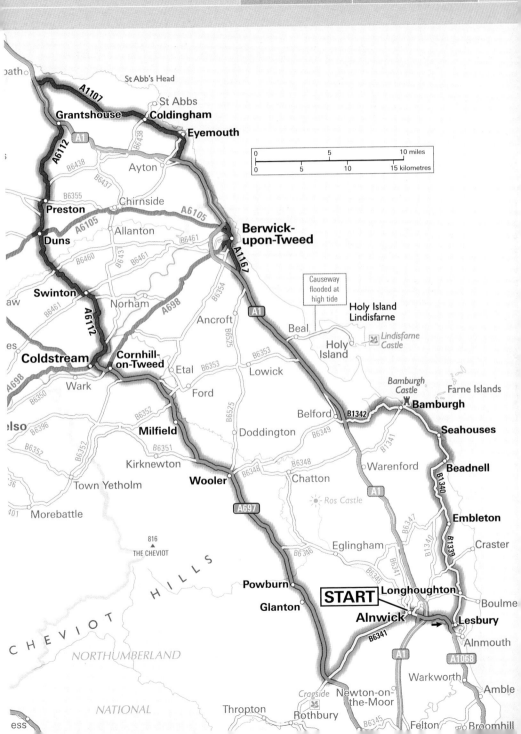

RIDE (44) North England Tour Day 1

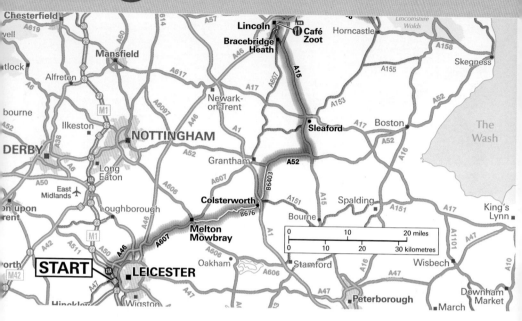

NORTH TOUR DAY 1
MORNING

IT'S CROSS-COUNTRY TO Lincoln – follow signs and park near the cathedral. Grab lunch in Zoot on Bailgate or Hobbsons on Steep Hill. After lunch, take the A1434 north to the Tesco petrol station and fill up there.

FROM M1 Leicester Forest East Services (north)
TO Lincoln, Lincolnshire
DISTANCE 73 miles
ALLOW 1.5–2 hours

Route Description

➤ **LFE Services** Head north on the M1 for one junction.
➤ **M1 Junction 21A** Leave the motorway for the A46 towards Newark-on-Trent.
➤ **A46** At the rbt with traffic lights, take the left-hand sliproad to stay on the A46 towards Newark-on-Trent.
➤ **A46** 1 mile after the rbt, take the exit for the A607 to Melton Mowbray.
➤ **Melton Mowbray** Enter the town centre, initially following signs for the A607. At the traffic lights after the safety camera, take the centre lane for the B676 to Colsterworth.
➤ **Colsterworth** As you come into the village, turn left onto the High Street (the junction is on easy-to-spot red tarmac).
➤ **Colsterworth** As you leave the village, turn right on the B6403 following signs for RAF Cranwell.
➤ **Grantham** Go straight across the roundabout on the A52 towards Boston.
➤ **A52 roundabout** Turn left on the A15 to Sleaford.
➤ **Holdingham roundabout** Take the second exit for the A15 to Lincoln.
➤ **Bracebridge Heath** Go right at the second set of lights on the B1131 to Canwick.
➤ **Mill Lodge** Turn left on the B1188 into Lincoln. The route ends on the A15 in Central Lincoln.

| ROUTE TYPE Tour | DISTANCE 73 miles morning | 124 miles afternoon |

NORTH TOUR DAY 1 **AFTERNOON**

THERE'S SOME GREAT seafood in Whitby – try Hadley's Fish & Chip Restaurant on Bridge Street, Trenchers on New Quay Road or The Magpie Café on Pier Road. There's a petrol station on Upgang Lane, where the next day's route begins.

FROM Lincoln, Lincolnshire
TO Whitby, North Yorkshire
DISTANCE 124 miles
ALLOW 2.5–3.5 hours

Route Description

> **Lincoln** Leave the city on the A158 towards Wragby.
> **Look out** About 7 miles past Wragby on the A158, take the easy-to-miss left-hand turn on the B1225 to Caistor.
> **Caistor** Straight across x-roads on A1173 towards Immingham. Where road bends sharply right, carry on straight (effectively a left turn) on back road towards Great Limber.
> **A18** Turn left towards Scunthorpe.
> **M180 roundabout** Carry straight across on the A15 for the Humber Bridge.
> **Hessle roundabout** Go straight across the roundabout after the Humber Bridge on the A164 towards Beverley.
> **Look out** About 7 miles from the Humber Bridge, on the A164, take the easy-to-miss left turn on the minor road to Walkington. Carry on straight over two crossroads.
> **Beverley** Straight across roundabout on the A1035 towards Bridlington.
> **Cherry Burton** At the next roundabout, take the first exit on the B1248 to Malton.
> **Bainton** When the road joins the A614, go straight on. Then at the roundabout, go straight across, to get back on the B1248.
> **Wetwang** Turn left on the A166 towards York. After leaving the 30mph limit, take the first right to get back on the B1248 to Malton.
> **Travel through** Norton-on-Trent, go into Malton town centre and turn right to pick up the A169 to Pickering.

> **Pickering** Ride straight through town on the A169, following signs for Whitby.
> **A171 roundabout** Turn right towards Whitby. After ¼ mile, keep forward on the B1460 to Whitby. Route ends in central Whitby.

RIDE (44) North England Tour Day 2

NORTH TOUR DAY 2 MORNING

SOME GREAT RIDING this morning – after the coast road from Whitby, swiftly onto the so-called North York TT, between Stokesley and Helmsley. It's a challenging road and well policed, so don't get carried away. It's a great run into the Yorkshire Dales, then on to Hawes with lunch at the popular Penny Garth Café. Top up with fuel in Ripon, Leyburn or Hawes.

FROM Whitby, North Yorkshire
TO Hawes, North Yorkshire
DISTANCE 108 miles
ALLOW 2.5–3.5 hours

Route Description

> **Whitby** Leave town on the A174 towards Sandsend.
> **Mickleby** Turn left on the B1266 towards Guisborough.
> **A171** At the T-junction, turn right on the A171 to Guisborough.
> **Guisborough bypass** Turn left at the roundabout on the A173 for Great Ayton.
> **Stokesley** Turn left at rbt on the B1257 through Great Broughton. When you get there, carry on straight across the mini-rbt to Helmsley.
> **Helmsley** Turn right on the A170 to Thirsk.
> **Thirsk** Go straight through town, taking the A61 to Ripon.
> **Ripon** Go straight into town and turn right at the clock tower, on the A6108 through Masham.
> **Leyburn** Turn left on the A684 to Hawes.
> **Bainbridge** Turn left to stay on the A684 to Hawes. The route ends in Hawes, on the main street, by the Penny Garth Café.

WHAT TO SEE AND DO

Thirsk Birds of Prey Centre More than 70 birds and three flying displays every day. Your chance to hold a falcon.
falconrycentre.co.uk

Masham brewery tours Both Theakston's and Black Sheep Brewery are in Masham – the former offers the chance to see some of the country's few remaining coopers (barrel-makers) at work. Book well in advance.

NORTH TOUR DAY 2 AFTERNOON

FROM THE TIGHT, challenging Buttertubs Pass out of Hawes to the awe-inspiring Hartside Pass between Hawes and Penrith, this is a staggering afternoon's ride. Do try to make time to visit the High Force waterfall outside Middleton-in-Teesdale before descending the spectacular Hartside Pass, with views all the way to the coast. There's accommodation in Penrith to suit all budgets. The next day's route starts from the A592 in Penrith.

FROM Hawes, North Yorkshire
TO Penrith, Cumbria
DISTANCE 82 miles
ALLOW 2–3 hours

Route Description

➤ **Hawes** Leave town carrying on along the A684 towards Sedburgh.

➤ **Look out** Take the first, easy-to-miss right turn off the A684, about 1 mile out of Hawes, signed for Hardraw. ½ mile later take the left turn, signed for Simonstone, for Buttertubs Pass.

➤ **B6270** When Buttertubs joins the B6270, turn left for Kirkby Stephen.

➤ **Nateby** Turn right on the B6259 to Kirkby Stephen.

➤ **Kirkby Stephen** Turn right on the A685 to Brough.

➤ **Brough** Turn right at the clock tower on the B6276 to Middleton-in-Teesdale.

➤ **B6277** At the T-junction with the B6277, go straight (effectively a left-turn) into Middleton-in-Teesdale. At the high street, turn left to take the B6277 to Alston.

➤ **Alston** Go straight down the steep, cobbled high street and turn left on the A686 to Penrith, Hartside Pass.

➤ **Penrith** At the A66 rbt, turn right for the town centre. Route ends in Penrith town centre.

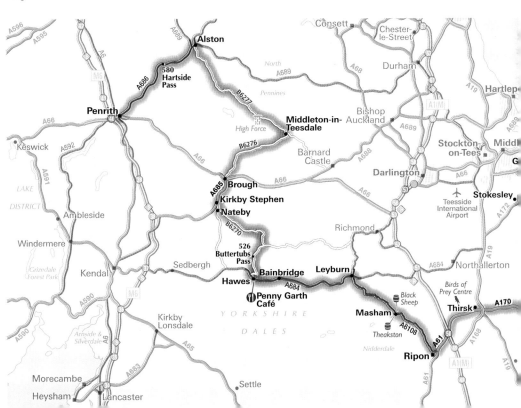

RIDE (44) North England Tour Day 3

NORTH TOUR DAY 3 MORNING

A STUNNING RIDE: WHINLATTER and Honister Passes are good, Wrynose Pass is better, then the infamous Hardknott Pass is a real challenge – tight, twisty and very steep. It's rewarding but demands confidence and caution. If you don't fancy it, stay on the A593 to Coniston. Lunch is at The Bluebird Café on the shores of beautiful Coniston Water. The garage is by the turn for the café: fill up here for the next part of the tour.

FROM Penrith, Cumbria
TO Coniston, Cumbria
DISTANCE 116 miles
ALLOW 2.5–3.5 hours

Route Description

➤ **Penrith** Leave town on the A66 towards Workington.
➤ **Braithwaite** After 20 miles, take the exit for the B5292 to Lorton and Whinlatter Pass.
➤ **B5289** At the T-junction, turn left on the B5289 to Low Lorton.
➤ **Look out** After about 3 miles, take the easy-to-miss left turn, signed to Buttermere. Stay on the road over Honister Pass.
➤ **Keswick** Enter the town centre and turn right, picking up the A591 to Ambleside.
➤ **Ambleside** Fight your way round the one-way system, following signs for A593 Coniston.
➤ **Look out** About 2 miles outside Ambleside on the A593 take the easy-to-miss right turn signed for The Langdales and Wrynose Pass. Note If you're concerned about the challenging Wrynose and Hardknott Passes, don't take this turn: stay on the A593 from Ambleside to Coniston and grab an early lunch, or maybe visit the beautiful village of Hawkshead.

➤ **Cockley Beck** Turn right over the bridge for Hardknott Pass.
➤ **Eskdale** Turn right by the pub, towards Holmrook, then left to Irton (look for brown signs for The Woodlands Tea Rooms).
➤ **A595** At the T-junction turn left on the A595 towards Barrow-in-Furness.
➤ **Silecroft** Turn left to stay on the A595 to Barrow.
➤ **High Cross Inn** Turn left on the A593 to Coniston.
➤ **Coniston** Into the village and turn right on Lake Road, to Coniston Water. The route ends at The Bluebird Café on Lake Road, Coniston.

NORTH TOUR DAY 3 AFTERNOON

A FTER A GREAT afternoon's riding, we'd grab a curry in the Voujon Indian restaurant in Hawes.

FROM Coniston, Cumbria
TO Hawes, North Yorkshire
DISTANCE 111 miles
ALLOW 2.5–3.5 hours

Route Description

➤ **Coniston** Leave the village on the A593 towards Broughton-in-Furness.
➤ **Torver** Turn left on the A5084 to Greenodd.
➤ **Lowick Green** Turn left on the A5092 towards Kendal.
➤ **Greenodd** Turn left on the A590 towards Kendal.
➤ **Newby Bridge** Turn left at the roundabout on the A592 to Windermere.
➤ **Windermere** Ride straight through town, following signs for the A592 Kirkstone Pass.
➤ **Pooley Bridge** Continue forward on the B5320. In village centre bear left at the rbt for Kendal.
➤ **Eamont Bridge** Right on the A6 through Shap.

➤ **Kendal** Go into the town centre and pick up the B6254 to Oxenholme – look out for signs for Westmorland General Hospital.
➤ **Kirkby Lonsdale** Turn left on the A65 towards Skipton.
➤ **Ingleton** Turn left on the B6255 Hawes.
➤ **Hawes** Turn right on the A684 into the town centre.

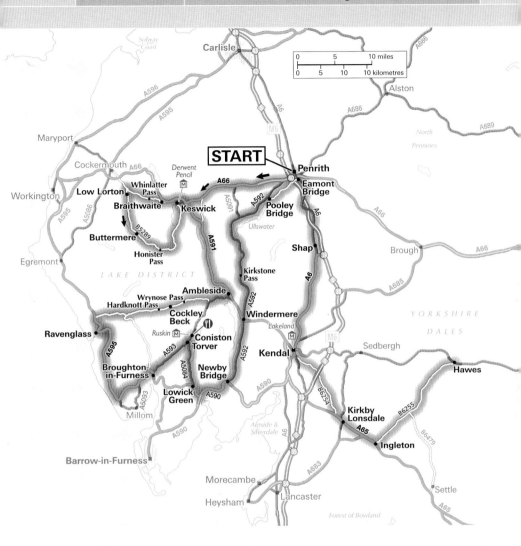

WHAT TO SEE AND DO

Derwent Pencil Museum
This museum is more interesting than you might think. An exploration of something we all take for granted. **derwentart.com/en-gb/c/about/company/derwent-pencil-museum**

The Ruskin Museum, Coniston John Ruskin was an artist and political thinker, but petrolheads may be more interested in viewing the museum's Donald Campbell *Bluebird* exhibits. **ruskinmuseum.com**

Museum of Lakeland Life, Kendal Local history, furniture, industry, crafts etc, as well as an Arthur Ransome Room, which will interest *Swallows and Amazons* aficionados. **lakelandarts.org.uk/lakeland-museum**

RIDE (44) North England Tour Day 4

NORTH TOUR DAY 4 MORNING

SOME SPECTACULAR ROADS – and some urban irritation to avoid in the centre of Halifax and Huddersfield.

Take care, as road signs aren't plentiful (particularly around Saddleworth), but the wonderful ride over Holme Moss more than repays the effort of finding it.

FROM Hawes, North Yorkshire
TO Glossop, Derbyshire
DISTANCE 112 miles
ALLOW 3 hours

Route Description

➤ **Hawes** Leave town on the A684 towards Aysgarth.
➤ **Bainbridge** Turn right to stay on the A684 to Aysgarth.
➤ **Aysgarth** Turn right on the B6160 signed for West Burton.
➤ **Threshfield** Continue straight on the B6265.
➤ **Skipton** Turn right along the A65, then at the next rbt turn left on the A629 to Keighley.
➤ **Keighley** Go across town, staying on the A629 for Halifax.
➤ **Cross Roads** Go right at the Cross Roads rbt on the A6033 to Hebden Bridge.
➤ **Hebden Bridge** When the road meets the A646 go straight (a left turn) towards Halifax.
➤ **Mytholmroyd** Turn right on the B6138 towards Rochdale.
➤ **Blackstone reservoir** Turn left on the A58 towards Halifax.
➤ **Ripponden** Turn right – almost doubling back on yourself – on the A672 towards Oldham, passing under the M62.
➤ **Look out** Tricky junction in Denshaw: turn left then immediately right onto Delph Road – follow the brown tourist sign. Go straight across the staggered x-roads.
➤ **Dobcross** Go right at the rbt on the A670, passing under the viaduct. Turn left just after the train station, then left on the A635 to Holmfirth.
➤ **Holmfirth** Turn right on A6024 to Holme Moss.
➤ **Woodhead reservoir** Turn right on the A628 towards Manchester.
➤ **Hollingworth** Turn left at the lights onto the A57 towards Sheffield. The route ends in Glossop.

NORTH TOUR DAY 4 AFTERNOON

AFTER SO MUCH glorious riding – Snake Pass, Hope Valley, the Via Gellia – it's an anticlimax to land on the dual carriageway of the A50, leading to the M1 and a return to the start. However, a bit of multi-lane covers the ground quickly – which can be very handy.

FROM Glossop, Derbyshire
TO M1 Leicester Forest East services (south)
DISTANCE 112 miles
ALLOW 2.5–3 hours

Route Description

➤ **Glossop** Continue on the A57 towards Sheffield.
➤ **Ladybower Reservoir** Turn right at the lights, across the bridge, on the A6013 to Bamford.
➤ **Bamford** Turn right on the A6187 to Hope.
➤ **Continue** along minor road and turn right at T-junction to Chapel-en-le-Frith.
➤ **Chapel-en-le-Frith** Turn left on the A6 to Buxton.
➤ **Buxton** Into the town centre and pick up the A515 to Ashbourne.
➤ **Look out** Don't miss the left turn at Newhaven (by a garage) for the A5012 to Cromford.
➤ **Cromford** Turn right onto the B5036 signed Wirksworth.

1 mile later, turn right onto the B5035 to Ashbourne.
➤ **Ashbourne** Enter the town centre to rejoin the A515, following signs for Lichfield.
➤ **A50 roundabout** Turn left on the A50 towards Derby.
➤ **M1** At the end of the A50, join the M1 southbound.
➤ **M1 J21A** Leave the motorway for the services. The route ends at Leicester Forest East Services, M1 southbound.

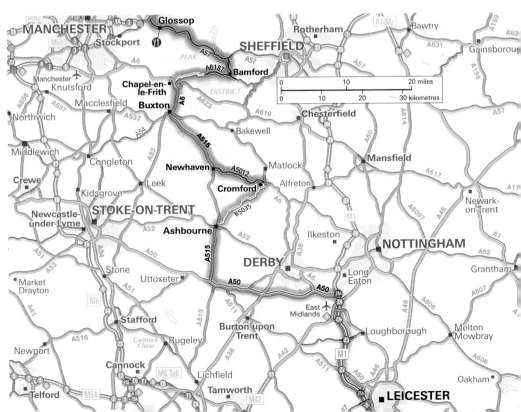

Wales

Wild mountains, spectacular shores, historic castles and miles of amazing roads. Croeso y Gymru – Welcome to Wales

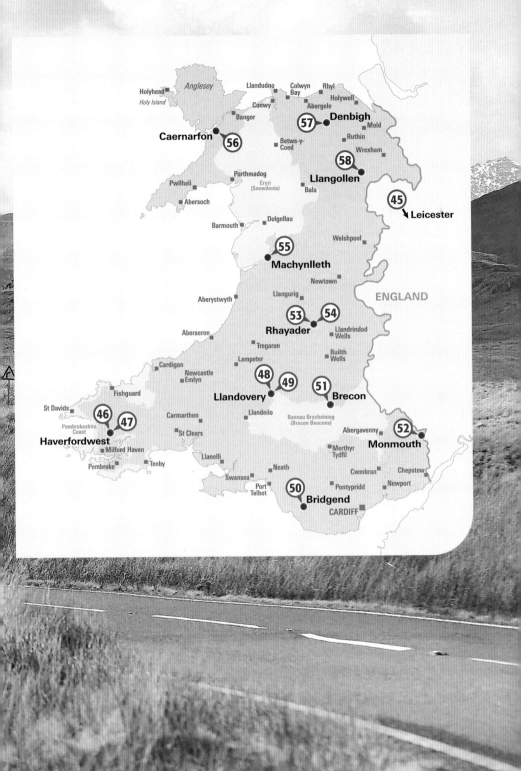

RIDE 45 Wales Tour Day 1

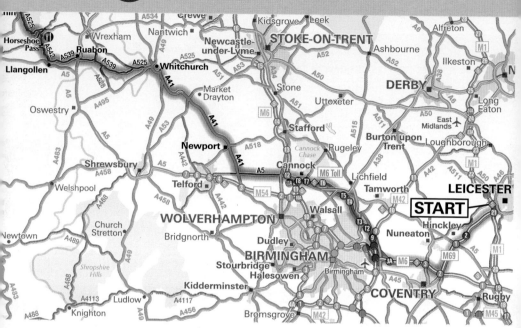

DAY 1 MORNING

TO GET US going quickly first thing, the morning route includes a chunk of motorway – with a toll to pay. If you want to avoid it you can take the A47 from Leicester Forest East Services and then the A5, picking up the route at the A41 roundabout. However, it's no more fun and is slower. Once you're on the A41 the real riding begins, building up to the spectacular Horseshoe Pass.

FROM M1 Leicester Forest East Services (south)
TO Horseshoe Pass, Denbighshire
DISTANCE 120 miles
ALLOW 2.5 hours

Route Description

➤ **M1 LFE Services** South-bound on M1 for one junction.
➤ **M1 J21** Right on the M69 to Coventry.
➤ **Coventry** Left on M6, then take the M6 Toll to rejoin M6.
➤ **M6 J12** Left on the A5 towards Telford.
➤ **A5/A41 rbt** Right on A41.

➤ **Whitchurch ring road** Left on the A525.
➤ **Look out** After 4 miles, take the easy-to-miss left turn on the A539, towards Hanmer. There's a second easy-to-miss left turn, 9 miles later (after the Cross Foxes pub), to stay on the A539.
➤ **Ruabon** Skirt the town, staying on the A539 following signs for Llangollen.
➤ **Llangollen** Straight through town on this road, which becomes the A542 as it climbs to Horseshoe Pass. Route ends at the Ponderosa Café on the Horseshoe Pass.

WHAT TO SEE AND DO

Conwy Castle Magnificent 13th-century fortress. Part of the town walls of Conwy. **cadw.gov.wales/visit/ places-to-visit/castell- conwy**

Great Orme, nr Llandudno Bronze Age copper mine, cable-operated street tramway, and impressive scenery. **greatormetramway.co.uk/ en/great-orme**

ROUTE TYPE Tour | DISTANCE 120 miles morning | 117 miles afternoon

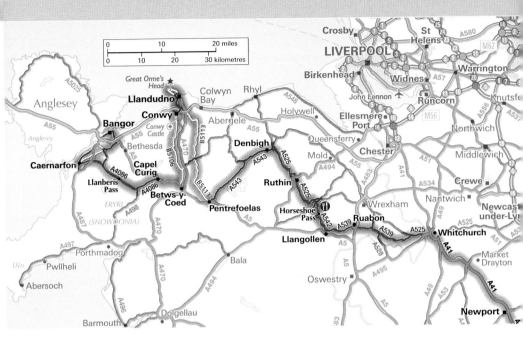

DAY 1 AFTERNOON

THE AFTERNOON'S RIDING takes in everything from fast and sweeping A-roads to tight and challenging B-roads. The route stops in Bangor – a vibrant university town with plenty of affordable accommodation. If you have time, nip over the Menai Bridge and visit Beaumaris Castle. Notice the services on the A4244/A5 roundabout on the way into Bangor: that's where to fill up next morning.

FROM Horseshoe Pass, Denbighshire
TO Bangor, Gwynedd
DISTANCE 117 miles
ALLOW 2.5–3 hours

Route Description

➤ **Ponderosa Café** Right, down Horseshoe Pass, staying on the A542 and then A525 to Ruthin.
➤ **Ruthin** Left at rbt, into town, then right on A525 to Denbigh.
➤ **Denbigh** Left on the A543 for Pentrefoelas.
➤ **Pentrefoelas** Right on A5, then first right turn for B5113.

➤ **A548** Left then right over a very staggered x-roads, staying on B5113.
➤ **Before Bryn-y-Maen** Left on B5381 towards Llansanffraid.
➤ **Llandudno Junction** Straight over roundabout, for Llandudno. At the seafront, turn left and stay left, beside the sea, riding around Great Orme's Head (toll road).
➤ **Llandudno** Carry straight on when returning to Llandudno, taking the A546 towards Conwy.
➤ **Llandudno Junction** Right at the roundabout, passing over

the A55, towards Conwy.
➤ **Conwy Castle** Left on B5106. By Gwydir Castle, turn right to stay on the B5106 to Betws-y-Coed.
➤ **Betws-y-Coed** Turn right on the A5 towards Bangor.
➤ **Capel Curig** Turn left onto the A4086. Take the right turn 5 miles later, to stay on the road through Llanberis Pass.
➤ **Caernarfon** Right at the rbt, on the B4366 towards Bethel.
➤ **Roundabout** Straight over on the A4244 towards Bangor.
➤ **A5** Turn left and stay on A5 all the way to Bangor.

RIDE (45) Wales Tour Day 2

DAY 2 MORNING

WHAT A RIDE! If you're concerned about time, you don't have to do the loop around Lake Vyrnwy – but it is spectacular and beautiful, so we highly recommend it. There are plenty of places to eat in Dolgellau – treat yourself to the deli/bakery Popty'r Dref on Finsbury Square. If you're worried about tank range, there is a petrol station at the A458/A470 roundabout. Otherwise, wait until after lunch and return to the Esso station just before the turning to Dolgellau.

FROM Bangor, Gwynedd
TO Dolgellau, Gwynedd
DISTANCE 124 miles
ALLOW 2.5–3 hours

Route Description

> **Bangor** Leave Bangor on the A4244 past Pentir and take the B4366 to Caernarfon.
> **Caernarfon** Into the town centre, go onto the elevated A487 for one junction, then bear left on the A4085 towards Beddgelert.

> **Beddgelert** Turn right on the A498 to Porthmadog.
> **Look out** Take the easy-to-miss left turn at Pont Aberglasyln, on the A4085.
> **Penrhyndeudraeth** Left on the A487 towards Dolgellau.
> **Look out** Don't miss the left turn after Trawsfynydd, for the A4212 to Bala.
> **Bala** Over staggered x-roads on B4391 to Llangynog.
> **Penybontfaw** Right turn on B4396 towards Llanwddyn.

> **Abertridwr** Turn right towards Llyn Vyrnwy, to do a lap of the lake on the B4393, returning past this junction. If worried about time, though, just turn left towards Llanfihangel.
> **T-junction** Right on B4395.
> **A458** Right towards Dolgellau.
> **Mallwyd** Right at roundabout on A470.
> **A470** Left for Dolgellau. Route ends in Dolgellau centre.

DAY 2 AFTERNOON

A DETOUR INTO ABERYSTWYTH for a stroll along the prom is recommended – it's a popular bike meet at weekends. An afternoon of flowing, sweeping roads brings you to the charming Victorian spa town of Builth Wells. It's a quiet place, unless you go when the Royal Welsh Show is on (best dodge that, really). Turning left at the showground roundabout will take you into town, past a petrol station: that's where you'll want to fill up in the morning.

FROM Dolgellau, Gwynedd
TO Builth Wells, Powys
DISTANCE 105 miles
ALLOW 2–2.5 hours

Route Description

> **Dolgellau** Leave town on the A470, retracing your steps towards the Mallwyd rbt.
> **Cross Foxes pub** Turn right on A487 to Machynlleth, continue through town towards Aberystwyth.
> **Bow Street** Turn left on A4159 towards Capel Dewi.
> **Roundabout** Left on A44 to Llangurig.
> **Llangurig** Left onto A470 towards Dolgellau.
> **Level crossing** Carry straight on, along the A489 to Newtown.
> **Newtown** Pick up the A483 to Builth Wells.
> **Royal Welsh Showground** Left at roundabout for Builth Wells. Route ends in Builth Wells town centre.

WHAT TO SEE AND DO

Ffestiniog Railway
Originally built to carry slate from the quarries at Blaenau Ffestiniog to the harbour at Porthmadog, the little trains now carry passengers through the beautiful scenery of the national park.
festrail.co.uk

RIDE (45) Wales Tour Day 2

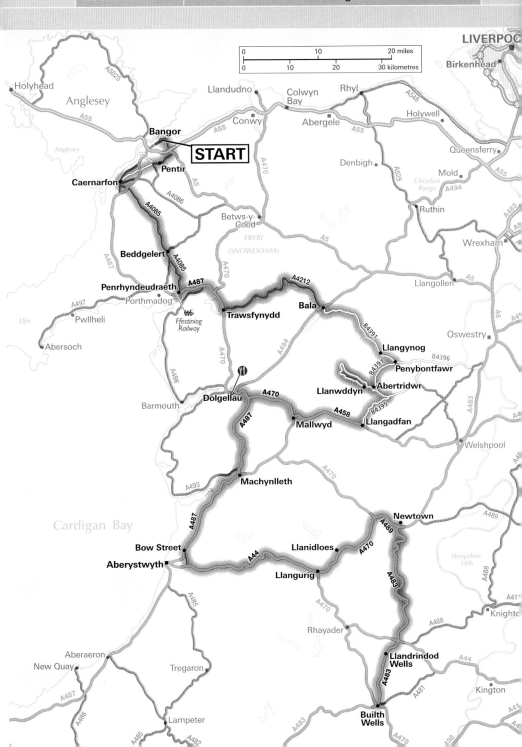

RIDE (45) Wales Tour Day 3

DAY 3 MORNING

FROM SWEEPING, OPEN roads, the route enters tighter, more challenging roads through the stunning countryside around Newcastle Emlyn, ending in the pretty seaside town of Cardigan. There are plenty of decent tea rooms and cafés but we'd favour Food For Thought Café on Pendre (the main street) or the excellent Castle Café. Find somewhere to park and work out how to get back to the roundabout on the edge of town. That's where the afternoon's route begins.

FROM Builth Wells, Powys
TO Cardigan, Ceredigion
DISTANCE 79 miles
ALLOW 2 hours

Route Description

➤ **Builth Wells** Leave town on the A470, towards Rhayader.
➤ **Newbridge-on-Wye** Turn left on B4358 to Beulah.

➤ **Beulah** Turn right on the A483 to Llandovery.
➤ **Llandovery** Turn right on the A40 towards Llandeilo.
➤ **Llanwrda** Turn right on the A482 to Lampeter.
➤ **Lampeter** Carry straight on through town, across the mini-rbt (it becomes the A475). Go straight over the staggered

x-roads, still on the A475, to Newcastle Emlyn.
➤ **Newcastle Emlyn** Turn right in the town centre, taking the A484 to Cardigan.
➤ **Cardigan ring road** Go straight across the A487 roundabout, into the town centre. The route ends in Cardigan town centre.

DAY 3 AFTERNOON

THE FINAL STRETCH between Llandovery and Brecon is one of the best rides ever. Top up with petrol before setting out to tackle the majestic A4069 over the Black Mountain. There are dozens of places to stay and eat in Brecon. Be warned, though: the town gets very busy when the Jazz Festival is on. As you rode into town, you passed a petrol station: that's where the morning's route will start.

FROM Cardigan, Ceredigion
TO Brecon, Powys
DISTANCE 137 miles
ALLOW 2 hours

Route Description

➤ **Cardigan** Leave town on the A487 towards Fishguard.
➤ **Look out** At Penfro, take the easy-to-miss left turn on the B4329 to Haverfordwest.
➤ **Haverfordwest** Turn left on the A40 towards St Clears.
➤ **Canaston Bridge** Turn right at rbt, on the A4075 to Tenby.
➤ **Carew** Left on A477.
➤ **St Clears** Go straight at the roundabout, rejoining the A40 to Carmarthen.

➤ **Carmarthen** Stay on the A40 as it skirts the town, following signs to Llandeilo.
➤ **Llandeilo** Turn right on the A483 towards Swansea.
➤ **Ammanford** Turn left at the end of the high street on the A474 (past the Old Cross, going in the opposite direction to the M4).
➤ **Lower Brynamman** Turn left just before the level crossing, on the A4069 to Brynamman.
➤ **Brynamman** Turn left at the mini-roundabout, on the A4069 to Llangadog.
➤ **Llangadog** Turn right in the centre of the village on the A4069 to Llandovery.

➤ **Llandovery** Straight along High Street, on A40 to Brecon.
➤ **Brecon bypass** Turn left at the roundabout on the B4601 into Brecon. The route ends in Brecon town centre.

WHAT TO SEE AND DO

Mwnt Beach Cardigan Bay
Sheltered sandy beach owned by the National Trust. Steep steps lead to beach, car park in a field above.

Poppit Sands, nr Cardigan
Gorgeous open blue flag beach with sand dunes. Great for power kiting.

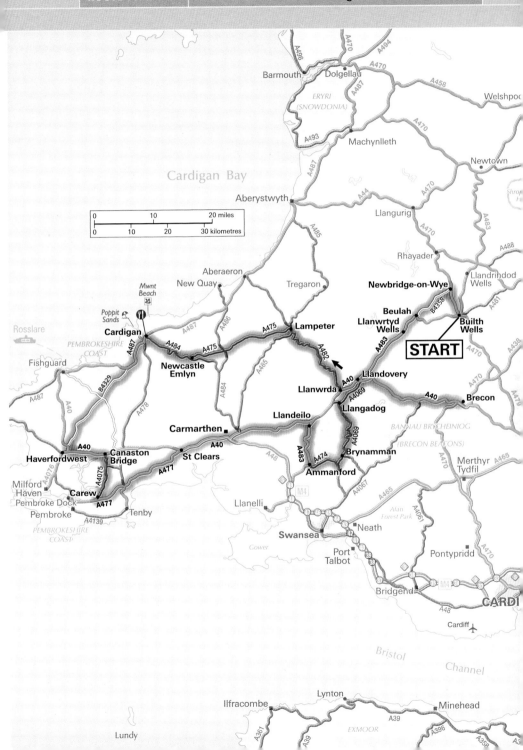

RIDE (45) Wales Tour Day 4

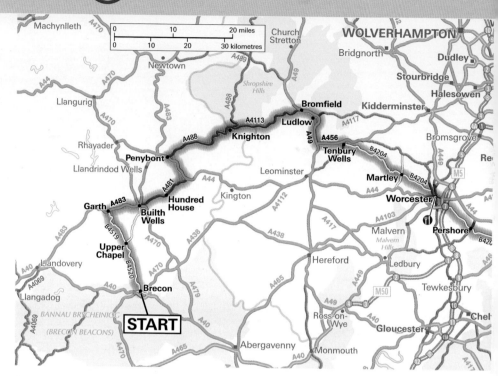

DAY 4 MORNING

AFTER SOME CLASSIC Welsh roads, it's time to return to England. It's a good ride, with a lunch stop in Worcester – there are plenty of cafés and restaurants to choose from. Once you've eaten, rejoin the Worcester one-way system.

FROM Brecon, Powys
TO Worcester
DISTANCE 100 miles
ALLOW 2–2.5 hours

Route Description

➤ **Brecon** Leave town on the B4520 to Upper Chapel.
➤ **Upper Chapel** Turn left on the B4519 to Garth.
➤ **Garth** Turn right on the A483 to Builth Wells.
➤ **Builth Wells** On one-way system follow signs for A483 towards Llandrindod Wells. After Royal Welsh Showground, turn right on A481 to Hundred House.
➤ **A44** Turn left at the Fforest Inn, following signs for A44 Rhayader.

➤ **Penybont** Turn right on the A488 to Knighton.
➤ **Knighton** Turn right on the A4113 to Bromfield.
➤ **Bromfield** Turn right on the A49 towards Leominster.
➤ **Woofferton** Left on the A456 towards Kidderminster.
➤ **Tenbury Wells** Right on the A4112 for Tenbury Wells town centre. Where the high street turns sharp right, go straight on (technically making a turn left) on the B4204, signed Clifton upon Teme.
➤ **Martley** Turn left to stay on the B4204 to Worcester.
➤ **Worcester** Turn right on A443 to the city centre. Route ends in Worcester city centre.

| ROUTE TYPE Tour | DISTANCE 100 miles morning | 98 miles afternoon |

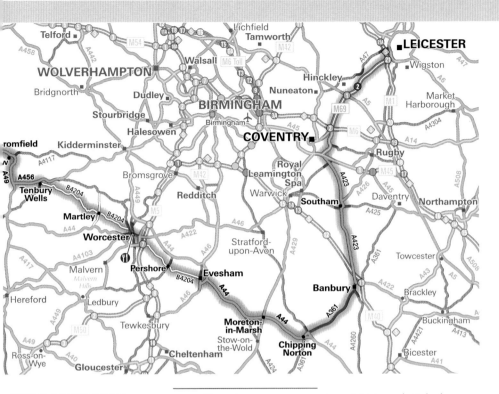

DAY 4 AFTERNOON

A LOVELY RUN IN across the Cotswolds – with the option of tea stops in quaint towns like Chipping Norton and Banbury. It's only on the urban fringes of Coventry that the plain side of riding in Britain reappears, with some dual-carriageway bypass leading to the final motorway leg on the M69 and M1.

FROM Worcester
TO Leicester Forest East Services (north)
DISTANCE 98 miles
ALLOW 2–2.5 hours

Route Description

➤ **Worcester** Leave the city on the A44 towards Evesham.

➤ **M5 roundabout** Go straight across, taking the B4084 through Pershore.

➤ **Evesham** Skirt town, following signs for the A44 (Oxford). From the ring road, turn right at the roundabout onto the A44 towards Wickhamford.

➤ **Moreton-in-Marsh** Straight across staggered x-roads to stay on A44 towards Oxford.

➤ **Chipping Norton** Turn left on the A361 to Banbury.

➤ **Banbury** Enter the town centre to pick up the A423 to Southam.

➤ **Southam** Around the town on the A423 to Coventry.

➤ **A45 roundabout** Go straight at the roundabout on the A45 to Coventry, going right at the ring road until the A46 leads onto the M69.

➤ **A46/M69** Take the motorway all the way to Leicester, joining the M1 Northbound for one junction. Route ends in Leicester Forest East Services, M1 northbound.

RIDE (46) West Wales 1

SPREAD OUT OVER 243 square miles, the spectacular Pembrokeshire coastline is laced with golden beaches, fringed with quiet islands and studded with sleepy villages. It's the kind of landscape that creates fabulous days on a bike, whether you want to meander down scenic lanes or pause to admire the giant ships sailing to the deepwater harbour of Milford Haven, the rich local wildlife or the many historic buildings. That's why we've provided two rides in this part of the country: this route and another on the following pages.

This ride allows you to stop and discover engaging towns like Tenby, leaving scope for further exploration and selecting the quietest roads for a day of rewarding riding.

FROM/TO Haverfordwest, Pembrokeshire
DISTANCE 115 miles
ALLOW 4 hours

Route Description

➤ **From Haverfordwest** Take B4327 towards Dale.
➤ **Approaching Dale** Turn left at T-junction for lane to St Ishmael's. Continue, crossing A4076, to turn right onto the A477 towards Pembroke Dock.
➤ **Pembroke Dock** Turn left then right to the A4139 to Pembroke.
➤ **Pembroke** Turn right onto the B4320 towards Angle.
➤ **B4320** Turn left onto the B4319 towards Castlemartin and continue beyond.

➤ **Just before St Petrox** Take right turn down lane towards Stackpole. Navigate coast roads to Freshwater East.
➤ **Turn left** up B4584 to Lamphey. Turn right to take A4139 towards Tenby.
➤ **Tenby** Pick up A478 to Narberth. Continue through the town on the B4313.
➤ **Go straight** across A40 to continue on B4313 all the way to Fishguard.
➤ **Fishguard** A487 St Davids. Shortly take A40 towards Haverfordwest.
➤ **Letterston** Turn right on B4331 to St Davids, turning left when road reaches A487.
➤ **Croes-goch** Turn left on B4330 back to Haverfordwest.

WHAT TO SEE AND DO

Dale Point For sheer coastal splendour, the deepwater harbour of Milford Haven takes some beating. Well worth a slight detour to the viewpoint at Dale Point.

Stone Circle, Trefin There are some fabulous beaches between St David's Head and Strumble Head… but we favour those near Trefin, watched over by an ancient stone circle Carreg Samson.

Tenby This superbly picturesque seaside town is the perfect place for a seaside coffee break and a wander.
aroundtenby.co.uk

below *Glorious Welsh countryside enhances any ride*

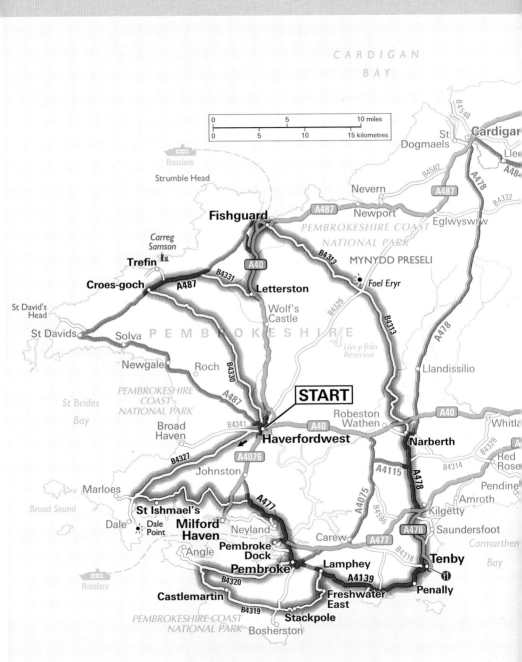

CARDIGAN BAY

Rosslare
Strumble Head
St Dogmaels
Cardigan
Llec
B4582
A487
A478
A48
B4332
Nevern
Newport
Eglwyswrw
Fishguard
PEMBROKESHIRE COAST
NATIONAL PARK
Carreg Samson
Trefin
A40
B4313
MYNYDD PRESELI
Foel Eryr
Croes-goch
A487
B4331
Letterston
B4329
B4313
A478
St David's Head
Wolf's Castle
St Davids
Solva
PEMBROKESHIRE
Llys-y-frân Reservoir
Newgale
Roch
B4330
A487
Llandissilio
St Brides Bay
PEMBROKESHIRE COAST NATIONAL PARK
Broad Haven
B4341
START
Robeston Wathen
A40
Whitla
Haverfordwest
A40
Narberth
B4328
Red Rose
B4327
A4076
Johnston
A4115
A478
B4314
Pendine
A4075
Amroth
Marloes
B4536
Kilgetty
Saundersfoot
Carmarthen
Broad Sound
Dale
Dale Point
St Ishmael's
Milford Haven
A477
Neyland
Carew
A477
B4318
A478
Tenby
Bay
Angle
Pembroke Dock
Lamphey
Penally
Pembroke
A4139
B4320
Freshwater East
Rosslare
Castlemartin
B4319
Stackpole
PEMBROKESHIRE COAST NATIONAL PARK
Bosherston

| 0 | | 5 | | 10 miles |
| 0 | 5 | | 10 | 15 kilometres |

RIDE (47) West Wales 2

THRUSTING FINGERS OUT into the storm-wracked Celtic sea, the Pembrokeshire Coast is one of three National Parks in Wales – jewels in the crown of the nation's countryside. You're always close to the coast – often within 10 miles – as the freshness of the air reveals. As you venture further inland, the hedges and trees close in before the land rises to open hilltops once more. Lose yourself in the maze of shady lanes and rolling hills between Carmarthen and Newcastle Emlyn. Discover Welsh bard Dylan Thomas' old haunts – plus the old boathouse where he wrote his intricate poems – at his home town of Laugharne, or visit Pendine Sands, where Sir Malcolm Campbell set his speed records.

FROM/TO Haverfordwest, Pembrokeshire
DISTANCE 133 miles
ALLOW 4 hours

Route Description

> **From Haverfordwest**
Take the A487 to St Davids. Follow the road all the way to Cardigan.
> **Cross the river** at Cardigan, then turn right at the roundabout on the A484 to Carmarthen.
> **Join the A40** at Carmarthen, heading west towards Fishguard and St Clears.
> **After 10 miles** Take the exit for the A4066 to St Clears. At the end of the slip road turn right on the A4066 to Pendine.
> **Stay on the road** through Pendine as it becomes the B4314 to Red Roses.
> **In Templeton** Turn left on the A478 towards Tenby.
> **After 3 miles** Turn right at the second roundabout on the A477 to Pembroke Dock.
> **At the A4076** Turn right to return to Haverfordwest.

WHAT TO SEE AND DO

Museum of Land Speed
For years, British daredevils and petrolheads came to Pendine Sands to chase the land-speed record.
cofgar.wales/venues/
museum-of-land-speed

St Davids Cathedral
Britain's smallest city has a spectacular cathedral, resting place of the principality's patron saint.
stdavidscathedral.org.uk

Carreg Coetan Arthur Chambered Tomb Just one example of the standing stones that litter the area. ½ mile walk from Newport car park.
cadw.gov.wales/visit/
places-to-visit/carreg-
coetan-arthur-chambered-
tomb

left Group riding in West Wales

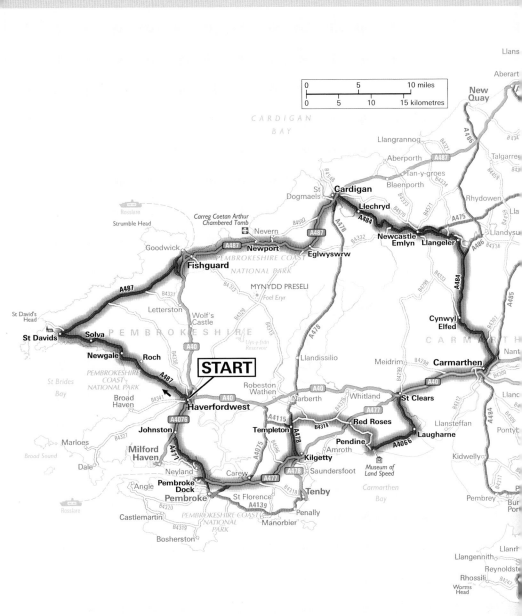

RIDE (48) Llandovery North Loop

EVERYONE LAUGHED AS Martin pretended to collapse off the bike. I'd taken some friends to see my favourite roads in Wales and while it had been a challenging ride, it wasn't that extreme… was it? Well, perhaps – the back roads between Tregaron and Llandovery, around the beautiful Llyn Brianne Reservoir, suit an adventure bike better than Martin's Suzuki SV1000S. Tight, narrow, occasionally broken up or strewn with gravel, they slice through the wooded hills around the lake as if travelling back in time, rather than just across the Cambrian Mountains. But for all the challenge, it's a rewarding ride. Even Martin was laughing as we picked him off the ground. 'That has to be the maddest road I've ever ridden,' he grinned.

FROM/TO Llandovery, Carmarthenshire
DISTANCE 59 miles
ALLOW 2.5 hours

Route Description

> **At Llandovery** Take the A40 southwest towards Llandeilo.
> **At Llanwrda** Turn right on the A482 towards Lampeter and ride through Pumsaint.
> **Turn right** onto the B4343 at Cwmann, continuing all the way to Tregaron.
> **In Tregaron** Turn right at the Talbot Hotel, onto a road that passes the Memorial Hall. Continue on the lane up the valley.

> **At a fork** Turn right onto a lane towards Llyn Brianne and Rhandirmwyn. Follow the lane to a bridge at the very head of Llyn Brianne, and a T junction.

below Spillway at Llyn Brianne

> **Turn right** towards Rhandirmwyn and the Dinas Nature Reserve.
> **Continue** through Rhandirmwyn and down the valley to return to Llandovery.

WHAT TO SEE AND DO

Dolaucothi Gold Mines

These unique gold mines are set amid wooded hillsides overlooking the beautiful Cothi Valley. Guided tours take you back to experience the conditions of the Roman, Victorian and 1930's underground workings.
nationaltrust.org.uk/visit/ wales/dolaucothi

RSPB Gwenffrwd-Dinas

Wales' answer to Robin Hood is shrouded in legend. A brisk walk through the beautiful Gwenffrwd-Dinas RSPB reserve, just south of Llyn Brianne, takes you to Twm Siôn Cati's Cave that supposed to have been his hideout.
rspb.org.uk/days-out/reserves/ gwenffrwd-dinas

Llyn Brianne Reservoir

Built in the late 1960's, 1970's, 300 metres above sea level, holding around 64 million cubic litres, with a 91-metre stone dam, this is largest of its kind in Europe. The spillway which powers a hydroelectric plant is very impressive when in full flow.

RIDE (48) Llandovery North Loop

ROUTE TYPE Loop | **DISTANCE** 59 miles

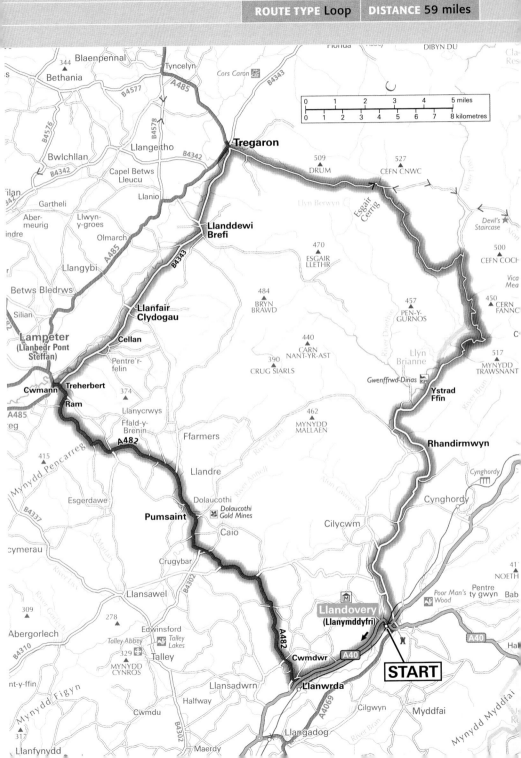

RIDE (49) Llandovery South Loop

I REMEMBER SITTING IN the passenger seat of the family car as a very young lad, while my dad drove us up the Black Mountain road, the A4069. It was the closest I ever saw him come to crashing because, as we neared the top, where there should have been a spectacular view across the countryside, there was a Hercules aircraft. We were level with the cockpit, staring at the flight crew. For a second, all we could do was gaze at them in amazement – not ideal when there's another corner coming up.

You're less likely to find low-flying aircraft there these days. There was a time when you might have met road testers – from TV shows like *Top Gear* as well as bike mags – but now there's a speed limit on the A4069 it's less popular for testing. It's still a great ride, but it's more about taking in views than hitting apexes these days. Mind you, the rest of the ride really flows – especially the A4067 and the crazy wooded section of the A40 near Halfway. It must be one of my favourite stretches of road. Never seen a plane there, though…

above *The Black Mountain at Brynamman*

FROM/TO Llandovery, Carmarthenshire
DISTANCE 52 miles
ALLOW 1.25 hours

Route Description

> **From Llandovery** Take the A4069 south to Llangadog.
> **Turn left** in the centre of Llangadog village, by The Castle Hotel, to continue on the A4069.
> **Follow the road** all the way across the Black Mountain to Brynamman.

> **On reaching the mini-rbt** at Brynamman, turn left onto the A4068 towards Ystalyfera.
> **At the large roundabout** turn left again to join the A4067 towards Ystradgynlais – home of the BMW Off-Road Skills Centre.
> **Continue on the A4067** through Glyntawe and up across the Brecon Beacons.
> **When the road meets the A40** turn left through Sennybridge to return to Llandovery.

WHAT TO SEE AND DO

Henrhyd Falls The highest waterfall in South Wales is a sight not to be missed. Take the guided walk down the beautiful Nant Llech valley, passing the site of a landslide and also a disused watermill.
nationaltrust.org.uk/visit/ wales/bannau-brycheiniog-brecon-beacons/henrhyd-falls-and-nant-llech-walk

Dan-yr-Ogof: The National Showcaves Centre for Wales Mainly for kids, but the caves are pretty impressive. Also there are life-size dinosaur models, and who would want to miss them?
showcaves.co.uk

Llandovery Castle This castle is an imposing sight with impressive views. Watch out for the statue of Llywelyn ap Gruffydd Fychan. This amazing steel statue of the 'Welsh Braveheart' was erected in 2001, the 600th anniversary of his death.
breconbeacons.org/poi/ castles-llandovery-castle

RIDE 49 Llandovery South Loop

ROUTE TYPE Loop | **DISTANCE** 52 miles

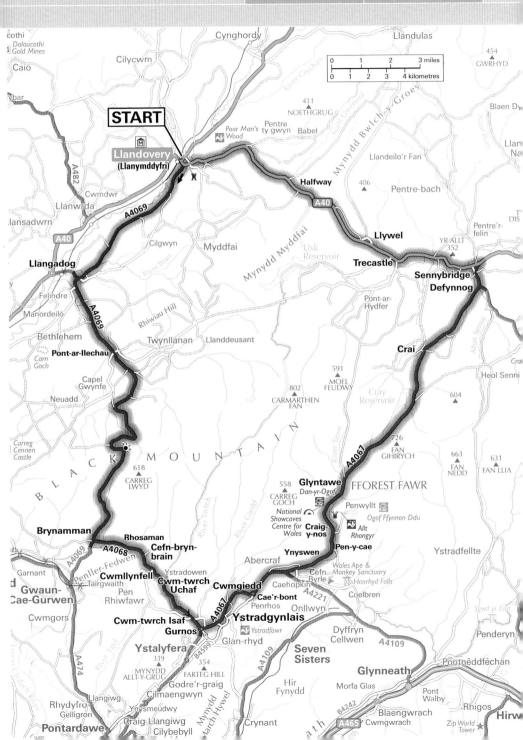

RIDE (50) Bridgend Twin Loop

THE WELSH VALLEYS have a proud history, powering the Industrial Revolution with the coal from the pits. There's no mining there now – but that's not the attraction for motorcyclists, anyway. Bikers come for the valleys – or to be more accurate, the hills and the roads that span them, dropping down in glorious cascades of corners, including the occasional hairpin.

The best thing about the riding in this area, though, is that once you're out of the villages, the roads are so quiet – the lack of heavy industry means a lack of heavy traffic. Instead we get broad lanes of decent tarmac slicing through a fresh, green landscape and plenty of time to enjoy it.

This ride through the valleys and up into the Brecon Beacons is based around Bridgend – but it's easily started and finished from J36 of the M4 if you're rushing into the area to ride it.

FROM/TO Bridgend
DISTANCE 87 miles
ALLOW 3 hours

Route Description

> **From Sarn Park Services at Bridgend** Take the A4061 towards Pontycymer and Ogmore Vale.
> **After ½ mile** Turn left on A4065 towards Abergarw.
> **In another ½ mile** Turn right on the A4064 to Llangeinor.
> **In Llangeinor** Turn right on A4093 towards Ogmore Vale.
> **Turn left** (going straight) in Lewistown, rejoining the A4061 towards Ogmore Vale.
> **In Treorchy** Turn right at the lights on A4058 towards Pontypridd.
> **At the mini-roundabout** Turn left on B4512 to Penrhys.
> **Join A4233** to Ferndale and Aberdare.
> **Cross Aberdare** Following signs for Merthyr Tydfil until picking up the B4276 to Llwydcoed.
> **At the A465** Turn right towards Merthyr Tydfil.
> **At roundabout** Turn

above *Astonishing riding in South Wales – just get north of the M4*

left on the A470 towards Brecon.
> **After 7 miles** Turn left on the A4059 to Hirwaun.
> **Go straight across** the A465 roundabout, on the A4061 to Treherbert. At the next roundabout turn left to stay on this road.
> **At the lights in Treorchy**

Turn right to stay on the A4061 (the stretch you rode earlier).
> **After 3½ miles** Turn right on the A4107 towards Port Talbot.
> **After 13 miles** Turn left at the light on the B4282 to Maesteg and Bryn.
> **In Maesteg** Pick up the A4063 to return to Bridgend.

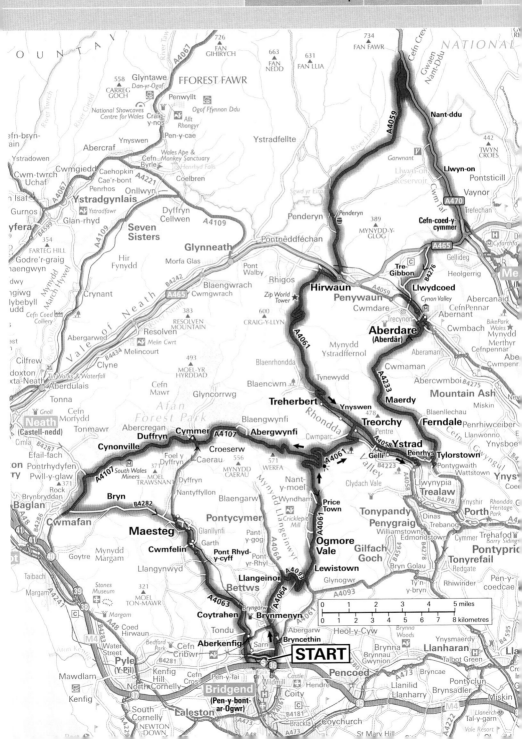

RIDE 51 Brecon Loop

WHEN A TOWN becomes a byword for biking and other outdoor activities, when even the major roads around it are quiet and thrilling to ride, it's easy to overlook the smaller roads. With Brecon, that would be a huge mistake. There are some fabulous rides to be had, hidden behind the high hedges and out on the open moors of the Beacons. The trick is finding them… and local knowledge is everything.

I had thought I knew the area pretty well until I went riding with my pal Ieuan. Leaving the beaten track for the path less travelled, he sprang a series of unexpected turns on me, slicing past tranquil reservoirs and across unspoilt hills I never knew existed. Some of the roads were tight, others were open and flowing; some he introduced me to were rough and bumpy while others had surfaces to shame Silverstone's GP circuit.

Even dipping onto the busy Head of the Valleys route didn't spoil the ride and, as we got back on roads I knew around Builth Wells, the pace didn't slacken. We barely burned a tankful of fuel, yet it was one of the best rides I'd had in ages. I came away realising that, even when you think you know where to go, there are always other great roads to be found – especially if you have a good local guide.

FROM/TO Brecon, Powys
DISTANCE 110 miles
ALLOW 3 hours

Route Description

> **Brecon** Take the A40 towards Abergavenny, soon turning right onto the B4558 towards Pencelli.

> **Talybont-on-Usk** Turn right to take a lane up to the reservoir. Continue up the valley and bend round to the left, to ride alongside Pontsticill Reservoir.

> **Keep straight ahead** down the valley towards Merthyr Tydfil.

> **At the A465** Turn left towards Abergavenny.

> **Beyond Tredegar** Exit onto the A4281 and at Garnlydan, turn left onto the B4560 to Llangynidr and carry on towards Bwlch.

> **Join the A40** towards Brecon, shortly turning right and back onto the B4560 towards Llangors.

> **At Talgarth** Join the A479 north, bearing right on the Bronllys ring road towards Builth Wells.

> **Keep straight on** as the road becomes the A470 to Builth Wells.

> **Just past Erwood** Turn right on B4567 towards Aberedw.

> **Take the first right** for the B4594 to Painscastle and stay on it for 16 miles.

> **A44** Turn left to Rhayader.

> **Crossgates** Turn left at the roundabout on the A483 to Builth Wells.

> **Builth** Pick up B4520 and follow it back to Brecon.

WHAT TO SEE AND DO

Brecon Mountain Railway
Swap the bike for a seat in a steam train for a different view of the Pen-twyn reservoirs in a route that runs from Pant to Dolygaer. Good café at Pontsticill too.
bmr.wales

Big Pit National Coal Museum, Blaenavon The UK's leading mining museum. Hundreds used to work in the colliery here. It includes underground tours, exhibitions and mining machinery.
museum.wales/bigpit

Royal Welsh Regiment Museum, Brecon The South Wales Borderers distinguished themselves in many military campaigns. This museum is full of fascinating related memorabilia.
royalwelshmuseum.wales

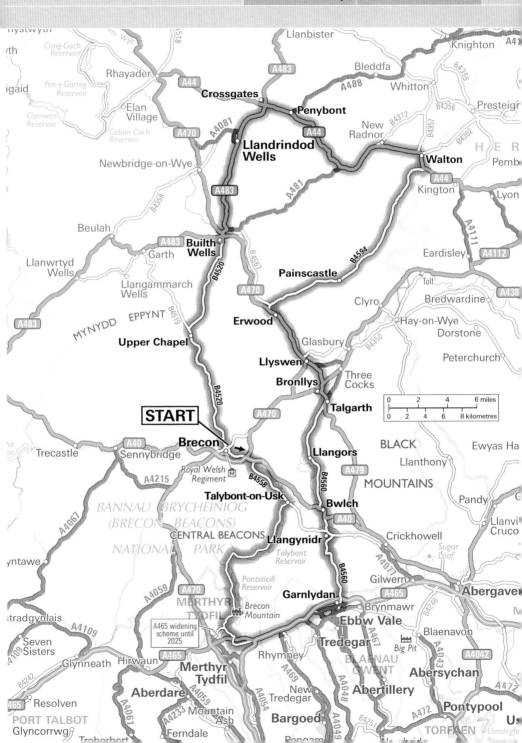

RIDE 52 Monmouth Loop

THE HIGHEST ROAD in Wales isn't in Eryri/Snowdonia. It's not even in the Brecon Beacons or the Cambrian Mountains. It's in the Welsh Marches, within spitting distance of the English border. Gospel Pass isn't famous like the more northerly Horseshoe Pass or the Llanberis Pass, but it has its own wild, twisty beauty and is arguably a lot more challenging than the more-well-known passes. It's just one of dozens of brilliant roads on this four-hour ride, which heads south along the border from Monmouth before looping inland for some high-quality Beacons riding.

FROM/TO Monmouth, Monmouthshire
DISTANCE 118 miles
ALLOW 4 hours

Route Description

> **Leave Monmouth** Take the A466 to Chepstow.
> **From Chepstow** Take the B4235 to Usk.
> **Join A472 into Usk** and stay on it all the way to the A4042. Follow the road to Pontypool.
> **At Pontypool** Turn right onto the A472 then right again on the A4043 to Blaenavon.
> **In Blaenavon** Turn right on B4246 towards Abergavenny. Cross the mountain and turn left at the T-junction through Govilon, still on B4246.
> **Join the A465** to Merthyr Tydfil. After 5½ miles exit for the A4281 towards Ebbw Vale.
> **Take the first exit** from the A4281 and turn right at the top of the sliproad on the B4560 to Llangynidr.
> **At the end of the road** Turn left towards Talybont-on-Usk.

> **Don't miss** the right-hand fork in the road in Llangynidr village, signposted for Bwlch still on the B4560. Turn left on A40 into Bwlch.
> **At the war memorial** in Bwlch turn right on the B4560 to Llangors. Stay on it all the way to Talgarth.
> **In Talgarth** Pick up A4078 to Aberllynfi and Three Cocks.
> **At the A438** Turn right towards Hereford.
> **In Glasbury** Go straight on (where the A438 turns left by the garage) on the B4350 to Hay-on-Wye.
> **Don't miss** the right turn, coming into Hay, signed for Capel-y-ffin (Forest Road). Stay on it as it becomes Gospel Pass.
> **In Llanvihangel Crucorney** Pick up the A465 towards Abergavenny.
> **When the A465** becomes a dual-carriageway turn left on B4521 towards Skenfrith, then left again.
> **After 10 miles** Take the easily missed right turn for B4347 and follow it all the way back to Monmouth.

left Have you seen a better road than the B4560 recently?

RIDE (52) Monmouth Loop

ROUTE TYPE Loop | **DISTANCE** 118 miles

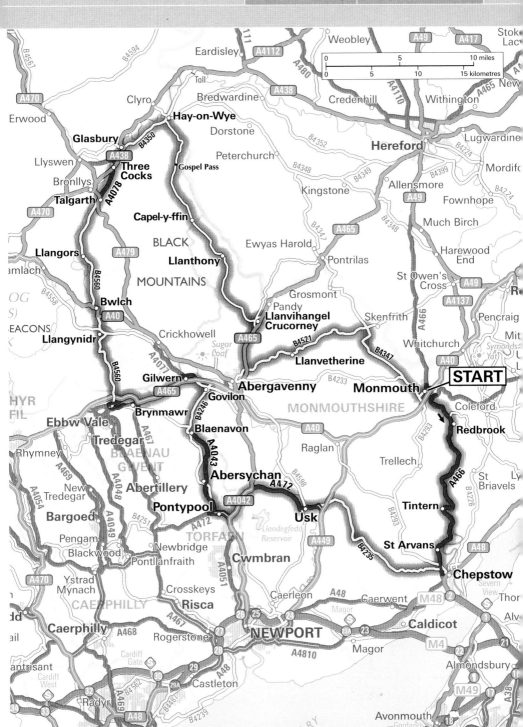

RIDE (53) Rhayader West Loop

THE FIRST TIME I visited the Elan Valley, you could probably have heard the sound of my mind being blown from as far away as Swansea. I'd thought I knew Wales pretty well. After all, I'd spent a good chunk of my childhood holidays in the Brecon Beacons and then a healthy portion of my formative motorcycling years sneaking over to play on the Principality's fabulous roads. Yet somehow I'd consistently ridden past without ever discovering this beautiful corner of the country. Turning left by the clock tower in Rhayader – rather than carrying straight on, as I always had before – was like discovering a secret door in a rather grand relative's home that leads to a whole new wing of the house, or maybe to Narnia… There's nothing fantastical about this ride through the Elan Valley and on other marvellous mid-Wales roads, though: it's just unbelievably fantastic.

FROM/TO Rhayader, Powys
DISTANCE 93 miles
ALLOW 2.5 hours

Route Description

> **From Rhayader**
Take the B4518 into Elan Valley. Follow the road through Elan Village and around the reservoirs.

> **When it meets** the mountain road (which will become B4574 after Cwmystwyth), turn left towards Aberystwyth.

> **At Devil's Bridge** Turn right on A4120 to Ponterwyd.

> **After 3 miles** Turn right on A44 to Llangurig.

> **Turn left** at Llangurig roundabout on A470 to Llanidloes.

> **Go into Llanidloes** and pick up B4569 to Trefeglwys.

> **In Caersws** Turn left on A470 towards Dolgellau.

> **In Llanbrynmair** Turn left on B4518 to Staylittle. Stay on this road all the way to Llanidloes. Turn right after crossing the river.

> **Don't miss** the left turn in Llanidloes – signed for Tylwch (Bryn-Du Road), to stay on B4518 all the way back to Rhayader.

below The Elan Valley is wild and breathtakingly beautiful

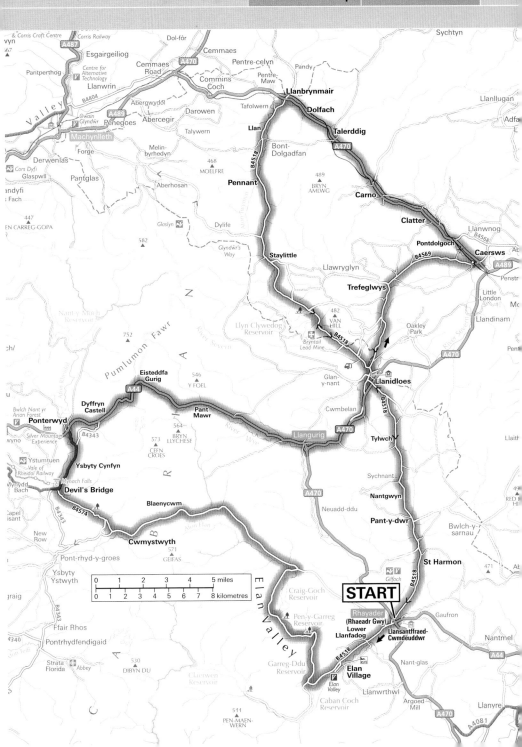

RIDE (54) Rhayader East Loop

THIS SECOND ROUTE around Rhayader features so many outstanding roads it seems almost unfair to single one of them out, but there's no doubting that the A483 between Newtown and Crossgates is something special (indeed, the whole length of the road to Llandovery is great). It's a road that draws riders from miles around – especially with the bike-friendly café by the petrol station at Crossgates.

Mind you, all of the roads on this route east from Rhayader are memorably great in their own ways – from the serpentine stretch of the A44 to the spectacular vistas from the Garth Hill viewpoint on the B4519 and the rollercoaster crests of the B4358. Any one of them would be worth a trip to ride on their own – but rolled up together with the A470 and A483? It's an unmissable circuit.

FROM/TO Rhayader, Powys
DISTANCE 100 miles
ALLOW 3 hours

Route Description
> **From Rhayader**
Head north on the A470 towards Newtown.
> **At the Llangurig roundabout** Turn right on A470 towards Llanidloes.
> **Keep straight on** as the road becomes the A489 towards Newtown.
> **At roundabout** Turn right on A483 to Llandrindod Wells.
> **At the Crossgates roundabout** Turn left on the A44 towards Leominster.
> **After 7 miles** Turn right on the A481 to Hundred House.
> **Go into** Builth Wells town centre. At the end of the high

street turn left on the B4520 towards Upper Chapel.
> **Don't miss** the right turn after 7 miles: the B4519 to Garth.
> **In Garth** Turn left on the A483 towards Llandovery.

> **In Beulah** Turn right on the B4358 to Newbridge-on-Wye.
> **In Newbridge-on-Wye** Turn left on the A470 to return to Rhayader.

below *A hairpin bend on the A483*

WHAT TO SEE AND DO

Thomas Shop Museum
Extraordinary museum that allows you to indulge in memories of a time in the 1800's.
thomas-shop.com

Café Express, Crossgates
A popular meeting point that will be thronged with bikes and their riders on any sunny weekend. The handy petrol station makes it a very efficient stop-off.

Elan Valley Visitor Centre
Great visitor centre set in a fantastic location against spectacular backdrop of the dam. **elanvalley.org.uk/visit/visitor-centre**

RIDE (54) Rhayader East Loop

ROUTE TYPE Loop **DISTANCE** 100 miles

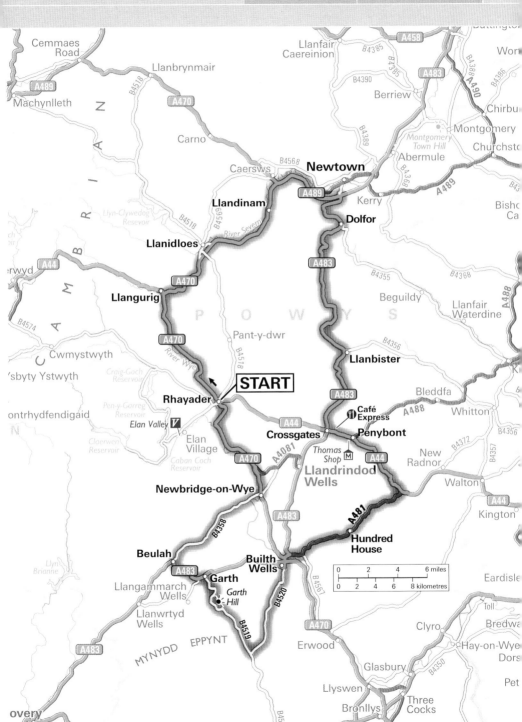

RIDE (55) Machynlleth Loop

THE PROBLEM WITH writing about routes in Wales is that it's possible to start the description of most by gushing, 'This could be the best route you ride this year...' Trouble is, that really could be true – especially of this route. It's one of the longer rides in the book and is a full day in every sense. It warms up with a coastal jaunt, out past Aberdyfi and Harlech. But it's not all about beaches as there are lakes too: Celyn, Tegid (Bala) and Vyrnwy. There are miles and miles of open moorland and shady woods, narrow lanes flanked by high hedges and glorious swoops down wide-open valleys. It has everything, all set in the most beautiful scenery imaginable – it really could be the best route you ride this year.

FROM/TO Machynlleth, Powys
DISTANCE 160 miles
ALLOW At least 5 hours

Route Description

➤ **Take the A487** towards Dolgellau.

➤ **Turn left** on the A493 to Aberdyfi.

➤ **At the A470** Turn left.

➤ **At the roundabout** Turn left on A496 to Barmouth.

➤ **At the A487** Turn right towards Dolgellau.

➤ **After 2 miles** Turn left on A470 towards Betws-y-Coed.

➤ **In Llan Ffestiniog** Turn right on the B4391 to Bala.

➤ **At A4212** Turn left to Bala.

➤ **In Bala** Go straight over staggered crossroads on B4391 to Llangynog.

➤ **Don't miss the right turn** in Penybontfawr for B4396 to Lake Vyrnwy and Llanwddyn.

➤ **At the shop in Llanwddyn**, turn right to do a lap of Lake Vyrnwy – then return

to continue on the B4393 to Llanfyllin.

➤ **At the T-junction** Turn right (almost doubling back on yourself) on the B4395 to Llwydiarth.

➤ **At the A458** Turn right towards Dolgellau.

➤ **At the Mallwyd roundabout** Turn right on the A470 towards Dolgellau.

➤ **After 7½ miles** Turn left on the A487 to return to Machynlleth.

below *The B4391 is just one of the amazing roads on this route*

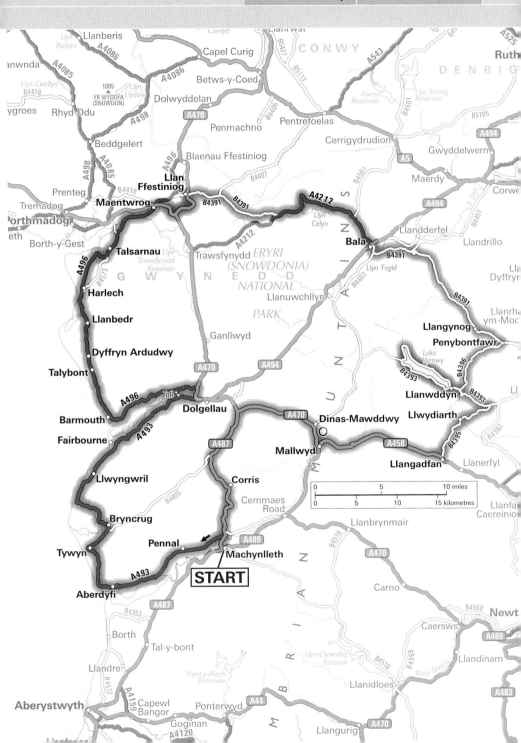

RIDE (56) Eryri/Snowdonia Loop

IF YOU WANT dramatic scenery, it's hard to beat Yr Wyddfa (Snowdon). The highest peak in Wales offers dramatic views – and dramatic riding – in every direction. It's easy to get to the top, if you take the summit railway from Llanberis (best booked in advance). In fact, there's loads to see and do in Eryri (Snowdonia) – from hillwalking and mountaineering to tourist attractions like the Zip World ziplines, the museums and numerous mines.

In other words, this is a popular area with visitors so pick your time to ride it with care. Sunny weekends – especially in the school holidays – will see more traffic about. If you're able to enjoy the ride on a weekday, chances are you'll have even popular roads like the Llanberis Pass more or less to yourself.

FROM/TO Caernarfon, Gwynedd
DISTANCE 80 miles
ALLOW 3 hours

Route Description
> **Leave Caernarfon** on A4086 to Llanberis. At the T-junction at the end of the pass, turn left to Capel Curig.
> **At the A5** Turn right to Betws-y-Coed.
> **Don't miss the left turn** on Betws-y-Coed high street: B5106 towards Trefriw.
> **At the T-junction** Turn right on B5106 into Llanrwst.
> **In Llanrwst** Cross the bridge and turn right, then turn left by the garage on B5427 to Nebo.
> **At the T-junction** Turn right on B5113 to Nebo and A5.
> **In Pentrefoelas** Turn right on A5 to Betws-y-Coed.
> **After one mile** Turn left on B4407 to Ysbyty Ifan (also signed for B4391 to Ffestiniog).
> **At T-junction** Turn right on B4391 to Ffestiniog.
> **Llan Ffestiniog** Turn right on A470 to Betws-y-Coed.
> **In Blaenau Ffestiniog**

above *Llanberis Pass (A4086)*

Turn left at the mini-roundabout on A496 signed to Dolgellau and Porthmadog.
> **At A487** T-junction turn right then take the second right: B4410 to Rhyd.
> **In Garreg** Turn right on A4085 to Beddgelert. Turn right when it meets A498 to go into Beddgelert.
> **In Beddgelert** Cross the river and follow the road round to the left and follow A4085 to return to Caernarfon.

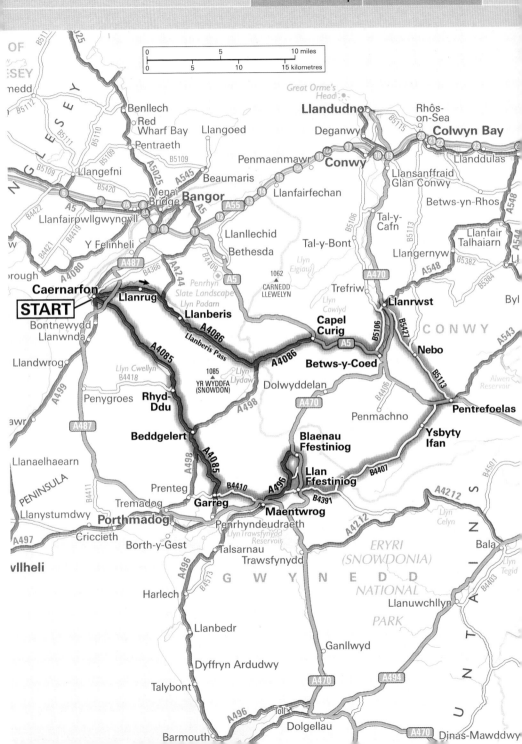

RIDE (57) Denbigh Loop

DENBIGH MAKES A great base for exploring the north of Wales. Handy for a run to the heart of Eryri (Snowdonia), it also has some superb riding on its doorstep. You can't go wrong with gentle day-trip to the seaside, with an ice cream in Penrhyn Bay and trip around the geological marvel of Great Orme's Head. Treat yourself to a day in Denbigh and you'll soon agree: it really does pay to take the roads less travelled.

FROM/TO Denbigh, Denbighshire
DISTANCE 100 miles
ALLOW 3 hours

Route Description

➤ **From Denbigh** Take the A543 to Bylchau.

➤ **At Bylchau** Turn right, onto the A544 towards Llansannan.

➤ **Continue** through Llanfair Talhaiarn, then turn right to take the A548 towards Abergele.

➤ **Turn left** at a x-roads onto the B5381 towards Betws-yn-Rhos.

➤ **At Dolwen** Turn right onto the B5383 to Old Colwyn.

➤ **Turn left** onto the A547, crossing the A55 at J20 to pick up the B5115 to Llandudno.

➤ **Turn right** on Llandudno's seafront Parade. Go right at end to take Scenic Drive around Great Ormes Head.

➤ **Leave Llandudno** on the A546 towards Conwy. At Llandudno Junction, on the A55 roundabout, pick up the B5381.

➤ **South of Bryn-y-Maen** Turn right at T-junction. Join the B5113 south towards Llanrwst.

➤ **Cross the A548** via x-roads to continue on the B5113 to Pentrefoelas.

➤ **In Pentrefoelas** Turn left on the A5 then left again on the A543 to Denbigh.

➤ **Don't miss** the right turn after 7½ miles: the B4501 to Cerrigydrudion and Llyn Brenig.

➤ **In Cerrigydrudion** Rejoin the A5 to Corwen.

➤ **After 8 miles** Turn left on the A494 to Ruthin.

➤ **In Ruthin** Pick up the A525 to return to Denbigh.

below *The Ogwen Valley with the Tryfan mountain beyond*

WHAT TO SEE AND DO

Denbigh Castle
Dominating the Denbigh skyline, the impressive ruins of the 13th-century castle and town walls make fascinating viewing for history buffs. **cadw.gov.wales/visit/places-to-visit/denbigh-castle**

Great Orme's Head
The spectacular views from this limestone headland make it well worth a trip – especially if you take the cable car from Happy Valley. **greatorme.org.uk**

RIDE (57) Denbigh Loop

ROUTE TYPE Loop | **DISTANCE** 100 miles

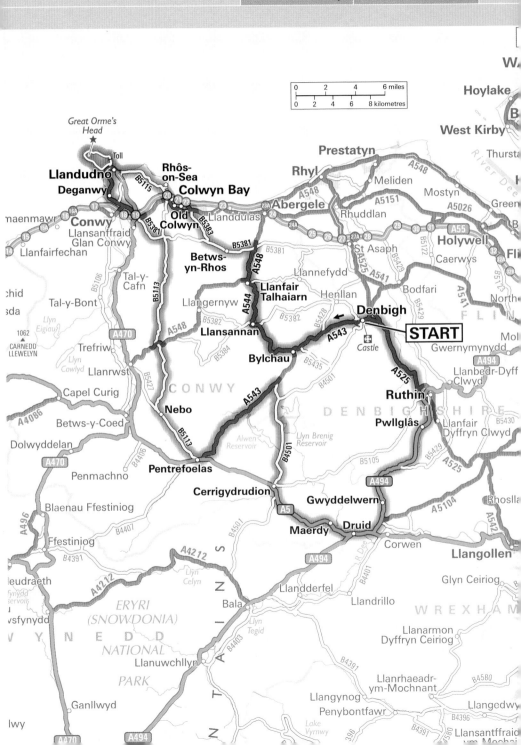

RIDE (58) Llangollen Loop

MENTION LLANGOLLEN TO most motorcyclists who know the area and they'll nod sagely: 'Horseshoe Pass and the Ponderosa,' they'll probably say, naming the local pass and biking café. Two great attractions – but there's so much more great riding around here. Not that the local council necessarily wants you to enjoy it: this area's been blighted by an outbreak of lowered speed limits. While this route avoids those as much as possible, it's important to understand that it's not an unrestricted opportunity for shenanigans. It's still a great ride, but the emphasis is on enjoying a laid-back blast through beautiful scenery.

FROM/TO Llangollen, Denbighshire
DISTANCE 135 miles
ALLOW 4 hours

Route Description

➤ **Leave Llangollen** on A542 to Ruthin (Horseshoe Pass). Continue ahead on A525 through Ruthin and Denbigh.
➤ **In Trefnant** Turn right at the lights on A541 to Mold.
➤ **After 3 miles** Turn right on B5429 to Llanbedr-Dyffryn-Clwyd and Llandyrnog.
➤ **In Llanbedr DC** Turn left on A494 towards Mold.
➤ **After 3 miles** Turn right on B5430 to Llanarmon-yn-Ial.

➤ **At the A525** Turn left to Wrexham.
➤ **Entering Wrexham** Turn right on A483 to Oswestry.
➤ **Leave the A55** at the 2nd exit: B5426, turning left at the end of the sliproad to Bangor-on-Dee.
➤ **At the roundabout** Turn right on A528 to Overton.
➤ **Don't miss** the right turn in Overton (by the chapel) to stay on A528 to Ellesmere.
➤ **In Ellesmere** Turn left at the roundabout on A495 towards Whitchurch.
➤ **Stay on the road** as it becomes A528 towards Shrewsbury.

➤ **In Burlton** Turn right on the B4397 to Baschurch. Turn right at the T-junction and follow the road, going straight over the A5.
➤ **At B4396 T-junction** Turn right to Knockin.
➤ **Continue on B4396** and in Llynclys go straight over crossroad on A495 towards Llansanffraid-ym-Mechain. Keep on road as it becomes B4396 again.
➤ **At B4391 T-junction** Turn right to Bala.
➤ **In Bala** Turn right on A494 to Llangollen.
➤ **At traffic lights** Turn right on A5 to return to Llangollen.

below *The Horseshoe Pass (A542) is short but glorious*

RIDE (58) Llangollen Loop

ROUTE TYPE Loop | **DISTANCE** 135 miles

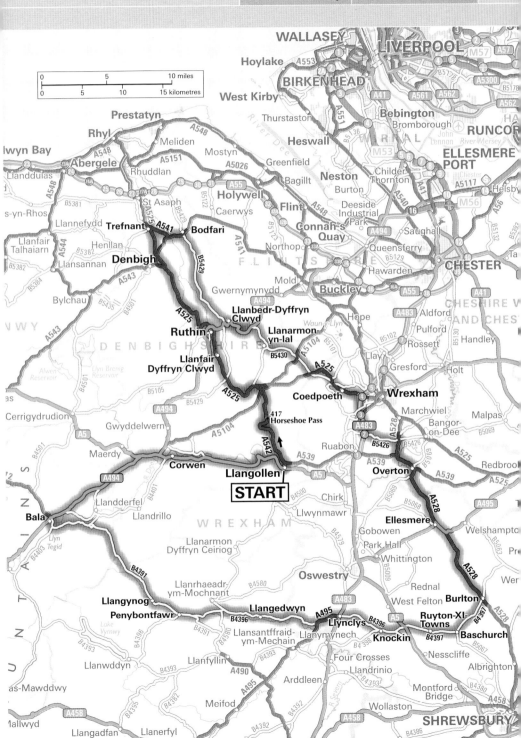

Scotland

Towering mountains, open moors, quiet glens and beautiful lochs –
and possibly the best riding in Britain

RIDE (59) Scotland Tour Day 1

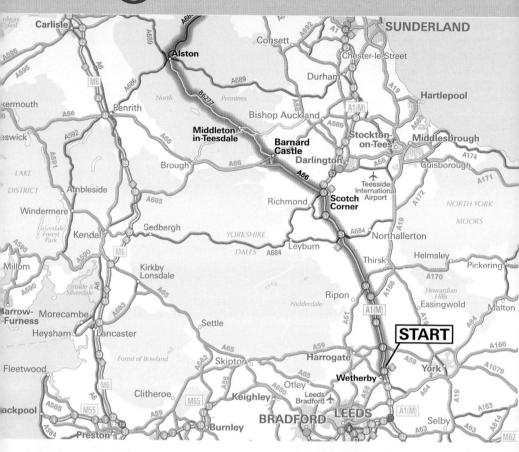

DAY 1 MORNING

THIS TOUR STARTS from Wetherby Services on the A1(M). If you have time for sightseeing, the High Force waterfall just outside Middleton-in-Teesdale is a great place to stop. Watch out for sheep on the high moors between there and Alston – a lovely town. For your lunch-stop, find somewhere flat to park the bike, ideally with wonderful views out towards the Lake District, and grab a bite to eat.

FROM Wetherby Services
TO Alston, Cumbria
DISTANCE 83 miles
ALLOW 3–3.5 hours

Route Description

➤ **Wetherby Services** Head north on the A1(M).

➤ **Scotch Corner** Leave the A1(M) at Scotch Corner, following signs for A66 Brough.

➤ **Look out** After a dozen miles on A66, turn right onto the B6277 to Barnard Castle.

➤ **Barnard Castle** Continue forward through the town centre to continue with B6277 to Middleton-in-Teesdale.

➤ **Middleton-in-Teesdale** Turn left on B6277 to Alston.

➤ **Alston** Go straight ahead into the town centre.

RIDE 59 Scotland Tour Day 1

ROUTE TYPE Tour | **DISTANCE** 83 miles morning | 118 miles afternoon

DAY 1 AFTERNOON

THE AFTERNOON ROUTE winds its way into Scotland past Hadrian's Wall – the Chesters Fort site at Chollerford, just outside Hexham, makes a fascinating detour if you have the time. It crosses the border at Carter Bar, before heading to Hawick and Selkirk. The final leg on the A708 is a fabulous, involving run – but treat it with respect if you're tired. The route ends in Moffat, opposite the Buccleuch Arms Hotel. Petrol is 200m to the right, on the A701 south.

FROM Alston, Cumbria
TO Moffat, Dumfries & Galloway
DISTANCE 118 miles
ALLOW 2.5–3 hours

Route Description

> **Alston** Turn right at the bottom of the main street, taking the A686 to Haydon Bridge.
> **Haydon Bridge** Turn right on the A69 to Hexham.
> **Hexham** Turn left on the A6079 towards Acomb.
> **X-roads** Turn left onto the A68 towards Jedburgh. When it reaches a T-junction, turn left and continue on the A68.
> **Carter Bar** After crossing the Scottish Border, take the first left onto the A6088 to Hawick.
> **Hawick** Left for town centre, then right to pick up A7 to Selkirk.
> **Selkirk** Into town centre and when main road turns right, carry on straight, following sign for Peebles. After the rugby club on edge of town, turn left on A708 to Moffat. Route ends in town centre.

WHERE TO STAY

The Buccleuch Arms Hotel Reasonably priced, comfortable and a great menu.
buccleucharmshotel.com

WHAT TO SEE AND DO

Chesters Roman Fort & Museum Superb museum on Hadrian's Wall.
english-heritage.org.uk/visit/places/chesters-roman-fort-and-museum-hadrians-wall

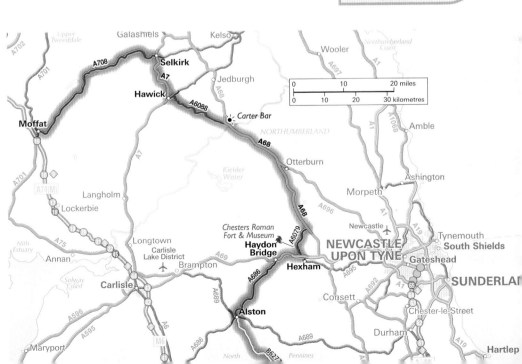

RIDE (59) Scotland Tour Day 2

DAY 2 MORNING

GRAB LUNCH IN St Andrews – we like Taste on North Street – but if you want a more substantial meal try The Rule on South Street. The petrol station is on City Road, so head back to fill up for the afternoon's route.

FROM Moffat, Dumfries
& Galloway
TO St Andrews, Fife
DISTANCE 106 miles
ALLOW 2–2.5 hours

Route Description

> **Moffat** Leave town on the A701 towards Edinburgh.

> **Look out** After about 30 miles, turn left onto the A721 towards Glasgow.

> **Carnwath** Turn right on the A70 towards Edinburgh.

> **Kirknewton** Turn left by the airfield onto the B7031 to Kirknewton, then right to pick up the A71 to Edinburgh.

> **Look out** After about 1½ mile, turn left onto the B7030 Ratho. Pass under the motorway, go through the industrial estate, then follow the signs for the M9 and M90 Perth.

> **M9 J1** Join the motorway, following Stirling M9. Leave the M9 at Junction 1A for the M90 and Perth.

> **M90 J2A** Leave the motorway for the A92 towards Glenrothes.

> **Kirkcaldy** Leave the A92 at the Redhouse roundabout, taking the A921 then picking up the A915 towards Leven. Stay on this road all the way to St Andrews. The route ends in St Andrews town centre.

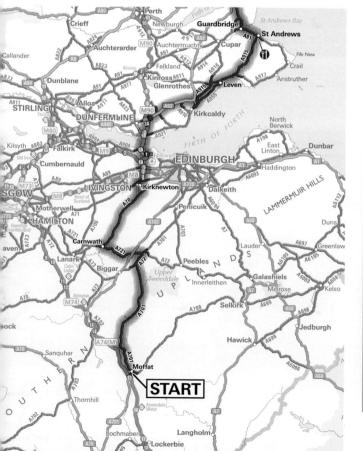

WHERE TO STAY

Strathness House Hotel Reasonably priced twin-bedded rooms.
strathnesshouse.com

Glenmoriston Town House Hotel A clean and comfortable overnight stop.
glenmoristontownhouse.com

WHAT TO SEE AND DO

Culloden Battlefield
Site of the last battle to be fought on mainland Britain in 1746. Regular re-enactments take place.
nts.org.uk/visit/places/culloden

| ROUTE TYPE Tour | DISTANCE 106 miles morning | 144 miles afternoon |

DAY 2 AFTERNOON

THERE IS NO shortage of things to see and do in the mighty, majestic Cairngorms National Park and also which from Blairgowrie, follows most of the Snowroads Scenic Route to Grantown-on-Spey heading then to Inverness.

FROM St Andrews, Fife
TO Inverness, Highland
DISTANCE 144 miles
ALLOW 2.5–3 hours

Route Description

> **St Andrews** Leave town on the A91 towards Dundee.
> **Guardbridge** Right at rbt on A919 for the Tay Road Bridge. Pick up the A92 to Dundee.
> **Dundee** Either go straight across the city, or right on the A85 then left on the A90, until you pick up the A923 to Coupar Angus.
> **Coupar Angus** Right on the high street to stay on the A923 to Blairgowrie.
> **Blairgowrie** Continue through the town then turn left on the A93 past Braemar.
> **Balmoral** Turn left on the B976 towards Tomintoul.
> **Gairnshiel Lodge** Turn left on the A939. When the road reaches a T-junction, turn left, still on the A939 through Tomintoul.
> **Grantown-on-Spey** Turn left on the A95 towards Perth.
> **Dulnain Bridge** Turn right on the A938 to Carrbridge.
> **A9** When the road comes to a T-junction, turn right on the A9 to Inverness.
> **Inverness** Take the A82 exit from the A9, turning left at the rbt for Inverness. The route ends in Inverness city centre.

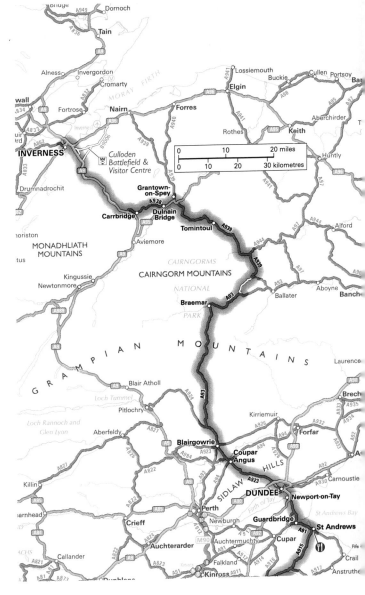

RIDE (59) Scotland Tour Day 3

DAY 3 MORNING

THE ROUTE TAKES you through one of the wildest landscapes in Britain. Much of the northern part of the A836 to Tongue is a single-track road with passing places. The scenery is astonishingly beautiful and, just when you don't think it could get any better, you turn onto the coast road. 'Spectacular' doesn't quite cover the views around Loch Eriboll.

The morning's route takes you to Durness: a tiny place, so lunch options are limited. If you're in a hurry, your best bet is a forecourt picnic with snacks from the Spar shop, but a short detour along the right-hand turn 100 yards from the Spar will take you to Balnakeil – the most northwesterly village on mainland Britain. There's a small bistro there, as well as the Cocoa Mountain Café (which makes and sells fabulous chocolates). If you have time when you're in Durness, the amazing Smoo Cave is well worth a visit. The shop is opposite the petrol station – which is the only one for miles around so after lunch, fill up there.

FROM Inverness, Highland
TO Durness, Highland
DISTANCE 115 miles
ALLOW 2.5–3 hours

Route Description

> **Inverness** Leave the city on the A9 heading towards Thurso.
> **Skiach Services** Turn left on B9176 towards Ardross.
> **A836** When the road reaches a T-junction, turn left (it's almost straight on) along the A836 towards Ferrycroft.
> **Bonar Bridge** Turn left towards Lairg on the A836. If you have a limited tank range, fill up in Lairg before continuing along the A836.
> **Tongue** Turn left at the T-junction, along the A838 to Durness. The route ends at the petrol station in Durness.

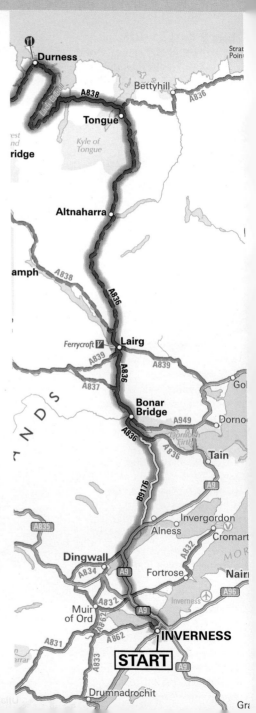

| **ROUTE TYPE** Tour | **DISTANCE** 115 miles morning | 95 miles afternoon |

DAY 3 AFTERNOON

THIS IS SOME of the finest riding – not just in Britain, but in Europe. When the sun beats down on the west coast of Scotland, it is truly magical. The A835 passes right by Knockan Crag – a great place to soak up this amazing landscape. The route ends in Ullapool, once voted the most romantic town in Scotland (not by hairy biker types, you understand). It's a quaint, quiet town built around its harbour. We'd stay in The Dipping Lugger near the ferry terminal, with an evening meal in The Arch Inn by the harbour – if you don't prefer buying some chips and eating them sitting on the quayside with your legs swinging over the water, that is.

FROM Durness, Highland
TO Ullapool, Highland
DISTANCE 95 miles
ALLOW 2.5–3 hours

Route Description

➤ **Durness** Continue along the A838 towards Rhiconich.
➤ **Laxford Bridge** Keep going straight towards Scourie, as the road becomes the A894.
➤ **Look out** Easy-to-miss right turn for B869 to Drumbeg, about 1 mile after the curved Kylesku Bridge.
➤ **Lochinver** Turn left on the A837 signed for Ullapool.
➤ **Ledmore Junction** Turn right onto A835 for Ullapool.
➤ **Ullapool** The route ends on the quayside in Ullapool.

WHERE TO STAY

The Dipping Lugger, Ullapool This 18th-century former manse has been transformed into a wonderful restaurant with rooms. **thedippinglugger. com**

The Arch Inn, Ullapool Friendly pub with decent rooms and excellent menu on the shore of Loch Broom. **thearchinn.co.uk**

WHAT TO SEE AND DO

Ferrycroft Visitor Centre A good place to stretch your legs would be the Ferrycroft Visitor Centre, which is an Information and Heritage Centre with a shop and toilets. **highlifehighland. com/ferrycroft-visitor-centre**

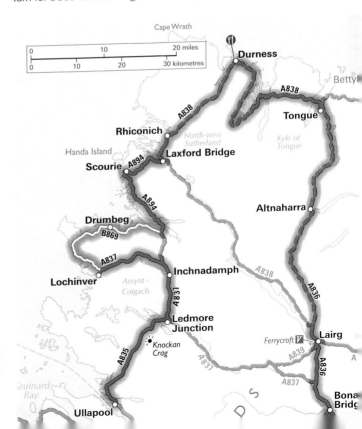

RIDE (59) Scotland Tour Day 4

DAY 4 MORNING

LEAVING ULLAPOOL, THE road cuts through a spectacular near-Alpine landscape, by Corrieshalloch Gorge – stop to see the Falls of Measach – then heads towards Kyle of Lochalsh. But mile-hungry riders wanting a serious challenge could detour along Loch Carron and Loch Kishorn on the A896, to find the road to Applecross – the famous Bealach na Bà, or 'Pass of the Cattle'. Alternatively, a great place to stop without adding any miles to the route is Eilean Donan Castle, a few miles after joining the A87, which also has a coffee shop. The morning route stops at the beautifully remote The Cluanie Inn, with the Landour Bakehouse – which makes a great lunch stop. However, if you've made good time and want to hold on for a later lunch, grab a late snack when you pass through Fort William.

FROM Ullapool, Highland
TO The Cluanie Inn, Highland
DISTANCE 101 miles
ALLOW 2–2.5 hours

Route Description

> **Ullapool** Leave town on the A835 towards Corrieshalloch Gorge.

> **Look out** About ½ mile before the village of Garve, take the right turn onto the A832 to Gairloch.

> **Achnasheen** Left at the roundabout on the A890 towards Kyle of Lochalsh.

> **Look out** Easy-to-miss left turn to stay on the A890, still signed for Kyle of Lochalsh.

> **A87** When the road gets to the A87 T-junction, turn left, signed for Fort William. Look for The Cluanie Inn, on the right, after about 20 miles. The route ends at The Cluanie Inn.

RIDE (59) Scotland Tour Day 4

| ROUTE TYPE Tour | DISTANCE 101 miles morning | 128 miles afternoon |

DAY 4 AFTERNOON

THE ROUTE PASSES straight through Fort William, at the foot of Ben Nevis. If the run into town beside Loch Lochy is impressive, the landscape only gets more magnificent as the A82 carries on through Ballachulish and up into Glen Coe, emerging between the mountains to roar across the prehistoric-looking Rannoch Moor. If you have any concerns about tank range for this afternoon leg, top up at the Tyndrum filling station (the famous Green Welly Stop – which also has an excellent café), a couple of hundred yards past the turning for the A85. The scenery around the A85 isn't quite so majestic as Glen Coe, but this is a splendid road and is usually fairly quiet. The route takes you into central Oban – a classic Scottish seaside resort town. It's another charming place to spend an evening, with plenty of restaurants to suit all tastes. Oban has hotels and B&Bs to suit all budgets, but we'd stay at the King's Knoll Hotel which is on the way into town, just a short stroll from the centre.

FROM The Cluanie Inn, Highland
TO Oban, Argyll & Bute
DISTANCE 128 miles
ALLOW 2.5–3 hours

Route Description

➤ **Cluanie Inn** Carry on along the A87 towards Fort William.
➤ **Look out** Take the easy-to-miss right turn to stay on the A87 to Fort William, about 10 miles from The Cluanie Inn.

➤ **Invergarry** Turn right on the A82 to Fort William.
➤ **Fort William** Carry on through the town, sticking with the A82.
➤ **Tyndrum** Turn right on the A85 to Oban. The route ends on Oban seafront.

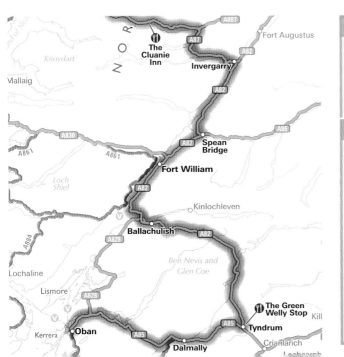

WHERE TO STAY

King's Knoll Hotel
Easy to find on the main road into Oban, with off-street parking.
kingsknolloban.com

WHAT TO SEE AND DO

The Green Welly Stop, Tyndrum Excellent self-service restaurant and Snack Stop offering home-made dishes. thegreenwellystop.co.uk

Eilean Donan Castle
One of Scotland's most iconic images, the castle sits on an island amid glorious countryside.
eileandonancastle.com

RIDE (59) Scotland Tour Day 5

DAY 5 MORNING

THE FIRST TASK of the day is to fill up at the petrol station on Soroba Road (the A816 heading south out of Oban). It's a great ride – south on the empty A816, then north along the shore of Loch Fyne, maybe with a coffee at Inveraray. At Tarbet on Loch Lomond the road becomes the A82 (there's no turn – just keep going straight) and gets busier as it heads towards Glasgow. The afternoon's riding starts with some dull roads to get around the city, so when filling up at Dumbarton it makes sense to either grab some grub for a forecourt picnic or go into the pub next to the petrol station for a meal.

FROM Oban, Argyll & Bute
TO Dumbarton, West Dunbartonshire
DISTANCE 106 miles
ALLOW 2–2.5 hours

Route Description

➤ **Oban** Leave town on the A816 towards Campbeltown.

➤ **Lochgilphead** Turn left on the A83 towards Glasgow. It becomes the A82 at Tarbet, but stick on this one road all the way to Dumbarton.

➤ **Dumbarton** The route ends at the Esso station on the A82 Dumbarton.

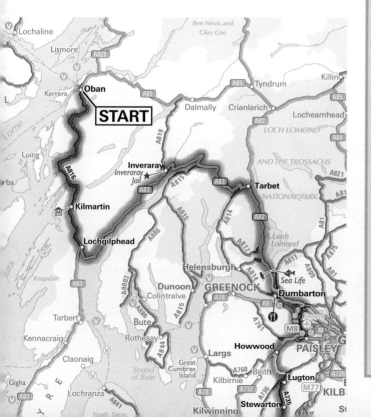

ROUTE TYPE Tour | **DISTANCE** 106 miles morning | 134 miles afternoon

DAY 5 AFTERNOON

A FTER DODGING THE urban sprawl, the scenic A713 from Ayr to Castle Douglas is a huge relief. It's a brilliant road, but the swooping A702 is slightly better. If you're concerned about your tank range, top up at the garage in St John's Town of Dalry, before the A702 turning.

FROM Dumbarton, West Dunbartonshire
TO Moffat, Dumfries & Galloway
DISTANCE 134 miles
ALLOW 2.5–3 hours

Route Description

➤ **Dumbarton** Continue along the A82 towards Glasgow, picking up the A898 for Erskine Bridge.
➤ **Erskine Bridge** Join the M898 and M8 towards Paisley.
➤ **M8 J29** Leave motorway, taking the A737 towards Irvine.
➤ **Howwood** Turn off A737 for B787 towards Howwood, take first lane on right and at T-junction with the B776, turn right, riding past Barcraigs Reservoir and crossing the B775.
➤ **A736** At the T-junction, turn right on the A736 towards Irvine.
➤ **Lugton** Turn left on the A735 to Dunlop, turning right at the lights in Stewarton following the signs for Kilmarnock.
➤ **Kilmaurs** Right at rbt on B751 towards the train station.
➤ **Crosshouse** Straight over staggered x-roads to stay on the B751 to Gatehead.
➤ **Gatehead** Turn right on the A759 to Troon.
➤ **Troon Bypass** Turn left on the A78 towards Glasgow Prestwick Airport.

➤ **Ayr** Skirt the town on the A78/A77 Ring Road until turning left on A713 to Castle Douglas.
➤ **Look out** Easy-to-miss left turn onto B729 towards Moniaive. Then take right turn for B7000 to St John's Town of Dalry.

➤ **St John's Town of Dalry** Turn left on the A702 towards Moniaive.
➤ **Thornhill** Turn left on the A76 towards Kilmarnock for 1 mile, then turn right to get back on the A702 towards Edinburgh.
➤ **Elvanfoot** Turn right on B7076 towards Beattock.
➤ **Look out** Don't miss left turn on B719 to Greenhillstairs.
➤ **A701** When the road reaches the T-junction, turn right on the A701 to Moffat.

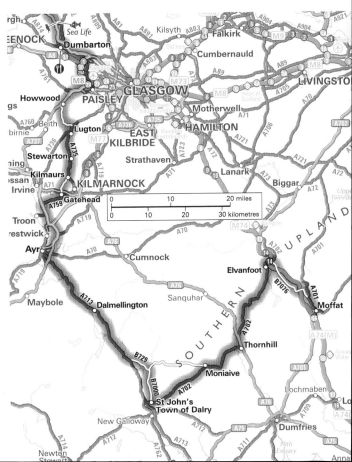

RIDE (59) Scotland Tour Day 6

DAY 6 MORNING

GETTING BACK INVOLVES a fair stretch of motorway – but it's not all dull multi-lane riding. Getting off the M6 as soon as it starts, a great road leads to Alston and then it's all the way over Hartside Pass before picking up the A6 to head south from Penrith. If your tank won't do the full 136 miles, get a quick top-up at the garage on the way into Kendal, then take the A684 into the heart of the Yorkshire Dales. Lunch stop is the Penny Garth Café. The petrol station is just opposite: when you're ready to move on, fill up here.

FROM Moffat, Dumfries & Galloway
TO Hawes, North Yorkshire
DISTANCE 136 miles
ALLOW 2.5–3 hours

Route Description

➤ **Moffat** Leave town on the A701, for the A74(M).
➤ **A74(M) J15** Join the motorway heading south.
➤ **M6 J44** Leave the motorway at Carlisle, taking the A689 to Brampton.
➤ **Brampton** Bypass the town on the A69 towards Hexham, turning off after 2 miles on the A689 through Hallbankgate.
➤ **Alston** Turn right on the A686 to Penrith.
➤ **Penrith** Straight across the rbt on the A6 towards Shap.
➤ **Kendal** Enter the town centre to pick up the A684 to Sedburgh (a left turn just before the bridge).
➤ **Sedburgh** Stay on the A684 to Hawes. The route finishes in Hawes town centre.

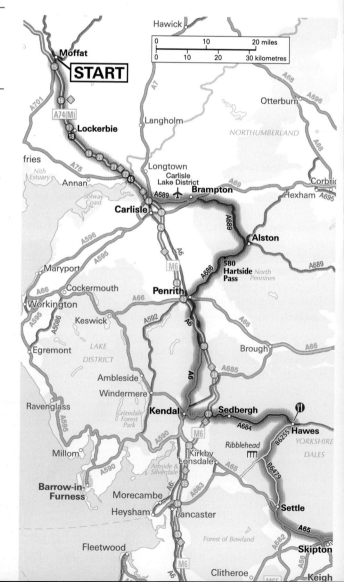

| ROUTE TYPE Tour | DISTANCE 136 miles morning | 69 miles afternoon |

DAY 6 AFTERNOON

THE IMMEDIATE POST-LUNCH ride is one of the best roads in the country, the B6255 from Hawes to Ribblehead. The B6479 from there to Settle isn't too shabby either. After that, though, the roads get busier. Staying on the route through Harrogate and Knaresbrough will take some concentration – the short-cut to Wetherby Services can be easily missed if you're not careful. All too soon we're filling up beside the M1 for the final run down the motorways. But looking back on the other roads, it's definitely worth it.

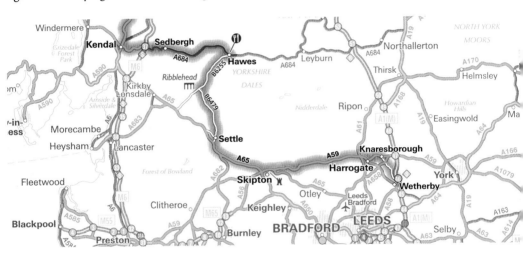

FROM Hawes, North Yorkshire
TO Wetherby Services
DISTANCE 69 miles
ALLOW 3–3.5 hours

Route Description

➤ **Hawes** Leave town on the B6255 to Ingleton.
➤ **Ribblehead** Turn left on the B6479 to Settle.
➤ **Settle** Go through town and pick up the A65 left to Skipton.
➤ **Skipton** Stay out of town on the A65 and at the third roundabout, carry straight on along the A59 to Harrogate.
➤ **Harrogate** Stick with the A59 to Knaresbrough.
➤ **Knaresborough** Follow the A59 for York, then turn right onto the B6164 to Wetherby.
➤ **Wetherby** Turn left on Deighton Rd, which will lead to the roundabout for the A1(M). The route ends at Wetherby Services on the A1(M).

WHAT TO SEE AND DO

Ribblehead Viaduct
Stunning piece of Victorian engineering in an iconic location that opened in 1876 and up to 100ft in height.
yorkshiredales.org.uk/places/ribblehead_viaduct

Penny Garth Café, Hawes
A popular biker meeting place for many decades, the café is open all day. Enjoy a butty, a mug of afternoon tea, a tasty pie or a pasty.
pennygarthcafe.co.uk

Skipton Castle
One of the most complete and well-preserved medieval castles in England. Built in Norman times, damaged in the English Civil War, then partially rebuilt.
skiptoncastle.co.uk

RIDE (60) Stranraer Loop

THERE AREN'T MANY advantages to missing a ferry. Let's be honest, it's normally an inconvenience of the very worst kind. However, if every cloud has a silver lining, I was determined to find it when I wound up in Cairnryan Port with the better part of four hours to kill until the next Belfast boat. If only all the roads you accidentally stumble upon were as good as these. The coast road north, the A77, was pleasant enough, but it was turning onto the A714 that really slackened my jaw: what a great road, loaded with spectacular corners but blissfully free from traffic. Heading back towards Stranraer, I realised I still had plenty of time, so I dived off towards Wigtown on the unexpectedly brilliant B733.

Time was starting to slip away as I rounded the coast on the A746 – such a scenic road it's a shame to rush it. Back on the A75, through Stranraer and onto the ferry… just in time. But as I strapped the bike down on the deck, I wondered – should I have got the next sailing, to ride the route again? I almost wish I had…

FROM/TO Stranraer, Dumfries & Galloway
DISTANCE 116 miles
ALLOW 3 hours

Route Description

> **From Stranraer** take the A75 towards Dumfries.
> **At Glenluce** turn right just beyond the village on A747 to Port William.
> **Continue through Port William** on A747. The road becomes the A746 through Whithorn and turns north towards Wigtown.
> **River Bladnoch** When main road curves right after the bridge on outskirts of Wigtown, carry on straight on the B7005 towards Newton Stewart.
> **At the x-roads** Turn left onto the B733 towards and through Kirkcowan. Turn right onto the A75, towards Dumfries.
> **Newton Stewart** Turn left onto the A714. Ride to the coast on the outskirts of Girvan.
> **Turn left onto the A77** and return to Stranraer.

below left *Cairnryan, Loch Ryan*

WHAT TO SEE AND DO

The Wicker Man The classic 1973 horror movie starring Christopher Lee, Edward Woodward and Britt Ekland was filmed in this area, but the climactic scenes, featuring the giant structure of the title, were filmed at Isle of Whithorn. The concrete stumps that held up the Wicker Man are still visible. Other locations include Newton Stewart, Whithorn, Creetown, Stranraer, Gatehouse of Fleet and Kirkudbright.

RIDE (60) Stranraer Loop

ROUTE TYPE Loop | **DISTANCE** 116 miles

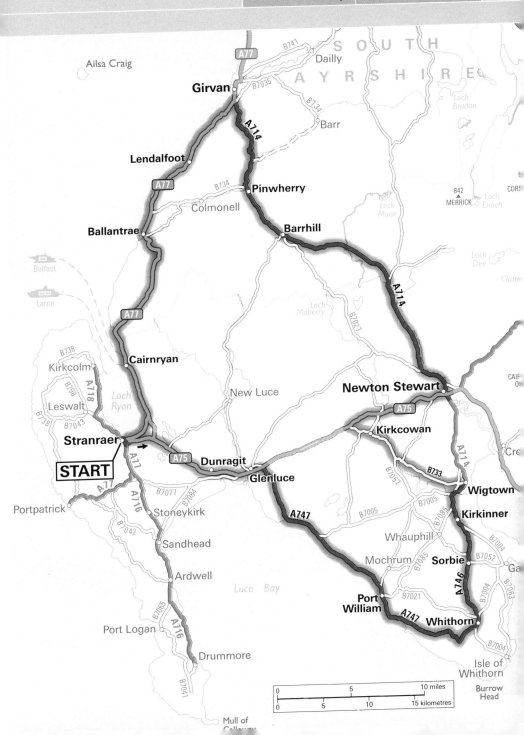

RIDE (61) Castle Douglas Daytrip

IF YOU WANT quiet roads, come to Dumfries and Galloway. It's a beautiful corner of Scotland that most people don't seem to know about. The towns and villages are small, there are miles of forestry and open moorland, and even the one main road – the A75 to Stranraer and the ferry to Northern Ireland – rarely see that much traffic.

This is an hourglass route, flowing constantly clockwise on some of our favourite roads – the sublime A702, the A713 and both stretches of the A712. The first stretch, from Crocketford, is involved and twisty, but the route turns away just before New Galloway, returning there to rejoin the A712 to Newton Stewart - a stretch known as The Queen's Way.

FROM/TO Castle Douglas, Dumfries & Galloway
DISTANCE 165 miles
ALLOW 4.5 hours

Route Description

> **Leave Castle Douglas** on the A75 towards Dumfries.
> **In Crocketford** Turn left on the A712 to Corsock and New Galloway.
> **At A713** T-junction turn right to St John's Town of Dalry and towards Ayr.
> **In St John's Town of Dalry** Turn right on A702 to Moniaive. Turn right in Moniaive to stay on the A702 to Thornhill.
> **At A76 Thornhill** T-junction turn left towards Kilmarnock.
> **In New Cumnock** Turn left at mini-roundabout on the B741 to Dalmellington.
> **In Dalmellington** Turn left on A713 to Castle Douglas.
> **Don't miss** the right turn after 18 miles for A762 to Glenlee and New Galloway.
> **In New Galloway** Turn right on the A712 towards Newton Stewart (The Queen's Way).
> **At A75** On outskirts of Newton Stewart turn left on the A75 to Dumfries.

above *Autumn hues on the A712*

> **After 17 miles** Turn right on the A755 to Kirkcudbright.
> **In Kirkcudbright** Turn right on the A711 to Auchencairn.

> **After 17 miles** Turn left at the lights on the A745 to return to Castle Douglas.

ROUTE TYPE Loop   **DISTANCE** 165 miles

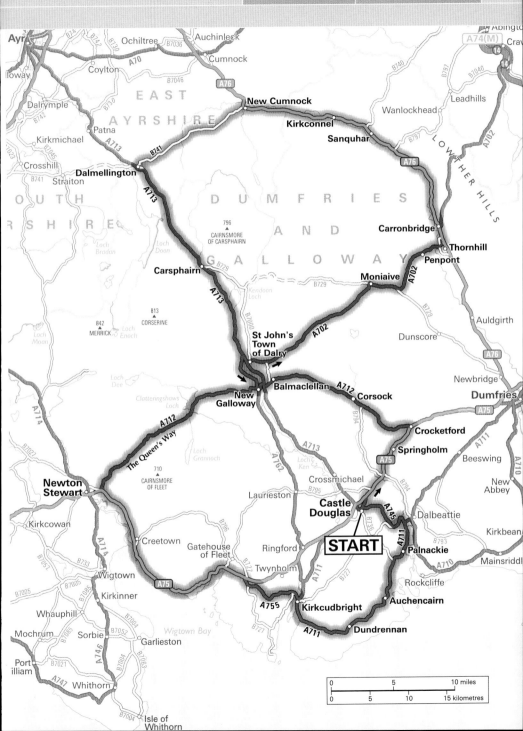

RIDE (62) Moffat Single Loop

A COLLEAGUE ASKED ME: 'What's the best ride in Britain?' Perhaps she thought I'd have trouble answering… but I didn't hesitate. 'Go to Moffat: A708, A72, A701.' Easy to trot out with absolute confidence – it's only three roads, after all. Thing is, out of all the routes in this book, this one might actually be the most perfectly balanced.

It doesn't take all day to ride, there's a full mix of corners, from the challenging rollercoaster of the A708 to the broader, sweeping turns of the A701, and the scenery is magnificent. It works equally well for steady two-up riding as it does for spirited scratching. And it's just three roads – it's as easy to follow as it is to enjoy.

Of course, this isn't really the best ride in the Britain… and with more than 80 other routes in this book alone, another one may suit you better: longer, shorter, twistier, faster. But is there one other route that could suit every rider so well? Certainly not!

FROM/TO Moffat, Dumfries & Galloway
DISTANCE 93 miles
ALLOW 2 hours

Route Description

➤ **Leave Moffat** on the A708 towards Selkirk.

➤ **On outskirts of Selkirk** Turn left, signed Peebles to join the A707.

➤ **At roundabout** Go straight over onto the A72 towards Peebles. Carry on through the town, in around 10 miles bearing left on the A72 when the A701 merges with it.

➤ **Where A72 turns right** signed for Skirling, keep ahead on the A701 to return to Moffat.

WHERE TO STAY

The Buccleuch Arms Hotel Redefines what you'll expect of a bike-friendly hotel, with individual garages for the bikes, washing kit and advice on routes. Great food, too.
buccleucharmshotel.com

WHAT TO SEE AND DO

Traquair House Scotland's oldest inhabited house includes an 18th-century working brewery.
traquair.co.uk

left *The view across St Mary's Loch*

RIDE (62) Moffat Single Loop

| ROUTE TYPE Loop | DISTANCE 93 miles |

RIDE (63) Moffat Double Loop

HOW MANY TIMES had I passed Moffat without stopping, head down on the M74, heading for the Highlands and never realising I was missing some of the best riding in Scotland? Dozens of times. That's dozens of missed opportunities… Now I know better and always try to stop in the bike-friendly Buccleuch Arms Hotel, with at least a day on the quiet roads of this most accessible area of outstanding riding beauty. There are so many possible routes round Moffat that the two we present here only scratch the surface. The essential, 'if-you-only-ride-one, ride-this' route is the triangle of A708, A72 and A701. But that's just the start. The route you see here is more flowing and sweeping, taking in the glorious Mennock pass.

FROM/TO Moffat, Dumfries & Galloway
DISTANCE 132 miles
ALLOW 4 hours

Route Description

> **Moffat** Head north on the A701 towards Edinburgh.
> **Devil's Beef Tub** At the edge of the huge gorge, take the left turn for the B719. When it ends at a T-junction, turn right on the B7076, running parallel to the A74(M).
> **A74(M) roundabout** Don't get on the motorway – take the A702 to Abington.
> **Abington** At the A74(M) rbt, take the B7078 to Douglas, parallel to the motorway but more pleasant.
> **At T-junction** Turn left onto A70 towards Douglas and Ayr.
> **Cumnock** Turn left on the B7083 then the A76 towards Dumfries.
> **Mennock** Turn left on the B797 through Wanlockhead.
> **Leadhills** Turn right on the B7040 to Elvanfoot.
> **Elvanfoot** At the T-junction turn right on the A702 towards Dumfries.
> **Carronbridge** Turn left on the A76 for Thornhill and Dumfries.
> **Dumfries** Take A75 ring road round the town, then turn left on A701 to return to Moffat.

WHAT TO SEE AND DO

Drumlanrig Castle
Spectacular home of the Duke of Buccleuch, with impressive gardens and art collection.
drumlanrigcastle.co.uk

Wanlockhead Scotland's highest village? No, it's not in the Highlands. It's Wanlockhead, which also has a fascinating museum dedicated to the village's lead-mining past.
leadminingmuseum.co.uk

Dumfries & Galloway Aviation Museum
They have a fantastic collection of aircraft, including the Battle of Britain veteran Loch Doon Spitfire, a supersonic Lightning fighter and a wartime assault glider collection.
dumfriesaviationmuseum.com

left Group riding on the route

RIDE (63) Moffat Double Loop

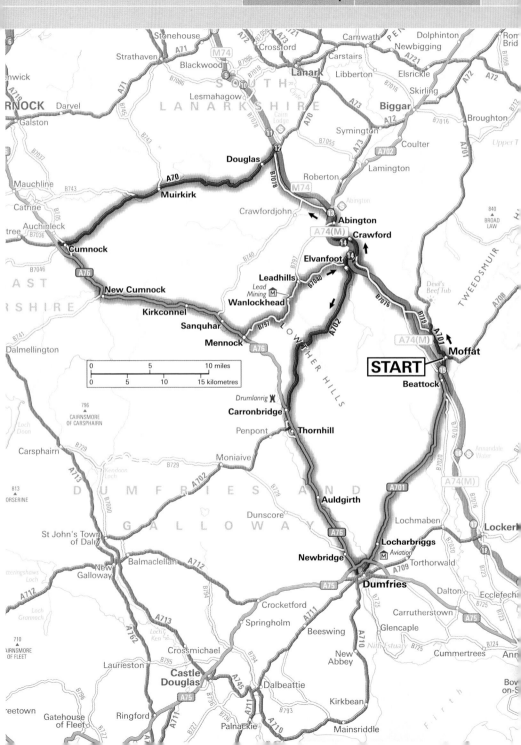

START

RIDE (64) Hawick Loop

THE LATE, GREAT Steve Hislop – TT racer and superbikes star – hailed from Hawick and, if you're prepared for a bit of a walk, there's a memorial statue to him in the park that surrounds the town museum. When you get out on the roads, the surprise isn't that the town produced a great TT racer – it's amazing it hasn't produced dozens of them.

This is proper biking country, but these aren't roads to be taken lightly. The corners come thick and fast, there are plenty of elevation changes… and surface changes too. A little caution is needed when riding or every crest becomes a launch pad and there's no way of knowing if the landing will be on more perfect tarmac or a patch of gravel or sheep poo or a pothole. Better to flow along at a sensible speed, enjoying the involving roads and beautiful, well-forested scenery – and leave the road racing to the TT boys and girls.

FROM/TO Hawick, Scottish Borders
DISTANCE 100 miles
ALLOW 2 hours

Route Description

➤ **Head south** from Hawick on A7 to Langholm and Carlisle.
➤ **Don't miss** the right turn in Langholm (by the big church) for B7068 to Lockerbie. Turn left a few hundred yards after crossing the bridge to stay on this road.
➤ **In Lockerbie** Turn right by the war memorial. At the mini-roundabout turn right on the B723 to Boreland.
➤ **At the T-junction** in Eskdalemuir, turn left on the B709 to Ettrick.

➤ **Don't miss** the left turn after 15 miles to stay on the B709 towards Innerleithen.
➤ **At A708 crossroads** Turn right to Selkirk on the A708.
➤ **Take A707** into Selkirk and pick up A7 to return to Hawick.

below *Look out for the Buddhist temple on the B709*

RIDE (64) Hawick Loop

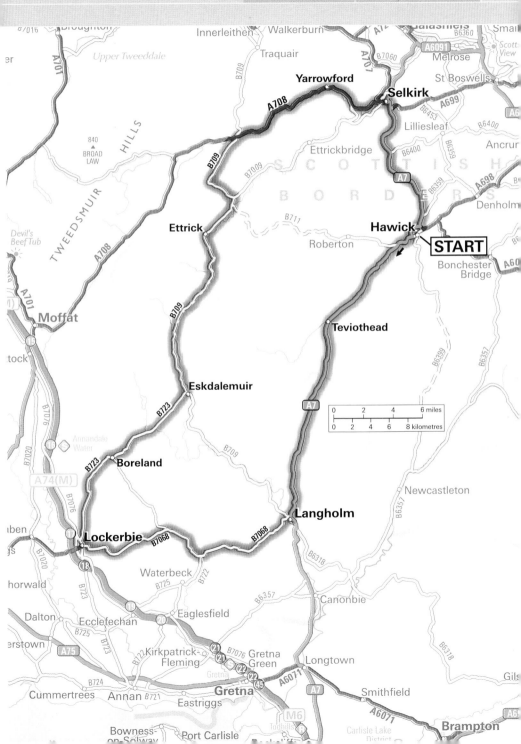

RIDE (65) North Berwick Blast

AS A GENERAL rule, the rides in this book avoid major trunk roads – usually there's a more interesting alternative to ride instead. But in this quiet corner of Scotland, nestled between Berwick-upon-Tweed on the border and Edinburgh, there simply aren't that many roads… so this route starts with a short stretch of the A1.

After that, though, things change. The riding goes up a gear as the roads get smaller and tighter – narrower B-roads blasting through the Scottish Borders. The B6355 past Whiteadder Reservoir has long been one of my favourite roads, but there are plenty of other quiet, quality B-roads here to give it a run for its money. Which one's your favourite?

FROM/TO North Berwick, East Lothian
DISTANCE 107 miles
ALLOW 2.5 hours

Route Description

➤ **Leave North Berwick** on the A198 towards Dunbar.
➤ **At the A199** Turn left towards Dunbar and the A1.
➤ **At the Thistly Cross roundabout** Join the A1 southbound towards Berwick-upon-Tweed.
➤ **After 17 miles** Turn right on the B6437 to Chirnside.
➤ **Don't miss** the left turn 1 mile later to stay on the B6437 to Chirnside.
➤ **At the T-junction** Turn right to stay on the B6437 to Coldstream. Turn right again on the A6105 to Coldstream.
➤ **Don't miss** the left turn at The Waterloo Arms pub for the B6437 to Allanton and Coldstream.
➤ **At the crossroads** Turn right on the B6461 to Swinton.
➤ **In Swinton** Turn left on the A6112 to Coldstream.
➤ **In Coldstream** Turn right on the A698 to Kelso. Don't miss the left turn 1 mile out of town to stay on this road.

➤ **In Kelso at roundabout** Turn right, following signs for the A6089 towards Edinburgh.
➤ **½ mile** out of Kelso turn right on the B6364 to Stichill.
➤ **At the A6105** Turn right to Greenlaw. Turn right to go into the village then left to stay on the A6105 to Duns.
➤ **In Duns** turn left on the A6112 to Preston.
➤ **In Preston** turn left on the B6355 to Cranshaws.

➤ **In Gifford** Turn right (by the church) on the B6369 to Haddington.
➤ **Cross Haddington** following signs for the A1, then cross the A1 and take the A199 towards North Berwick.
➤ **After 1½ mile** Turn left on the B1347 to Athelstaneford. At the T-junction turn left, then turn right to continue on the B1347 to return to North Berwick.

below *If you want brilliant, quiet B-roads, come to the Scottish Borders*

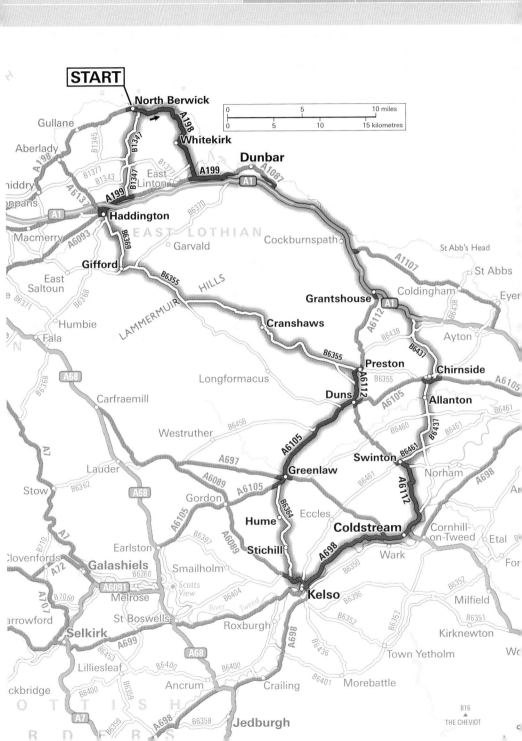

RIDE (66) Stirling Standards

STIRLING IS ONE of Scotland's treasures – an attractive old-stone town crowned with a gem of a castle. It's also the gateway to some fabulous riding – which locals know, especially riders from the nearby cities of Edinburgh and Glasgow. Some popular biking roads get busy at weekends, so these routes may be better enjoyed on quiet weekdays. This loop heads north to join the epic A85 along the shores of Loch Earn, before heading through the Queen Elizabeth Forest Park to the heart of the Trossachs. Climbing the spectacular Duke's Pass, we skirt the Lake of Menteith before diving down quieter roads to the Carron Valley and returning to Stirling.

FROM/TO Stirling
DISTANCE 98 miles
ALLOW Half a day

Route Description

➤ **Leave Stirling** on the A9 towards Perth. When it reaches the end of the M9, turn right onto the B8033 to Dunblane.
➤ **Go through Dunblane** on the B8033, through Kinbuck and on to Braco.
➤ **At Braco** Turn left onto A822 for a short distance, then left again onto B827 to Comrie.
➤ **In Comrie** Turn left on the A85 to Loch Earn.
➤ **At Lochearnhead** Turn left on the A84 towards Stirling.
➤ **At Kilmahog** Turn right onto the A821 to Aberfoyle, bearing left around the end of Loch Achray to ride the Duke's Pass.

➤ **Go left in Aberfoyle** down through Main Street, continuing on the A821.
➤ **At roundabout** Take the left turn onto the A81, towards Stirling.
➤ **Turn right at Port of Menteith** on the B8034 to Arnprior.
➤ **Turn right at Arnprior** onto A811 and quickly turn left down lane signed Fintry.
➤ **At lane end** Turn right onto the B822, still signed for Fintry.
➤ **At Fintry** Turn left onto the B822 towards Lennoxtown and shortly turn left again, onto the B818 towards Denny. The road runs alongside Carron Valley Reservoir.
➤ **Reach Stoneywood** and ride under the M80 to a T-junction at Denny.

➤ **Turn left onto the A872** towards Stirling, turning left again a little further on to follow this road back to Stirling town centre.

WHAT TO SEE AND DO

Stirling Castle One of Scotland's best-preserved castles and one of the most rewarding to visit, with plenty to occupy all ages. historicenvironment.scot/visit-a-place/places/stirling-castle

SS Sir Walter Scott Swap the bike for a boat and enjoy the peace of Loch Katrine, in the heart of the Trossachs. lochkatrine.com

Queen Elizabeth Forest Park Enjoy iconic views of sparkling lochs, wooded hills and rugged mountains, or take to the Three Lochs Forest Drive. forestryandland.gov.scot/visit/forest-parks/queen-elizabeth-forest-park

left Stunning views across Queen Elizabeth Forest Park

RIDE 66 Stirling Standards

ROUTE TYPE Loop | **DISTANCE** 98 miles

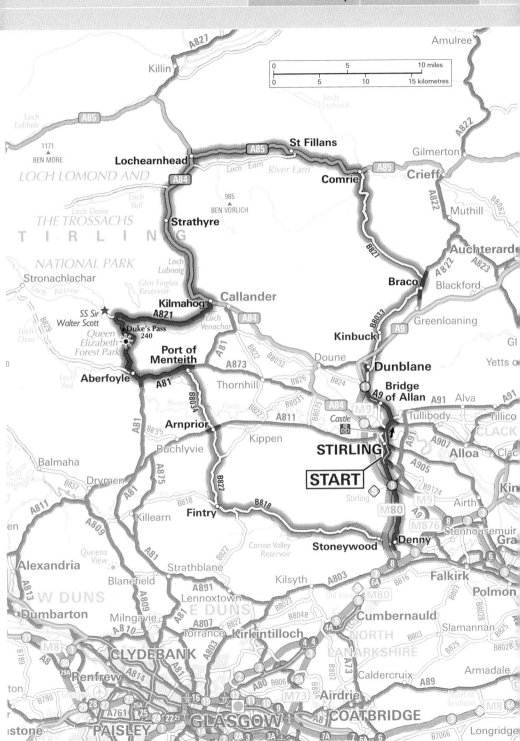

RIDE (67) Oban Loop

THIS REWARDING DAY'S ride is built around one road – the A83 – as it heads down the Kintyre Peninsula. Don't worry – you're not likely to bump into Paul McCartney, though apparently he still owns a house on the Mull of Kintyre. Instead, the route passes through Campbeltown to the chapel at Southend at the very tip of the peninsula. If you want a quiet, beautiful place – that's it.

The A83's far from the only great road you'll encounter on this ride, though.

The initial run on the A85 and A819 to Inveraray is enough to get the blood pumping before you even join the A83. It's possible to return from Campbeltown to Kennagcraig on the B842, with its fabulous views over Arran, but this is a long day anyway so the broader A83 makes more sense, and it's so good that riding it in both directions makes sense. Then from Lochgilphead, there's the spectacular A816 to close the loop to Oban. A full day, but a brilliant one.

FROM/TO Oban, Argyll & Bute
DISTANCE 220 miles
ALLOW 5.5 hours

Route Description

➤ **Leave Oban** on the A85 towards Crianlarich.
➤ **After 22 miles** Turn right on the A819 to Inveraray.
➤ **In Inveraray** Turn right on the A83 to Campbeltown.

➤ **In Campbeltown** centre pick up the B842 to Southend.
➤ **Keep going straight** from Southend and stay on the road as it runs past the beach and St Columba's Chapel. In about 3 miles it will loop back to the B842.
➤ **Turn left** on the B842 to Campbeltown.

➤ **Pick up** the A83 to retrace your steps.
➤ **At the roundabout** in Lochgilphead go straight on the A816 to return to Oban.

below *Early morning on Loch Fyne, Inveraray*

RIDE 67 Oban Loop

| ROUTE TYPE Loop | DISTANCE 220 miles |

RIDE 68 Fort William South Loop

OFFICIALLY, INVERNESS IS the capital of the Highlands… but Fort William's the heart. This small town on the shores of Loch Linnhe, in the shadow of Ben Nevis, is the gateway to so many outdoor activities that it's often fairly busy. There are climbers and walkers and sailors… and bikers. Especially when the Scottish Six-Day Trial is on, but more or less all year round, as the riding is so brilliant.

This long route works well in both directions, but I've put it down as a 'clockwise' route. That's because I never tire of the way the landscape unrolls before you as the A82 heads over Rannoch Moor and down through Glen Coe – it's a spectacular sight on any ride, even if there's often a bit of traffic. Don't worry, though – the rest of the ride is just as spectacular and mostly much quieter.

FROM/TO Fort William, Highland
DISTANCE 180 miles
ALLOW 4 hours

Route Description

➤ **From Fort William** Head north on the A82 towards Inverness.

➤ **In Spean Bridge** Turn right on the A86 towards Newtonmore.

➤ **In Laggan** Turn right on the A889 to Dalwhinnie.

➤ **At the A9** Turn right towards Perth.

➤ **After 17½ miles** Turn right to Tummel Bridge on the B847.

➤ **In a few hundred yards** Turn right to Struan on the B847.

➤ **Stay on the B847** until the T-junction with the B846. Turn left to Tummel Bridge.

➤ **At the lights** in Aberfeldy,

turn right on the A827 to Kenmore.

➤ **At the A85** Turn right to Crianlarich.

➤ **Continue through Crianlarich** and turn right at the roundabout on the A82 to return to Fort William.

below *The Three Sisters through Glen Coe*

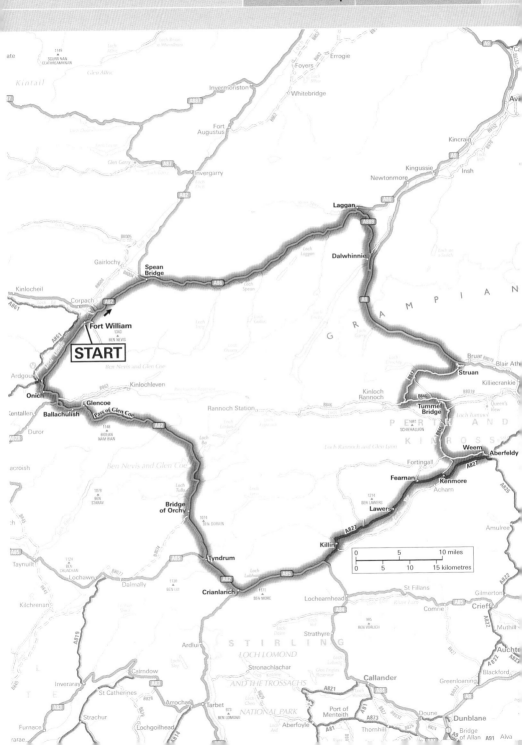

RIDE (69) Fort William North Loop

THIS ROUTE FEATURES two of the best roads in Scotland – sorry, to be clear, that's two of the best roads in Britain – and one ferry. I can't predict whether you'll prefer the A87 or the A830, but they're both amazing. They're absolutely packed with spectacular corners and majestic views – including historic structures (Eilean Donan Castle on the A87, the curving Glenfinnan Viaduct on the A830). They're both wide and swooping and utterly brilliant to ride.

So why pick favourites? At the end of the day, every mile of the route is a joy. But not that every mile is on tarmac. After crossing the bridge to reach Skye, you'll need to take the Mallaig ferry to return to the mainland. This can get busy in summer, so you may want to book in advance. If you plan to set off from Fort William at 10am, reserve a space on any crossing after 3pm (see calmac.co.uk) unless you plan on stopping to explore Eilean Donan – in which case better make that a 4.30-ish ferry.

FROM/TO Fort William, Highland
DISTANCE 143 miles
ALLOW 4 hours

Route Description
> **Leave Fort William** Take the A82 towards Inverness.
> **At Invergarry** Turn left on the A87 to Kyle of Lochalsh.
> **Turn left** at the T-junction to stay on the A87.
> **At the roundabout** after the Skye Bridge, turn right to Portree.
> **After 5½ miles** Turn left on the A851 to Ardvasar and Armadale.
> **Take the ferry** to Mallaig.
> **Roll off the ferry** and keep going straight: you are now on the A830, which returns to Fort William.

right On the A87 – possibly the best road in Scotland

RIDE (69) Fort William North Loop

ROUTE TYPE Loop | **DISTANCE** 143 miles

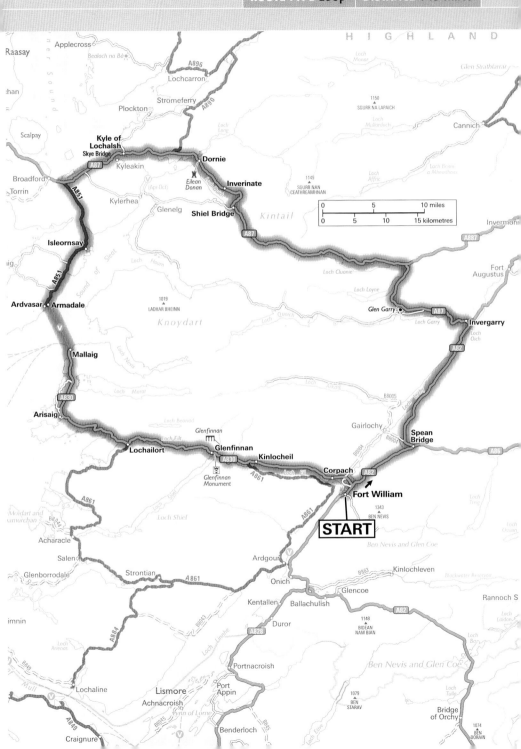

RIDE (70) Fort William West Loop

THE MOST WESTERLY point of the British mainland is a promontory on the Ardnamurchan peninsula – handily crowned by a lighthouse and reached by a road. A very narrow, very twisty road. This is the west and it is properly wild – and utterly beautiful.

This is not a route for high-speed hijinks – it's one for patient exploring. It's demanding riding, with lots of looping crests and blind turns on single-track roads. I reckon I've seen more deer on the roads here than in the rest of Scotland put together. Surfaces range from immaculate to rough and gravelly. Getting through all this safely to reach the lighthouse, perched on its rocky point, feels like a significant achievement.

Like the Fort William North Loop, this route uses the A830 and a ferry – in this case the Corran Ferry, crossing Loch Linnhe to speed you back to Fort William on the A82. You can carry on along the shores of the loch, to return on the A830 – but it's another beautiful but narrow road, so if time's pressing it's better to take the boat.

FROM/TO Fort William, Highland
DISTANCE 130 miles
ALLOW 5 hours

Route Description

> **From Fort William** Leave by the A82 towards Inverness, then at rbt turn left on the A830 towards Mallaig.
> **In Lochailort** Turn left on the A861 to Glenuig.
> **After 21 miles** Turn right to Kichoan on the B8007.
> **In Kilchoan** Turn right to stay on the B8007 – now signed for Portuairk and the lighthouse.
> **Don't miss** the left turn 4 miles later to reach the lighthouse.
> **After grabbing** a victory selfie or other picture with the lighthouse, retrace your steps through Kilchoan to the A861.
> **At the A861** Turn right to Strontian.
> **In Ardgour** (opposite the hotel) take the Corran Ferry to cross Loch Linnhe.
> **Take the A82** to return to Fort William.

below The road from Glenborrodale to Kilchoan

RIDE ⑦ Fort William West Loop

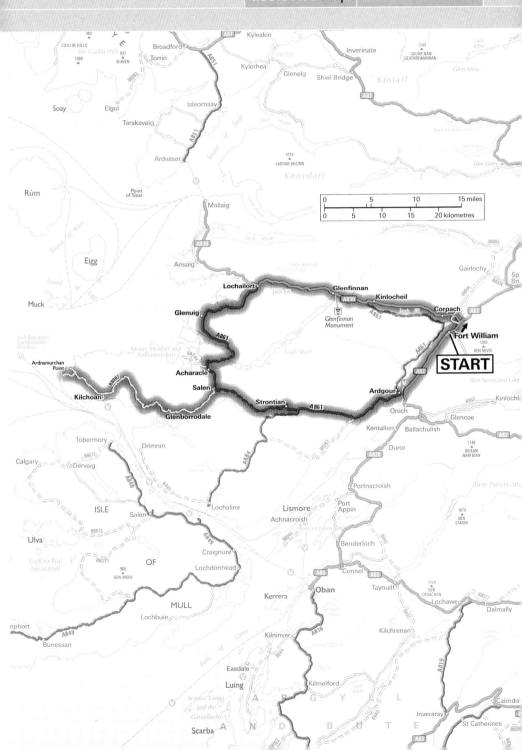

RIDE (71) Skye's the Limit

HEADING NORTH FROM Glasgow, it's only natural to take the A82 around Loch Lomond, across Rannoch Moor and through Glen Coe. This is wild Scotland at its most beautiful – right? Wrong. Wait until you get to Skye. It's magical. Of course, the A87 is fabulous, but taking the ferry is even better. It slows the journey, brings it home to you that this is real travel, almost an adventure. It helps that the A830 from Fort William to Mallaig, where you catch the Skye Ferry, is an amazing road as well… But real magic happens on Skye. There's an untamed quality to the towering Cullin Hills; a sense that you've stumbled into the land that time forgot. Pause beside a rocky inlet and it's easy to picture Viking raiders landing in a longboat, or mammoths stalking the high slopes of the hills. The roads on Skye are involving and a lap of the island can – just about – be done in a day from Fort William, though it's easier if the return leg is over the Skye Bridge to Kyle of Lochalsh. But this is an island to savour, not to rush. Far better to find a bed in Uig or Dunvegan, explore Skye slowly, lose yourself in the landscape and fall under its spell.

FROM/TO Armadale, Highland
DISTANCE 152 miles
ALLOW 4 hours

Route Description

> **From Armadale Ferry Terminal** Bear right, away from Ardvasar to follow the A851 towards Broadford.
> **At the A87** Turn left towards Portree on the A87.
> **Ride through Broadford** and along the coastal road to the junction at Sligachan.

> **Turn left onto the A863** Ride towards Dunvegan.
> **Continue** at Dunvegan, turn right to follow the A850 towards Portree.
> **At the A87** Turn left to Uig.
> **Follow the A87** through Uig as it becomes the A855 to Staffin, climbing round a hairpin.
> **Don't miss** the right turn just after the hairpin signed for Staffin via the Quiraing.

> **At the A855** Turn right for Staffin.
> **At Portree** Follow the road through town and emerge at the A87 junction.
> **Turn left onto the A87** Ride towards Kyle of Lochalsh.
> **Continue past Sligachan** Either retrace your outward route to the ferry, or stay on the A87 to the Skye Bridge and Kyle of Lochalsh.

WHERE TO STAY

Uig Hotel Easy to find, with a good restaurant and a decent rear car park to keep the bike out of sight of the road. **uig-hotel-skye. com**

WHAT TO SEE AND DO

Staffin Dinosaur Museum Houses an interesting collection of dinosaur footprints and fossils discovered in the local area. **staffindinosaur museum.com**

below Cuillin Hills beyond a bridge at Sligachan

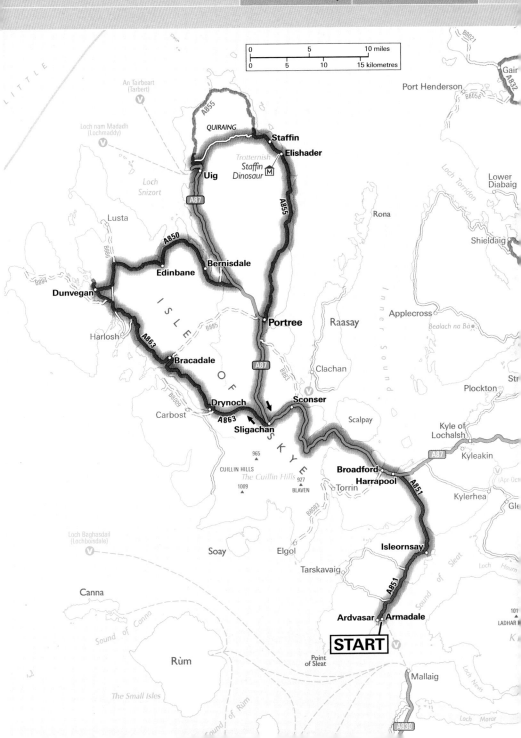

RIDE (72) Cairngorm Loop

THERE WERE FIVE of us on a short tour of Scotland, blessed with glorious weather but running late, heading south from Tongue on the very north coast of Scotland. Standing in the petrol station in Aviemore, we conferred. The A9's all well and good... but what's round the other side of the mountains? We decided to tear up the schedule and find out...

What a great decision. The eastern half of the Cairngorms is definitely where the best of the riding is. While the A9 is open and sweeping, the A939 is tighter, more challenging, more rewarding. Twisting through thick pine forests, it climbs steeply to burst out of the trees on the final ascent to the Lecht Ski Area. There's a staggering view out across the countryside... but not of the road, which drops as steeply as a rollercoaster with no view of where it's going until you're on it.

Down through Glen Shee, we were torn between admiring the spectacular views and concentrating on the challenging turns as the road writhed along the rock-studded valley floor. Hooking west to pick up the A924 provides one final jolt of adrenaline, before picking up the calmer A9 to return to Aviemore (just respect the average-speed cameras). So if you ever find yourself in Scotland's ski capital, wondering which way to go – don't debate. Do a lap of the Cairngorms: you won't regret the decision.

FROM/TO Aviemore, Highland
DISTANCE 173 miles
ALLOW 4 hours

Route Description

> **From Aviemore** Take the A95 to Grantown-on Spey.
> **Cross the River Spey** and turn right on the A939 to Tomintoul.
> **Don't miss** the right turn just after Tomintoul village to stay on the A939 to Cock Bridge.
> **5 miles** after the Lecht Ski Area, turn right to stay on the A939 to Ballater.
> **At A93** turn right to Braemar.
> **In Bridge of Cally** turn right on the A924 to Ballintuim.
> **In Pitlochry** turn right following signs for Inverness (A9).
> **Keep going straight** to Blair Atholl on the B8019 (which then becomes the B8079) parallel to the A9.
> **When the B8079** meets the A9 after Blair Atholl, turn right to Inverness.
> **After 18 miles** Turn left on the A889 to Dalwhinnie.
> **At A86 T-junction** Turn right to Laggan.
> **In Kingussie** Cross the A9, taking the B9152 to return to Aviemore.

WHAT TO SEE AND DO

Balmoral Castle Victoria and Albert first rented Balmoral in 1848, and Albert bought it soon after. The new castle was completed in 1856 and is still the Royal Family's Highland residence.
balmoralcastle.com

Ruthven Barracks, Kingussie Dating from 1721, these now-ruined barracks were part of the British government's attempt to quell the Jacobite rebellion. They were captured in 1746.
historicenvironment.scot/visit-a-place/places/ruthven-barracks

Corgarff Castle This rather small castle was besieged in 1571 and associated with Jacobite risings in 1715 and 1746. Also used as barracks to control whisky smuggling between 1827 and 1831.
historicenvironment.scot/visit-a-place/places/corgarff-castle

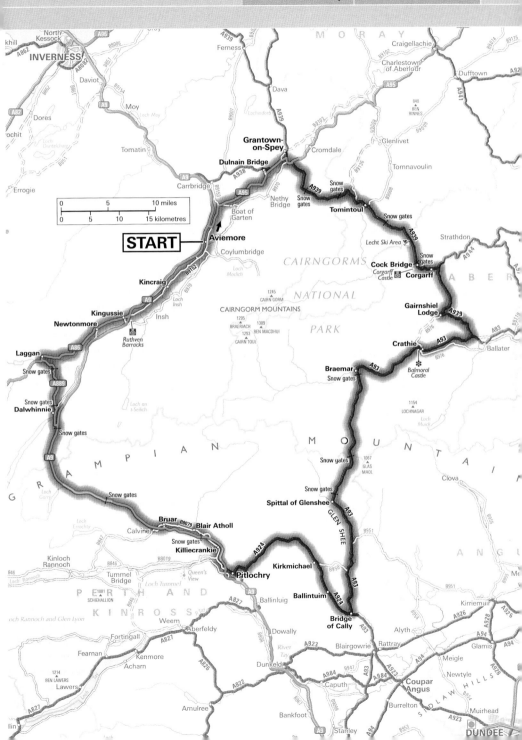

RIDE (73) Whisky Galore

DRINKING AND RIDING a bike don't mix – but there is something compelling about riding around the whisky heartland around Grantown-on-Spey. Mostly it's the outstanding roads that are so inviting, but the thought of bringing home a souvenir from a distillery or two (to be enjoyed at home) also has an appeal… The roads around Speyside have something for everyone. There are narrow, tight moorland B-roads and rolling, open A-roads, vast vistas across open countryside and shady, perfumed straights cutting through forests beside fast-flowing rivers. These Cairngorm foothills produce the kind of roads that can go to your head – never mind the local firewater.

If there's one thing these roads lack, it's traffic. Elgin's a fairly bustling town for this area and the coastal A98 can sometimes get a little busier, but it's worth it for the views and option of adding a detour for a seaside lunch (though if you really want to avoid traffic, take the A96/A95 detour through Keith to Banff). But it's as the route swings away from the coast again that it becomes truly intoxicating. Through Huntley, Dufftown and onto the majestic A95 along the banks of the Spey – it's a fabulous day's ride. Cheers!

FROM/TO Grantown-on-Spey, Highland
DISTANCE 170 miles
ALLOW 5 hours

Route Description

➤ **At Grantown-on-Spey** Take the A95 towards Aviemore.
➤ **At Dulnain Bridge** Turn right on the A938 to Duthil.
➤ **After Duthil** Just past the village, turn right on the B9007 towards Ferness.
➤ **A939** When the road meets the A939, turn right, back towards Grantown-on-Spey.
➤ **A940** After half a dozen miles, take the sharp left turn onto the A940 to Forres.
➤ **At Forres** Turn right at roundabout onto High Street B9011, then shortly right again on the B9010, through Rafford and Kellas on the way to Elgin.
➤ **Elgin** Join the A96 towards Aberdeen.
➤ **Fochabers** Turn left on the A98 towards Fraserburgh.
➤ **Banff** In the town centre, pick up the A97 through Aberchirder.
➤ **Huntly** Use the A96 bypass to avoid the town centre, then at next roundabout turn left on the A97.
➤ **Rhynie** Turn right on the A941, passing through Dufftown.
➤ **Craigellachie** Turn left on the A95 towards Aviemore, which will take you back to Grantown-on-Spey.

WHAT TO SEE AND DO

Glenfiddich Distillery
Set close to Balvenie Castle, the distillery was founded in 1887. Visitors can see the whisky-making process in its various stages and then sample the finished product.
glenfiddich.com

Rockpool Café
This great café is in Cullen, on the A98. You don't even need to divert from the route to make a pit stop – just park your bike in the square and dive in.
rockpool-cullen.co.uk

Duff House, Banff
Designed by William Adam for William Duff, later Earl of Fife. The roof went on in 1739 but the planned wings were never completed. However, it's still one of Britain's finest Georgian baroque buildings.
historicenvironment.scot/visit-a-place/places/duff-house

RIDE (73) Whisky Galore

ROUTE TYPE Loop | **DISTANCE** 170 miles

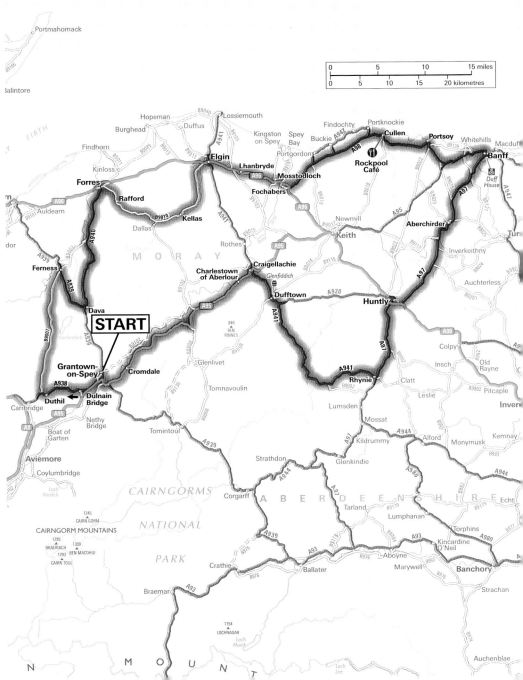

RIDE (74) The North East 250

SCOTLAND'S EMBRACED THE power of the number to market its brilliant roads to visitors. After the success of the North Coast 500 (see p206), the North East 250 was created to attract tourists to the Cairngorms, Deeside, Speyside and the Northeast and East Coasts. See the *northeast250.com* site for more information.

The official route is a 'balloon route' – a circular ride with a one-road detour, like the string on a balloon. Our version of the route starts from Aberdeen; a great base that makes it practical and easy to enjoy the ride. It's easily shortened by cutting off the tail of the balloon and skipping the jaunt to Glenshee – though that would be a shame as it's arguably the best part of the ride.

FROM/TO Aberdeen, Aberdeenshire
DISTANCE 250 miles
ALLOW 5.5 hours

Route Description
➤ **Leave Aberdeen** on the A93 to Braemar.
➤ **For the full route** Stay on the A93 all the way to the Glenshee Ski Centre – then turn around and return to the B976 then turn left. **(For the shorter version)** of the route, turn right after Balmoral Castle on the B976 to Tomintoul.

➤ **At Gairnshiel Lodge** Turn left on the A939 to Tomintoul. At the next T-junction, turn left to stay on this road.
➤ **In Tomintoul** Turn right on the B9008 to Dufftown.
➤ **At the A95 T-junction** Turn right towards Elgin. Stay on it as road becomes the A941.
➤ **In Rothes** Turn right at roundabout on the B9015 to Mosstodloch.
➤ **At A96 roundabout** Turn right, cross the river, then turn left at roundabout on the B9014 to Spey Bay.

➤ **From Spey Bay** Take minor road to Portgordon and Buckie. Keep following signs for these until joining the A990.
➤ **In Buckie** Pick up the A942 to Portknockie.
➤ **At the A98** Turn left to Fraserburgh.
➤ **Don't miss** the left turn in Portsoy (after the school) on the B9139 to Whitehills.
➤ **At the crossroads** Turn left to Whitehills.
➤ **In Whitehills** Turn right on the B9038 to Banff.
➤ **At the A98** Turn left to Banff.
➤ **Leaving Macduff** Turn left on the B9031 to Rosehearty. 2 miles after New Aberdour, turn left to stay on the B9031 to Fraserburgh.
➤ **From Fraserburgh** Take the A90 past Peterhead.
➤ **After Longhaven** Turn left on the A975 to Cruden Bay.
➤ **At the A90** Turn left to Aberdeen.
➤ **After 2½ miles** Turn right to Dyce and the airport on the B977. Turn right, then left, at the B999 to stay on this road. Keep following signs for the airport.
➤ **In Dyce** Pick up the A947 and A96 to return to Aberdeen.

below *Braemar mountain sunset*

RIDE (74) The North East 250

| ROUTE TYPE Loop | DISTANCE 250 miles |

RIDE (75) Wick Loop

THE GORSE WAS out when I first passed through Helmsdale – a riot of yellow flowers and healthy green grass sandwiched between the cloudless blue of the sky and the pewter mirror of the North Sea, glinting far below. Not that I had much time to admire the view: there were some proper corners demanding my attention.

This furthest northeastern corner of Scotland is full of contrasts: tight turns and hills on one hand or long, straight roads across flat farmland on the other; the crowds thronging the sign at John o' Groats and the empty hills of the quiet hinterland; the glorious riding when it's warm and sunny… and the cold rain and fierce winds that can batter you if you're unlucky with the weather. For a more original souvenir picture than the John o' Groats one, take the detour to Dunnet Head – the actual most northerly point of mainland Britain.

FROM/TO Wick, Highland
DISTANCE 148 miles
ALLOW 3.5 hours

Route Description

> **Leave Wick** on the A882 to Thurso.
> **After 14 miles** Turn left on the A9 towards Inverness.
> **Don't miss** the right turn in Helmsdale (by the hotel, before the bridge) for the A897 to Kinbrace. Turn right at the mini-roundabout to stay on this road.
> **Stay on A897** all the way to the north coast. Note that while it's an A-road, it's single-track and in places imperfectly surfaced.
> **At the A836** Turn right to Thurso.
> **In Thurso** Turn left at the lights on the high street. Cross the river and turn left at the next set of lights on the A836 to John o' Groats.
> **In Dunnet** Turn left on the B855 to Dunnet Head.
> **After visiting** the mainland's most northerly point, return to

above Don't forget to get your picture taken at John o' Groats

the A836 and continue to John o' Groats.
> **At the T-junction** Turn left to go into John o' Groats on the A99.

> **From John o' Groats** Take the A99 to return to Wick.

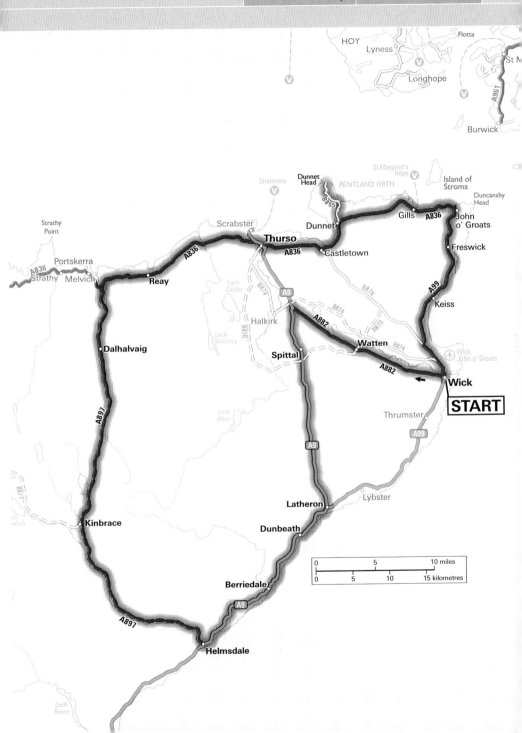

RIDE (76) West Highland Loop

THE WEST COAST of Scotland offers arguably the finest riding in Britain. Yes, cynics will tell you it's offset by the worst weather, but for many riders it's worth risking a bit of drizzle (or the occasional summer downpour) to get on these roads. And if it's sunny… well, you have a ride to beat anything else in Britain; one to rival Europe's finest biking roads. This loop gives a taste of the greatness – the spectacular scenery, the involving roads, the absence of traffic… The kind of ride that brings a bike to life. It includes the challenging Bealach na Bà (Pass of the Cattle) and the narrow, spectacular coast road round the Applecross peninsula to Shieldaig. It may be less than 200 miles, but this is a full day's riding. If you're travelling from outside Scotland, consider a two-night stop in Applecross: get up there one day, ride this loop the next, then ride home on day three. Perfect!

FROM/TO Garve, Highland
DISTANCE 179 miles
ALLOW A full day

Route Description

➤ **From Garve** Take the A835 north towards Ullapool. After 1½ miles, turn left onto the A832 towards Gairloch.

➤ **At Achnasheen** Turn left onto the A890 to Lochcarron, which becomes single track.

➤ **Stay on this road** as it becomes the A896 through Lochcarron.

➤ **At Tornapress** Turn left onto signed lane to Applecross. This will take you over the Pass of the Cattle, Bealach na Bà.

➤ **In Applecross** At the T-junction turn right on the single-track road that winds its way around the coast.

➤ **A896** When the coast road reaches a T-junction, turn left on the A896 through Sheildaig and past turning to Torridon.

➤ **In Kinlochewe** Turn left on the A832. Fill up at the petrol station. Carry on along the A832 through Gairloch and Dundonnell.

➤ **A835** When the A832 reaches the T-junction with the A835, turn right to return to Garve.

below *Dramatic Glen Docherty*

WHAT TO SEE AND DO

The Applecross Inn
A fabulous place to stay – not just for the journey there and the views, but also for the food and real ale. The associated campsite is equally good.
applecrossinn.co.uk

Torridon Countryside Centre Visitor centre with information about the local natural history. There's also a deer museum nearby.
visitscotland.com/info/see-do/torridon-countryside-centre-p255011

RIDE (76) West Highland Loop

| ROUTE TYPE Loop | DISTANCE 179 miles |

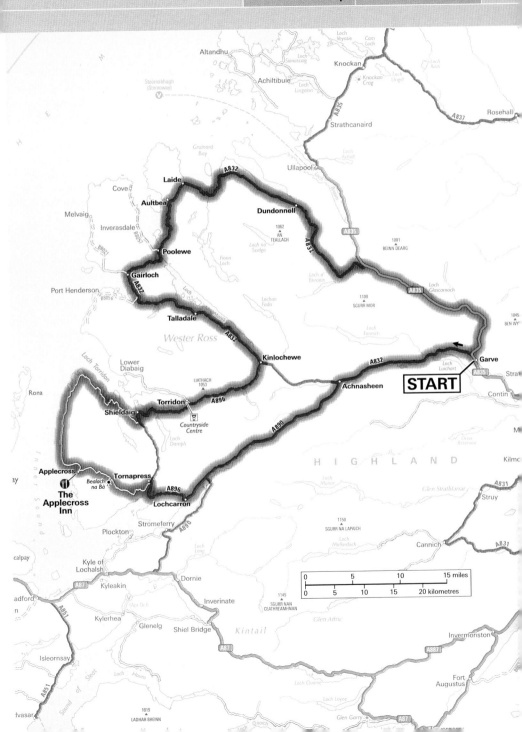

RIDE (77) On Top of the World

FULL TANK OF fuel? Absolutely. The far northwest of Scotland is not a place to play tank-range roulette. When people casually talk of 'wide, open spaces' or 'the wilderness' this is what they mean. It's one of the most enchanting landscapes on earth – and, while it's a delight to ride through, it's the last place you'd want to run out of fuel.

If the first leg of the A836 from Lairg is wildly beautiful, the stretch from Altnaharra to Tongue is like stepping back to another age. This single-track road balances on the banks of Loch Loyal, rushing between forest and across moorland with epic views to distant peaks.

The road just gets better and better. The A838 along the coast is generally wider, rushing across the spectacular Kyle of Tongue and then hugging the shore to the geological miracle of Loch Eriboll beneath towering cliffs. It goes round Durness – with its petrol station – and south along the shore.

Turning left at Laxford Bridge to stay with the A838, the road becomes a single-track affair as it rushes between the peaks of Ben Stak and Ben Screavie. It passes large lochs until it reaches the truly massive Loch Shin, following its banks to return to Lairg.

This is a truly unmissable route through the untamed furthest reaches of the Highlands. When people speak of 'adventure', this is what they should be talking about.

above *A838 in the Kyle of Durness*

FROM/TO Lairg, Highland
DISTANCE 124 miles
ALLOW 3 hours

Route Description
> **From Lairg** Take the A836 north towards Tongue, with Loch Shin on your left.
> **Carry straight on** The road becomes single track, all the way through Altnaharra and beyond, alongside Loch Loyal.
> **At Tongue** Turn left onto the A838, following the road round some tight turns through the village. Keep on the road across the Kyle of Tongue and round Loch Eriboll to tiny Durness.
> **Durness** There is a petrol station opposite the Spar shop. Continue on the A838 towards Rhiconich.
> **At Laxford Bridge** Turn left to stay on the A838 as you ride towards Lairg.
> **Stay on the single-track road** and rejoin the A836 just north of Lairg.
> **Turn right** to complete the ride or do the loop again in a clockwise direction.

WHAT TO SEE AND DO

Ferrycroft Visitor Centre, Lairg Find out about the history and ecology of the area in this resource centre with its award-winning loos. visitscotland.com/info/see-do/ferrycroft-visitor-centre-p1027901

Smoo Cave, Durness At 200ft long, 130ft wide and 50ft high, this amazing cave offers a waterfall, a boat trip and a guided tour. smoocavetours.com

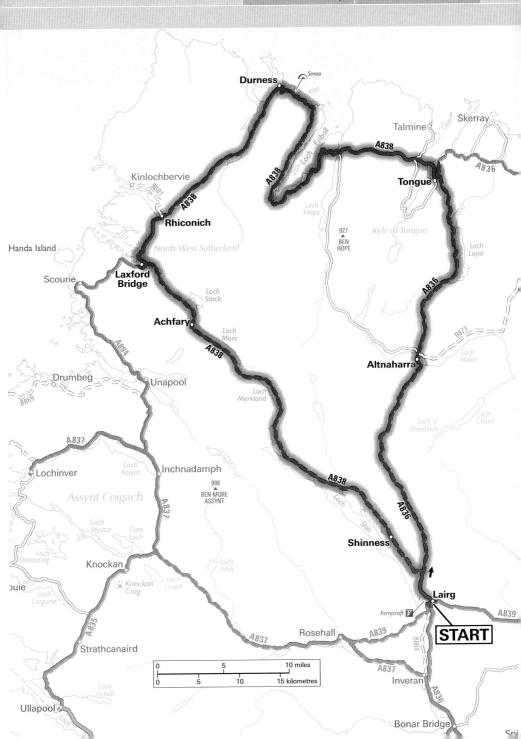

RIDE (78) The North Coast 500/600 Day 1

IT'S FAIR TO say that the North Coast 500 was a 'thing' before it became a 'thing'. Savvy British bikers have always headed for the west coast of Scotland and up to the northern shore for a brilliant ride – but marketing it as the North Coast 500 has drawn droves of tourists, eager to explore this spectacular landscape.

We present two versions of the ride here: the 'official' route (found on the great *northcoast500.com* site and shown in yellow on the map) and one developed more recently: our North Coast 600... because it's a shame to go to Scotland and not ride the A87. The routes can be ridden in either direction, but we favour going clockwise.

FROM Inverness
TO Kylesku, Highland
DISTANCE 255 miles (500)/ 290 miles (600)
ALLOW 5 to 6 hours

Route Description

> **Leave Inverness** on the A862 to Beauly.
> **For the NC600** Pick up the A833 to Drumnadrochit. Turn left at the A831.
> **In Drumnadrochit** Turn right on A82 towards Fort William.

> **In Invermoriston** Turn right on the A887. Continue onto the A87 towards Kyle of Lochalsh.
> **Look out for** Eilean Donan castle: 3 miles later, turn right on A890 to Lochcarron.
> **At the T-junction** Turn left on A896 to Lochcarron – rejoining the core NC500 route (below).
> **For the NC500** Stay on A862 to Muir of Ord and pick

up the A832 to Marybank.
> **At the A835** T-junction turn left to Contin and Ullapool.
> **½ mile** after Garve turn left on the A832 to Gairloch.
> **At the Achnasheen roundabout** Turn left on the A890 to Lochcarron.
> **For the NC500 and NC600** Follow the A896 through Lochcarron and round to Tornapress and turn left to Applecross (this is Bealach na Bà – the Pass of the Cattle).
> **In Applecross** Turn right and follow the road around the coast.
> **When it meets the A896** Turn left to Shieldaig.
> **Continue on A896** to Kinlochewe and then turn left on the A832 to Gairloch.
> **At the A835** Turn left for Ullapool on the A835. Stay on the road through Ullapool towards Kylesku.
> **At Ledmore Junction** Turn left on the A837 to Lochinver.
> **Stay on the road** round Loch Assynt for 18 miles, then turn right on the B869 towards Achmelvich.
> **At A894** Turn left to Kylesku.

left *Riding along the A832 at Second Coast*

RIDE ⑦⑧ The North Coast 500/600 Day 1

ROUTE TYPE Tour | **DISTANCE** 255 miles (500)/290 miles (600)

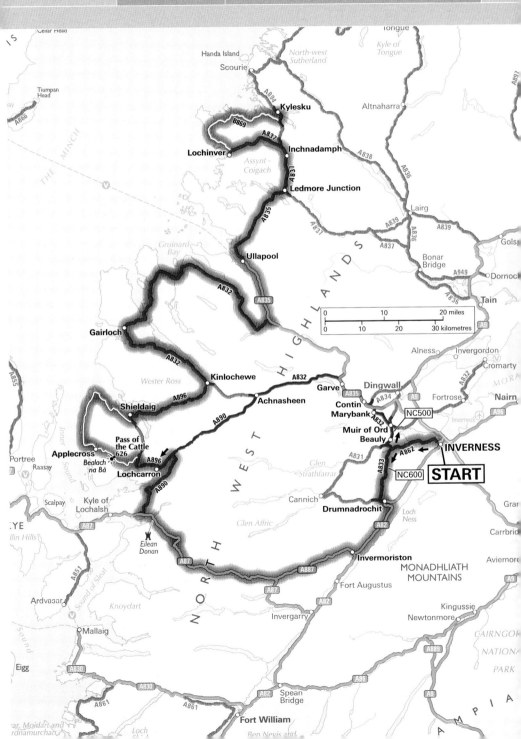

RIDE (78) The North Coast 500/600 Day 2

RIDING THE NORTH Coast is hugely satisfying. But it's not necessarily the easiest ride. It travels through one of the last great wilderness areas of Britain and the roads can be challenging: narrow, imperfectly surfaced, and occasionally with road-hogging traffic. So ride with a bit of caution and don't expect that vehicle coming towards you to stop at the passing place…

It is definitely worth the effort, though. This is all that's best about biking: out in the glorious Scottish landscape, soaking up the fresh, clean air and revelling in the sense of absolute freedom.

While the official route sticks firmly to the coast, our North Coast 600 version nips inland in certain strategic places in order to include a few of our favourite wild roads as well.

FROM Kylesku, Highland
TO Inverness
DISTANCE 260 miles (500)/
300 miles (600)
ALLOW 5 to 6 hours

Route Description

➤ **From Kylesku** Go north on the A894. The road becomes the A838 through Durness and along the north coast.
➤ **For the NC600** Leave the village of Tongue and turn right on the A836 to Altnaharra.
➤ **After 16 miles** Turn left on the B873 to Syre. Stay on the road as it becomes the B871 to Bettyhill.
➤ **At the A836** Turn right to Bettyhill, rejoining the core NC500 route.
➤ **In Thurso** Turn left at the lights on the A9 to Inverness, then left at the next lights on the A836 to John o' Groats.
➤ **At the T-junction** Turn left on the A99 to go into John o' Groats, then return taking the A99 to Wick. Continue on this road as it becomes the A9 to Inverness.
➤ **For the NC600** Turn right 3 miles after Golspie for the A839 to Lairg.

➤ **In Lairg** Turn left on the A836 to Bonar Bridge.
➤ **In Bonar Bridge** Turn right to Ardgay on the A836.
➤ **After 4 miles** Turn right on the B9176 towards Alness.

➤ **At the A9** Turn right towards Inverness, rejoining the core NC500 route.
➤ **At the Ardullie roundabout** Turn right on A862 to Dingwall. Stay on the A862 all the way to Inverness.

below *The spectacular curved bridge at Kylesku*

RIDE (78) The North Coast 500/600 **Day 2**

ROUTE TYPE Tour | **DISTANCE** 260 miles (500)/300 miles (600)

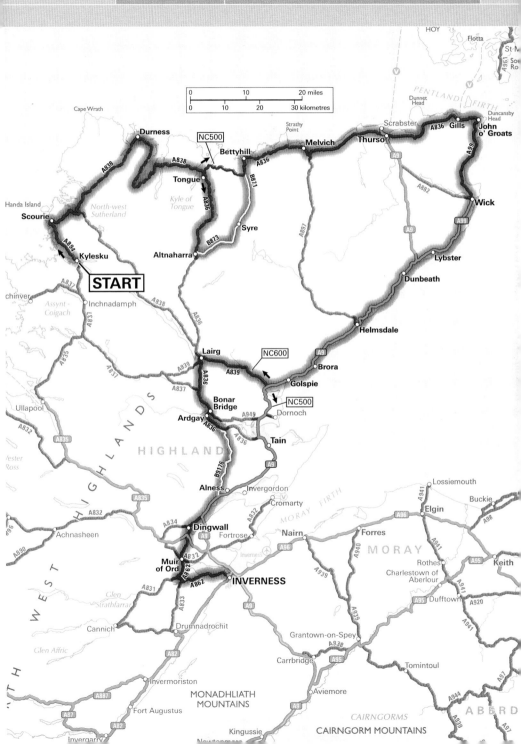

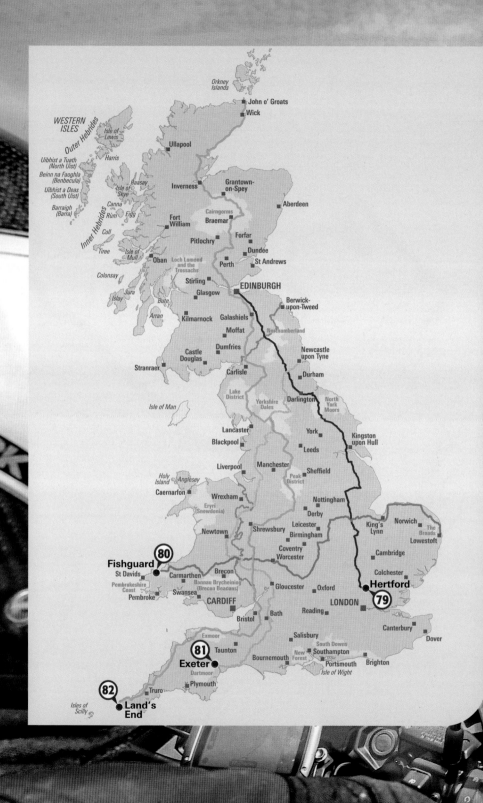

Crossing the Country

If you want to explore an entirely different region it doesn't have to mean spending a day on the motorway. Forget the A1 and the M1 – here's how to avoid the beaten track

RIDE (79) South to North

BRITAIN DOESN'T HAVE a Route 66... but if it did, it would probably be the Great North Road. Unfortunately, for a touring motorcyclist that's not such a great road. The A1 will get you rapidly from one end of the country to the other, it's true... but it's not much of a ride. Spending a day on dual carriageway and motorway isn't exactly a rewarding way to travel – you might as well be in a car. So here's our alternative route, broadly shadowing the Great North Road (in fact, nipping onto one short section south of Peterborough). It can get you from the South East to Scotland in a day, but it's probably better split over two more comfortable ones, breaking the journey in Hull.

FROM Hertford, Hertfordshire
TO Edinburgh
DISTANCE 400 miles
ALLOW One very long day or two relaxed ones

Route Description

> **Hertford** A10 north.
> **Royston** Left on A505 ring road to pick up A1198.
> **Huntingdon** Left onto the A14 to the A1(M) north.
> **Peterborough** J17 A1(M) for A1139 to the A15.
> **A15 Waddington** Right onto the B1178.
> **Potterhanworth** Left onto the B1202 then the B1190 to Bardney and Horncastle.

> **Horncastle** Left onto the A158 towards Lincoln.
> **Baumber** Right onto the B1225.
> **Caistor** Straight over x-roads onto A1173, then straight on at corner on minor road signed for Great Limber. Bear left.
> **Kirmington** Left onto the A18.
> **Barnetby le Wold** Straight over roundabout onto the A15 for the Humber Bridge.
> **Hessle** Straight over roundabout onto the A164.
> **Beverley** Left onto A1079 then go straight over Dog Kennel Lane roundabout onto the B1248.
> **Wetwang** Left onto the

A166, then right onto B1248.
> **Malton** Straight on at the High Street onto the B1257.
> **Sproxton** Right onto the A170 and into Helmsley.
> **Helmsley** Left in Market Place, then right onto B1257.
> **Stokesley** Straight over rbt onto A172 then straight over second rbt onto the B1365.
> **Middlesbrough** Left onto the A174, right onto the A19 then left onto the A66.
> **Darlington** Enter town centre to pick up the A68.
> **Corbridge** Left onto the A69 then take left sliproad onto the A68 all the way to Edinburgh. The route finishes at the Edinburgh Bypass.

below The Humber Bridge

RIDE (79) South to North

ROUTE TYPE Cross-country | **DISTANCE** 400 miles

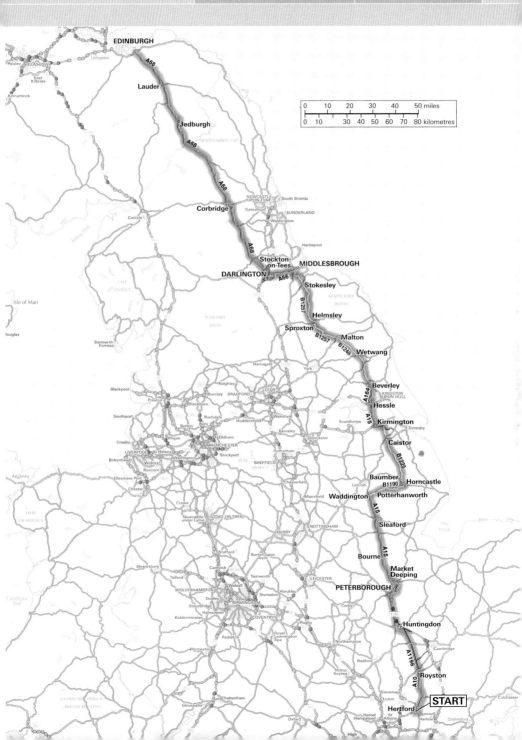

RIDE (80) West to East

THERE'S A LOT of fantastic riding to be had in Wales, everyone knows that. There's also some spectacular (if rather different) riding to be had in East Anglia. So how do you get from one place to the other? Well, we'd set about the journey like this. Now, we know that at first glance this route might not seem much use for those who live in West Sussex rather than West Wales. However, this isn't included for the particular pleasure of residents of the Pembrokeshire Coast National Park. We're sharing this route because, whichever way you're heading, there's a good chance you'll be able to pick up or adapt stretches of it to fit in with your own journeys from one side of Britain to the other. It's quick without being boring.

Of course, there's nothing actually wrong with the M4 or the M6 and the A14 when you're heading horizontally across the country. They're fine roads, everyone agrees, but frankly they're best left to the long-distance lorry drivers or time-pressed travellers rushing about, not enjoying their journeys. The route we present here is for anyone who wants to enjoy the travel as much as the destination.

FROM Fishguard, Pembrokeshire
TO Lowestoft, Suffolk
DISTANCE 435 miles
ALLOW One very long day or two relaxed ones.

Route Description
➤ **Fishguard** North on A487.
➤ **Cardigan** Right on the A484.
➤ **Newcastle Emlyn** Left on the A475.
➤ **Lampeter** Straight on A482.
➤ **Llanwrda** Left on the A40.

➤ **Llandovery** Left on A483.
➤ **Builth Wells** Right on A481.
➤ **T-junction** Right on A44.
➤ **Worcester** Take the A4440 bypass until picking up the A44 again (signed to Evesham).
➤ **Chipping Norton** Left on the A361.
➤ **Daventry** Left on the A45 then right on the A361 again.
➤ **DIRFT (International Rail Terminal)** Right for M1.
➤ **M1** Take motorway northbound for two junctions.

➤ **M1 J20 (Lutterworth)** Right on the A4304.
➤ **Market Harborough** Left in town centre for the B6047.
➤ **Melton Mowbray** Right for the B676.
➤ **Colsterworth** Straight on A151.
➤ **Spalding** Straight on through town centre on the A151.
➤ **Holbeach** Right on the A17.
➤ **King's Lynn** Left on the A149.
➤ **Great Yarmouth** Straight on the A47. The route finishes in Lowestoft town centre.

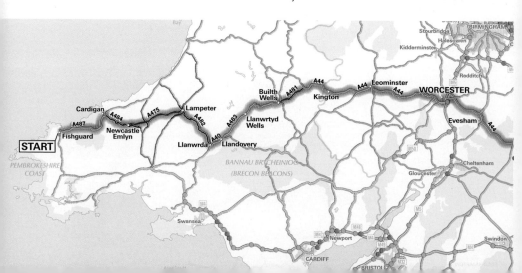

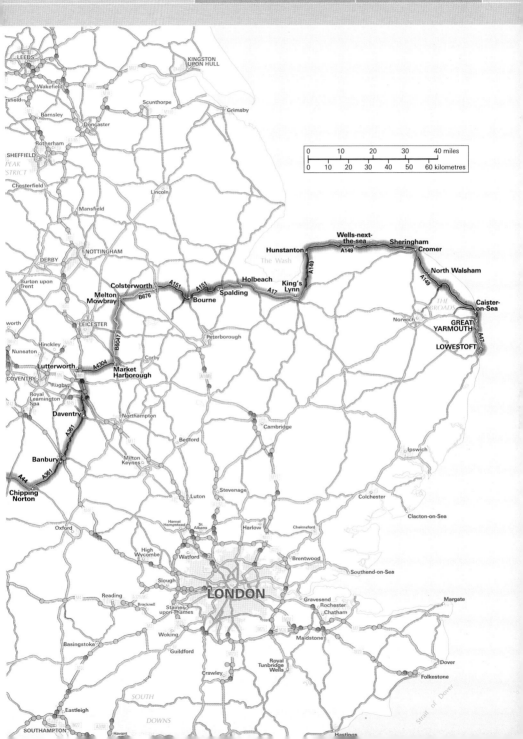

RIDE (81) Southwest to Northeast

ON PAPER, GETTING between the glorious Southwest and the rugged Northeast involves a tough choice: M5/M6 and the scant consolation of the A66; or M5/M4/M25/M1. It's like deciding if you'd rather have toothache or stomach ache… Actually, forget the major motorways and try this more relaxed ride, detouring through Wales, the Forest of Bowland, the Yorkshire Dales and the Pennines.

FROM Exeter, Devon
TO Newcastle upon Tyne
DISTANCE 490 miles
ALLOW One long day or two relaxed ones. Suggested overnight stop in Northwich or Preston

Route Description

➤ **Exeter** East on the A3052.
➤ **Lyme Regis** Left on B3165.
➤ **Crewkerne** Straight on A356, then right towards Andover when it meets the A303.
➤ **Sparkford** Left for the A359.
➤ **Nunney** Right on the A361 Frome Bypass.
➤ **Beckington roundabout** Straight on for Bath on A36.
➤ **Limpley Stoke** Right on the B3108.
➤ **Bradford-on-Avon** Left on the A363.
➤ **Bathford** Left on the A4, then straight on as it becomes the A46 for Stroud.
➤ **A46 north of Old Sodbury** Left to Hawkesbury on France Lane.
➤ **Wotton-under-Edge** Right on the B4058.
➤ **Nailsworth** Left on the A46.
➤ **Pitchcombe** Left on A4173.
➤ **Gloucester** A40 rbt. Straight on the A417 to Ledbury.
➤ **Ledbury** Left on the A438.
➤ **Willersley** Right on A4111.
➤ **Kington** Left on the A44.
➤ **Crossgates** Right on A483.

➤ **Oswestry Bypass** Right on the A495.
➤ **Whitchurch** Left for A49.
➤ **Stretton** Right on M56 for one junction; north on M6 towards Preston.
➤ **M6 Junction 31A** Left on B6243 (towards Longridge).
➤ **Clitheroe** Left on B6478.
➤ **Long Preston** Left on A65.
➤ **Roundabout** Right for the B6480.
➤ **Settle** Right on the B6479.
➤ **Ribblehead** Right on B6255.
➤ **Hawes** Right on the A684.

➤ **Leyburn** Left at Kings Head pub for Reeth.
➤ **Reeth** Straight by The Buck Hotel towards Langthwaite then turn right, then Barnard Castle.
➤ **A66** Right then immediately left on the B6277.
➤ **Barnard Castle** Left on A67, then left on the B6278.
➤ **Eggleston** Right to stay on the B6278.
➤ **Consett** Left on the A694. The route finishes on the A1 Newcastle Bypass.

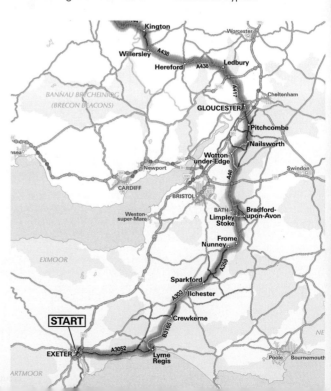

RIDE 82 Land's End to John o' Groats

THE TRADITIONAL ROUTE from Land's End to John o' Groats involves hundreds of miles of motorways and dual carriageways. Riders with buttocks of granite can just about do it in a day. We'd rather take more time and enjoy the trip.

DAY 1

FROM Land's End, Cornwall
TO Bristol
DISTANCE 230 miles
ALLOW 7 hours

Route Description

> **Land's End** East on the A30, then left on the B3306.
> **St Ives** Left on the A3074.
> **Hayle** Left on the A30.
> **Chiverton** Leave A30 for the A3075.
> **Newquay** Right on A392.
> **Trevarren** Left on A39.
> **Bridgwater** Right on A39.
> **Farrington Gurney** Straight on A37. Route ends in Bristol.

DAY 2 STARTS with some motorway to get clear of urban Bristol, before crossing the River Severn and heading up through the Welsh Marches and into the Peaks. Skirting Halifax, the day's ride ends in the charming town of Hebden Bridge.

DAY 2

FROM Bristol
TO Hebden Bridge, North Yorkshire
DISTANCE 234 miles
ALLOW 7 hours

Route Description

> **Bristol** North on M32, left on M4 to M48 Severn Bridge.
> **M48 J2** Right for A466.
> **After Wormelow,** turn left for the A49.
> **Shrewsbury** Right on bypass for the A5 and M54.
> **M54 J6** Left for Wellington, right on A442 towards Whitchurch.
> **Wellington** Right on A518.
> **Uttoxeter** Right on A50, then left on A515.
> **Buxton** Straight on A5004.
> **Whaley Bridge** Left on A6.
> **New Mills** Right on A6015.
> **Hayfield** Left on A624.
> **Glossop** Straight on B6105.
> **Woodhead Reservoir** Right on A628, left on A6024.
> **Honley** Left on the A616.
> **Huddersfield** Left on ring road, left on the A629.
> **Halifax** Left on the A646. Route finishes in Hebden Bridge town centre.

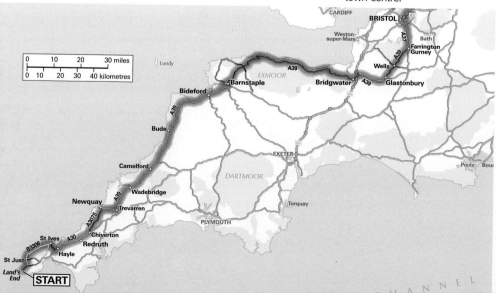

RIDE (82) Land's End to John o' Groats **Part 1**

| ROUTE TYPE Cross-country | DISTANCE 464 miles |

RIDE 82 Land's End to John o' Groats

OUR ROUTE LEAVES England in style, crossing the Yorkshire Dales, the Lakes and the Pennines. The scenic A7 leads over the Firth of Forth to Dunfermline.

DAY 3

FROM Hebden Bridge, North Yorkshire
TO Dunfermline, Fife
DISTANCE 264 miles
ALLOW 7.5 hours

Route Description

➤ **Hebden Bridge** North on the A6033.
➤ **Haworth** Left on the A629.
➤ **Skipton** Straight on at roundabout on the A65.
➤ **Cleatop roundabout** Right on the B6480.
➤ **Settle** Right on the B6479.
➤ **Ribblehead** Left on B6255.
➤ **Ingleton** Right on A65.
➤ **M6 roundabout** Straight on on the A590, which becomes the A591.
➤ **Windermere** Right on A592.
➤ **Ullswater** Straight on through

Pooley Bridge on B5320. At the A6, turn left to Penrith.
➤ **Penrith roundabout** 3rd exit on the A686.
➤ **Alston** Left on the A689.
➤ **Brampton** Straight on A6071.
➤ **Longtown** Right on the A7.

➤ **A720 roundabout** Left on the A720 Edinburgh Bypass.
➤ **Edinburgh** M8, M9 and M90 over Queensferry Crossing.
➤ **M90 J2** Left on A823(M) and right on A823. Route finishes in Dunfermline centre.

THE FINAL RUN up through the Highlands, skirting the wild Caringorms, is a real treat. Mileage is high on this final push for the line, but the lack of traffic and the flowing roads should make it easy to ride in a relaxed style.

DAY 4

FROM Dunfermline, Fife
TO John o' Groats, Highland
DISTANCE 308 miles
ALLOW 7.5 hours

Route Description

➤ **Dunfermline** North on the A823 through Gleneagles and passing over the A9.
➤ **A822 junction** Right to Crieff.
➤ **Crieff** Right on the A85, then left on the A822.
➤ **Dunkeld** Straight on A923.
➤ **Blairgowrie** Left on A93.
➤ **Bridge of Gairn** Left on A939.
➤ **Grantown-on-Spey** Left on

A95.
➤ **Dulnain Bridge** Right on A9.
➤ **Alness Services** Left on B9176.
➤ **AA Sentry Box #504** Left on A836.
➤ **Bonar Bridge** Right on A949.
➤ **Clashmore** Left on A9. (becomes A99). Route finishes at John o' Groats.

RIDE ⑧② Land's End to John o' Groats **Part 2**

ROUTE TYPE Cross-country | **DISTANCE** 572 miles

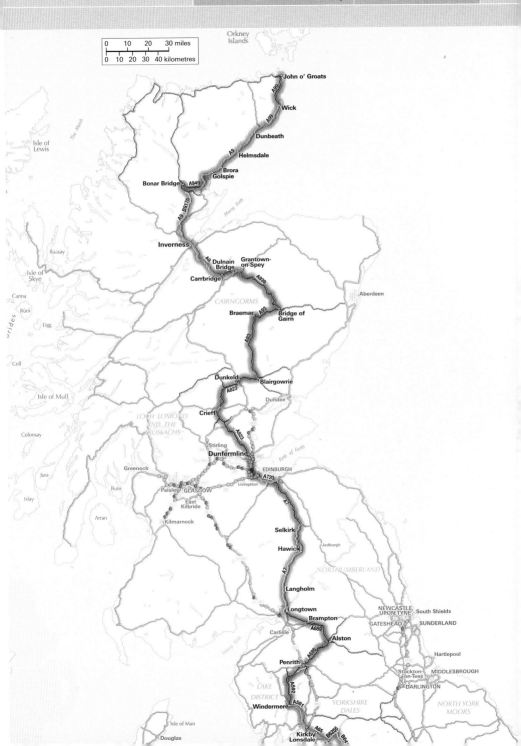

DISTANCE CHART and Journey Times

Journey times

Cities (diagonal axis): Aberdeen, Aberystwyth, Barnstaple, Birmingham, Brighton, Bristol, Cambridge, Cardiff, Carlisle, Carmarthen, Dorchester, Dover, Edinburgh, Exeter, Fort William, Glasgow, Gloucester, Guildford, Hereford, Holyhead, Hull, Inverness, Kendal, Leeds, Lincoln, Liverpool, Maidstone, Manchester, Middlesbrough, Newcastle, Northampton, Norwich, Nottingham, Oxford, Penzance, Perth, Peterborough, Plymouth, Portsmouth, Preston, Salisbury, Sheffield, Shrewsbury, Southampton, Stoke-on-Trent, Stranraer, Taunton, Wick, York, LONDON

The chart is a triangular distance/journey-time matrix. Distances in miles are given in the lower-left figures of each cell; journey times in hours and minutes are given as small raised figures.

Distance (miles) rows from Aberdeen downward:

- 473
- 597 213
- 426 124 178
- 599 264 204 178
- 508 129 96 89 158
- 456 219 250 100 119 168
- 527 107 126 109 191 43 200
- 231 242 366 194 367 276 262 296
- 511 50 189 163 253 106 259 68 282
- 568 198 94 150 118 62 179 111 339 174
- 573 300 271 201 86 196 120 228 379 290 199
- 122 337 461 289 461 371 357 391 94 375 433 473
- 579 195 42 160 172 78 224 109 349 171 54 244 443
- 154 444 568 397 569 479 464 498 202 482 540 580 136 550
- 148 339 463 292 464 374 359 393 96 376 434 474 47 444 108
- 474 111 124 56 153 35 131 61 245 124 96 190 338 106 445 340
- 556 209 175 136 44 105 89 137 327 199 99 96 420 148 527 422 100
- 476 80 149 58 183 54 154 58 247 87 142 219 340 148 447 342 30 129
- 454 109 331 160 332 242 256 193 225 158 303 356 318 313 425 319 209 290 168
- 365 236 317 138 259 228 146 247 171 283 290 263 239 299 371 266 194 218 196 216
- 104 497 620 449 621 531 517 551 254 534 593 633 158 603 66 170 498 579 500 478 424
- 277 198 321 150 323 232 246 251 48 236 293 346 141 303 248 143 199 281 178 132 301
- 323 182 286 119 258 208 153 228 130 220 284 269 198 279 330 225 175 216 177 163 60 383 72
- 377 199 260 88 214 171 101 196 184 233 244 217 251 243 384 279 148 217 146 88 437 143 72
- 354 120 270 99 271 181 194 173 125 158 243 294 218 253 325 220 148 229 116 94 128 379 79 73 139
- 534 261 232 162 66 156 84 189 341 251 161 42 397 205 541 436 151 57 181 318 223 594 306 229 177 256
- 351 143 258 87 259 169 168 188 121 181 230 282 214 240 321 216 131 42 83 87 34 374 75 43 87 34 244
- 284 251 354 175 314 264 204 284 94 289 341 320 158 336 294 189 231 273 233 232 89 320 83 71 123 142 281 113
- 230 284 386 208 347 297 236 316 59 322 373 353 104 368 238 153 264 305 266 264 148 266 91 103 156 174 314 146 39
- 474 173 208 79 105 89 105 219 188 146 143 199 281 101 178 132 301 175 216 177 163 60 383 72
- 475 278 312 159 175 230 63 252 283 302 241 176 349 286 483 377 193 151 215 315 150 536 241 170 103 254 128 251 254 117
- 382 163 230 51 191 141 94 160 189 197 217 210 256 212 389 284 108 149 110 174 92 443 159 71 39 109 172 82 128 161 64 119
- 496 158 168 79 109 73 89 105 270 162 89 146 363 151 469 64 78 234 190 323 100 523 45 152 103
- 691 307 108 273 284 189 336 221 462 283 166 356 554 111 662 557 219 261 244 401 412 715 415 391 358 365 318 352 448 481 303 398 324 263
- 88 386 509 339 511 421 406 440 144 424 482 523 44 492 103 59 388 469 389 367 314 113 191 326 268 484 264 208 169 389 424 331 412 604
- 423 203 248 84 154 155 41 190 229 227 201 158 296 231 429 324 126 113 140 235 118 483 188 117 65 159 119 132 168 200 42 77 58 86 343 371
- 621 238 63 203 214 120 266 151 392 214 96 286 485 46 592 487 149 191 194 332 341 646 346 322 288 295 249 283 379 411 233 329 255 193 80 534 273
- 579 221 162 159 51 116 134 148 349 211 74 140 443 129 549 446 111 46 140 314 262 603 303 249 216 253 103 240 306 339 133 196 183 82 242 492 156 173
- 318 156 278 123 280 190 203 209 89 193 251 303 182 261 289 184 172 214 105 35 244 360 254 141 183 143 159 66 413 118 35 48 81 205 42 99 131 98 148 38
- 353 184 265 85 224 174 129 194 160 230 251 244 227 246 360 254 141 183 143 159 66 413 118 35 48 81 205 42 99 131 98 148 38 137 358 302 94 289 217 78 204
- 406 76 201 48 219 112 143 109 176 110 173 243 269 183 375 270 71 178 53 106 163 688 139 104 121 296 319 127 226 183 89 146 109
- 564 206 142 144 63 102 131 134 336 196 54 151 428 109 536 430 96 52 126 300 256 589 289 236 200 238 113 226 293 325 111 193 169 68 242 478 153 153 19 248 23 203 169
- 383 118 217 41 219 129 142 148 349 211 74 140 242 146 209 208 353 248 96 177 98 122 129 407 107 91 92 56 204 44 160 193 97 171 51 120 313 296 98 243 200 66 163 50 39 185
- 233 348 468 296 469 378 364 398 101 382 439 480 131 450 186 86 340 451 361 350 278 91 200 325 298 536 329 208 229 246 382 303 384 541 44 460 244 588 492 252 438 328 422 526 313 607
- 549 164 49 130 168 48 202 79 319 141 46 223 413 32 519 414 76 127 101 259 269 573 273 249 216 223 185 210 306 338 160 264 182 120 144 462 200 75 114 231 71 216 154 94 170 419
- 206 598 721 551 723 633 618 652 356 636 694 734 259 704 166 271 599 681 601 579 526 103 403 485 538 479 696 476 423 384 601 636 543 623 816 214 583 747 704 443 666 513 530 689 508 358 674
- 330 209 312 133 273 223 162 242 118 248 299 278 204 294 318 213 189 231 192 191 47 371 91 29 72 101 240 71 49 85 146 180 86 185 406 252 123 338 265 96 252 57 142 250 119 218 264 473
- 541 239 203 121 54 121 58 153 311 216 131 76 382 176 511 406 105 32 102 190 165 265 196 144 214 38 202 254 286 69 114 130 61 289 454 84 219 76 223 88 145 163 83 163 412 155 666 214

Distances in miles (1 mile equals 1.6093km)

Distances and journey times

The distance chart above shows the distances in miles between two locations along AA-recommended routes. Driving on motorways and other major roads, this is normally the fastest route, though not necessarily the shortest. The journey times are shown in hours and the times given do not allow for unforseen traffic delays, rest breaks or fuel stops. For example, in optimum conditions the 377-mile journey between Glasgow and Norwich should take around 7 hours 18 minutes.

CITY AND TOWN Locator Map

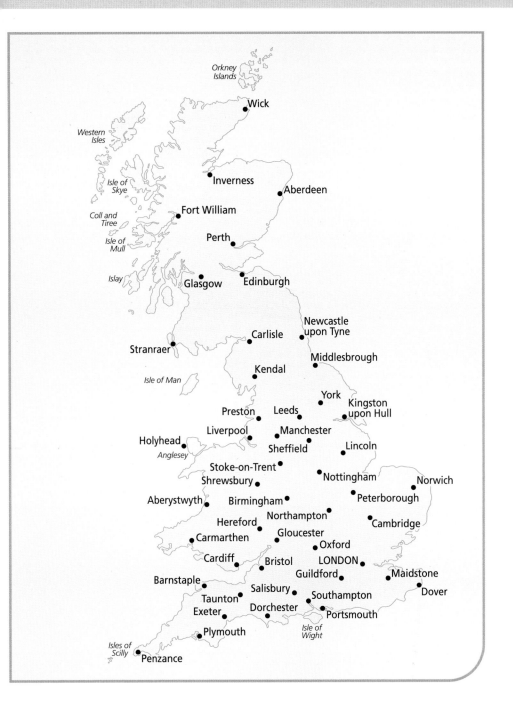

Orkney Islands

Wick

Western Isles

Isle of Skye

Inverness

Aberdeen

Coll and Tiree

Fort William

Isle of Mull

Perth

Islay

Glasgow

Edinburgh

Newcastle upon Tyne

Carlisle

Stranraer

Middlesbrough

Kendal

Isle of Man

York

Kingston upon Hull

Preston

Leeds

Liverpool

Manchester

Holyhead

Sheffield

Lincoln

Anglesey

Stoke-on-Trent

Shrewsbury

Nottingham

Norwich

Aberystwyth

Birmingham

Peterborough

Hereford

Northampton

Cambridge

Carmarthen

Gloucester

Cardiff

Oxford

Bristol

LONDON

Barnstaple

Guildford

Maidstone

Salisbury

Southampton

Dover

Taunton

Dorchester

Exeter

Portsmouth

Plymouth

Isle of Wight

Isles of Scilly

Penzance

ACKNOWLEDGEMENTS

AA Media would like to thank the following photographers, companies and picture libraries for their assistance in the preparation of this book. Every effort has been made to trace the copyright holders, and we apologise in advance for any unintentional omissions or errors. We would be pleased to apply any corrections in a following edition of this publication.

Front and Back cover © Simon Weir LTD/Mark Manning.

Inside pages:
1 RiDE/Bauer Media; 2 RiDE/Bauer Media; 3 RiDE/Bauer Media; 5 RiDE/Bauer Media; 7 © Simon Weir LTD/Mark Manning; 9 RiDE/Bauer Media; 11 RiDE/Bauer Media; 12 RiDE/Bauer Media; 14 RiDE/Bauer Media; 20 © BL Images Ltd/Alamy Stock Photo; 24 AA/Rupert Tenison; 26 © Guy Edwardes Photography/Alamy Stock Photo; 28 RiDE/Bauer Media; 30 AA/Caroline Jones; 32 RiDE/Bauer Media; 36 RiDE/Bauer Media; 44 RiDE/Bauer Media; 46 RiDE/Bauer Media; 48 RiDE/Bauer Media; 50 RiDE/Bauer Media; 52 © Cristian Prisecariu/Alamy Stock Photo; 56 © Rod Edwards/Alamy Stock Photo; 58 RiDE/Bauer Media; 60 RiDE/Bauer Media; 62 © Loop Images Ltd/Alamy Stock Photo; 64 RiDE/Bauer Media; 70 RiDE/Bauer Media; 72 AA/Caroline Jones; 74 © Edward Fury/Alamy Stock Photo; 76 RiDE/Bauer Media; 82 AA/Tom Mackie; 84 © Martyn Williams/Alamy Stock Photo; 86 RiDE/Bauer Media; 88 © Ian Dagnall Commercial Collection/Alamy Stock Photo; 92 RiDE/Bauer Media; 94 RiDE/Bauer Media; 98 © J. Schwanke/Alamy Stock Photo; 100 AA/Anna Mockford & Nick Bonetti; 102 © Glyn Thomas Photography/Alamy Stock Photo; 104 © Dan Tucker/Alamy Stock Photo; 106 RiDE/Bauer Media; 108 RiDE/Bauer Media; 110 RiDE/Bauer Media; 120 RiDE/Bauer Media; 130 © Stijn Verrept/Alamy Stock Photo; 132 RiDE/Bauer Media; 134 © joan gravell/Alamy Stock Photo; 136 © James Davies/Alamy Stock Photo; 138 RiDE/Bauer Media; 142 RiDE/Bauer Media; 144 RiDE/Bauer Media; 146 RiDE/Bauer Media; 148 RiDE/Bauer Media; 150 RiDE/Bauer Media; 152 © Realimage/Alamy Stock Photo; 154 RiDE/Bauer Media; 156 RiDE/Bauer Media; 170 © john briscoe/Alamy Stock Photo; 172 RiDE/Bauer Media; 174 © Wayne Linden/Alamy Stock Photo; 176 ©Matthew Totton/Alamy Stock Photo; 178 RiDE/Bauer Media; 180 RiDE/Bauer Media; 182 AA/Steve Day; 184 © Shine-a-light/Alamy Stock Photo; 186 Alan Novelli/Alamy Stock Photo; 188 RiDE/Bauer Media; 190 © Coatsey/Alamy Stock Photo; 192 AA/Jim Henderson; 198 © jazman/Alamy Stock Photo; 200 RiDE/Bauer Media; 202 © Rachel Husband/Alamy Stock Photo; 204 © Realimage/Alamy Stock Photo; 206 RiDE/Bauer Media; 208 RiDE/Bauer Media; 210 RiDE/Bauer Media; 212 © Sean Gladwell/Alamy Stock Photo.